RECOVERY READER

SECOND EDITION

Recovery Reader

Studies in AA, the Steps and the Process of the Program

Second Edition

Winter 2016

Recovery Reader – Second Edition

EDITORS
Joe A., Gary P., Rich T., and James W.

CONTRIBUTORS
Barefoot Bob H., Beth J., Fred S., Jack McC., Joe A., John H., Kate O., Kerry
K., Steve L., Ted D., and contributors identified within specific articles, and
those who asked to be left anonymous.

Additional material drawn from from:

sober.org

standupoet.net

barefootsworld.net

primarypurposegroup.org

Also see the list of suggested websites in Reference section for additional
information.

We would like to thank the estates of some contributors who have left a
significant contribution to the lore of Recovery. We have been unable to contact
the domain holders of some original websites and no claim against their work is
intended by inclusion in this volume. If anyone from those websites can contact
us, it would be much appreciated.

Revised Edition published by sponsormagazine.info

Winter 2016

Details available from:

sponsormagazine.info/reader.html

Release 2b

This guide may be downloaded without charge and in several formats from Sponsormagazine.info and may be shared with others provided that no fees are charged other than the cost of duplication and delivery.

Pass it on.

To honor the intent of many authors, living and dead, to keep this material available to anyone who wants it, all of the articles in this document remain available for free download as PDF documents. Downloads of the book as a whole and divided into its individual segments can be found at http://sponsormagazine.info

Table of Contents

Throughout this book references to page numbers without assignment to other titles will be from the book Alcoholics Anonymous, also known as the Big Book.

Page numbers in this PDF edition and the similarly sized 'print on demand' edition may not match. The ePUB version does not use the page numbering system and allows content to be resized according to the device and reader.

How to Use This Book

This book is intended to be used:

a) *to serve as a personal enrichment course-in-a-book on Recovery and AA History.*

b) *for a Sponsor who shares this information with someone they are attempting to help.*

c) *to create a new class as appropriate to your area's needs and opportunity by taking the suggestions and materials to assemble or revise as you see fit.*

It is not presented as the "only" way to do the work of sharing the Program, but it is a synthesis of work by over thirty authors with over half a century of effective AA Recovery.

This document is intended to be shared and may be downloaded in whole, in sections, or by individual articles through:

http://sponsormagazing.info/reader

This book may be shared so long as no fees are charged for the electronic file and that the associated credits, copyrights, and notices remain with the file.

The home page also provides a link to order a printed copy from a print-on-demand service. Print-on-demand is an outside service intended for convenience and price to compare with the printer, ink, and paper for printing out the pages of this document, or the costs of photocopies.

Dr. Ernie Kurtz, author of "Not God" and other books on AA and Recovery, had a suggestion for the use of Recovery Reader. He was familiar with the "sortes Virgilianae", a method he and other students used to find a topic for conversation by turning to a random page of Virgil's "Aeneid." He suggested the same exercise be used with Recovery Reader - as excursions into self education, study or discussion based on opening to a random page. It is also called 'bibliomancy' - book magic.

The same thing has been done with the Big Book as a topic for a meeting, and same thing done for "Daily Reflections" (random date), "As Bill Sees It" (random page), and other conference approved books as a starting point for group investigation.

Forward to the Second Edition

Origins of This Book

The idea for this book came about in 2007, after two years of volunteering to teach an "Introduction to Recovery" class at the Healing Place for Wake County, a public homeless shelter with a curriculum for alcoholic and drug addicted men. It began as a simple Big Book reading where one man came in and read from the Big Book to the clients at the center. The people attending the reading were men from the detox center, often still drunk or high from the streets, and the men in the shelter, who may or may not have an interest in getting sober.

When he decided he could not keep doing his reading, he asked one of the editors of this book to take over. On the first night the reading was from "To The Wives" - Chapter Seven. Many of the men attending had never heard of AA or the Twelve Steps, and their first exposure was from a part of the book dealing with Steps Nine and Twelve.

They had not heard about Step One yet, but they were being read to from Chapter Seven because they had not been there for the earlier parts of the book. Without a clear sense of what came before Steps Nine and Twelve, the attendees could not be expected to understand what was being said to them.

It was decided that from that point on, the class would focus on Steps One, Two and Three – it would be an introduction to the Twelve Step Program of Recovery every week. There would be new people arriving every week so the decision was made to make sure everyone coming in, for the first time, would be welcomed with a place to begin.

The class often had men who had already attended the introduction for a few times and, when there were no newcomers, we discussed the Inventory, Amends and lessons for later Steps.

But every week we asked if anyone was coming to the Twelve Steps to deal with alcoholism or drug addiction, and if anyone said they were, we spent the opening of the class on the first three Steps.

A curriculum was developed from the body of literature that had grown up around the Twelve Step Process - books, internet and the wealth of original recordings from the people who brought the message to the fellowship during its first eighty years.

It became important to never claim to represent a new "orthodoxy" for Recovery – a "one true way." We found a source, shared the information, and then compared that information with additional sources. When we found better information, we shared that. When we discovered we had stepped into a controversy between factions within the fellowship, we admitted that and presented the information from all sides.

The class was changed to mimic the process of Recovery. Show up, learn, share the best you can, learn more, share better, admit if you've made a mistake or discovered corrections to previous information. No secrets. No gossips. No continuation of old resentments, self-serving versions and personality over princples.

To the best of our ability.

Our Group Conscience

This anthology is not the thought or effort of one peson. This book was an expression of a group conscience. It is not the only, nor an 'orthodox', voice of Recovery. Some of the views may appear to be in conflict with other statements, but they are all expressions of the experience of our members across space and time.

It was not our purpose to tear away any of the viewpoints but to present what people found to help others find their own personal garden of living in Recovery.

Although it was not identified as part of our program the Twelve Traditions were adopted by the majority of the AA groups and have been part of our process as a collection of very different people, beliefs, customs and geography.

At the very beginning, the book Alcoholics Anonymous was the distribution of the 'Multilith' edition of the manuscript for what would become the Big Book. That version requested, and received, comments from members within the fellowship and our non-alcoholic friends outside that fellowship, in a variety of occupations and locations. Subtle tweaks in the wording shaped a book that has served us for more than 75 years as of this writing.

This collection represents authors sharing across eight decades of Twelve Step Recovery from cities all over the world.

Some authors have since died; the words they wrote continue after their deaths to share the message of hope they were given in life.

The authors made their contributions from several countries and almost all of the states within the United States.

The editors for this second edition have included people from North Carolina, Connecticut, Delaware, California, Florida, Virginia, Washington, Idaho, Texas, Georgia and people in transit between locations.

Take what you need, but don't leave the rest. Take it, too - you may need it later.

Free Access / Creative Commons

The class and the book have not been perfect and will never be perfect. But it is our hope this will provide a good foundation for any student of Recovery - newcomer, Sponsor, family member, academic or friend of people in Recovery.

It was decided that the material gathered for this class would be made available through the internet. There were a number of documents released as PDFs and later it was determined that all of the material released would be under the Creative Commons license. Creative Commons is an open-source system that allows material to be freely copied and shared. It can be printed and shared or it can be shared as an electronic files download. The license we offer states free duplication and sharing of documents and recordings, that these files cannot be sold (other than real costs of photo-copying, when that applies), and the files are not to be altered to hide the source or to claim the released material as an original work.

Where material is under the copyright of the original author, that statement is included and the rights of the author take priority over the Creative Commons license.

Today it is possible for the person new to the fellowship of Alcoholics Anonymous to become lost in the myriad of meetings, books, sayings, slogans, and, (at times) conflicting suggestions. It is also possible for the person new to reaching out to the newcomer to become confused as to the best approach. A Recovery Reader, and its associated projects, provide a simple and understandable introduction to the fellowship of Alcoholics Anonymous, the Program of Recovery. From there, the book takes the reader through many facets of Recovery.

In 1938, when the Big Book was written, Bill W. said:

> *"Our hope is that when this chip of a book is launched on the world tide of alcoholism, defeated drinkers will seize upon it, to follow its suggestions. Many, we are sure, will rise to their feet and march on. They will approach still other sick ones and fellowships of Alcoholics Anonymous may spring up in each city and hamlet, havens for those who must find a way out."*

Alcoholics Anonymous, page 153

No one could have imagined how large and widespread the fellowship of Alcoholics Anonymous would become. Fearing that they (the original members) would be overwhelmed with requests for help, the book Alcoholics Anonymous was published to provide a concise method of Recovery for the lone sufferer of alcoholism. While certainly the book inspired the formation of groups all over the world and has served as the foundational guide for Recovery, it could not provide one of the most essential ingredients to Recovery, one alcoholic working one-on-one with another alcoholic. The importance of this relationship is borne out in Bill W.'s telling of the story of his encounter with Dr. Bob and the founding of A.A. This relationship between alcoholics would later become known as the Fellowship.

The material is laid out so clearly that the newcomer can easily acquaint him/herself with all facets of the Recovery program, building naturally on the basics to the more advanced aspects of sobriety. For the Sponsor, each section is available for individual download and can be easily distributed to Sponsees for study and discussion.

For those that find themselves in an area where there may be a limited number of Sponsors available (or the Sponsor that is overwhelmed by Sponsees), A Recovery Reader includes a section on setting up classes to study the material.

By far, A Recovery Reader may be the most comprehensive collection of Recovery resource material available for the newcomer and old-timer alike.

Editing

The first edition was released in 2011 and proved to have been premature. The problems with spelling, grammar, punctuation, and sometimes with the actual information, made the first edition less than the resource we had hoped it would be.

Through the use of copy editing this new edition (begun in late 2014) presents the material cleanly, accurately and with due diligence. At that time we did not know that it would take more than eighteen months to accomplish.

Fresh information became available and, thanks to the internet, will continue to appear. We have included the information available at the time of publication.

This is not a final, or perfect, edition. It is possible an edit was missed in the volume of information provided. Progress not Perfection is not an excuse, but we have come to accept it as the reality for releasing this kind of research volume.

Anonymity

The question of names has been an issue in sharing these materials. Alcoholics Anonymous, and its dozens of descendant Programs, have a tradition of "anonymity" – at the level of press, radio and film.

This tradition has been the source of controversy from the introduction of The Twelve Traditions. First, alcoholics do not take well to being told what to do. Proponents wanted to protect Alcoholics Anonymous from public embarassment due to the actions of individuals who, in the public mind, represented the fellowship. This was based on celebrities in early days of Recovery, who had announced their sobriety in the press, and whose subsequent relapses were also covered, in detail, in newspapers and on radio. The purpose was not to discourage any individual from approaching AA because of the apparent failure of the Program – or because they did not like the public personality of the person associated with AA.

The anonymity also protected the newcomer. They did not come into the rooms dragging their job, their family or other issues with them. They began Recovery on an equal footing with everyone else in the room, united by their common problem.

Opponents said that they were anonymous because of shame and that, in Recovery, we are to be the equal of anyone else in the general society. Some insisted that their last name be used in and out of meetings.

Over time, as people moved into their professional lives, it was felt that public identifcation, if not as members of a specific Twelve Step program, but as a person in long term Recovery helped to establish that 'Recovery' was a real thing. Even in the early 21st Century, many people do not believe that real change and Recovery are possible – they believe that all members of the recovering community will eventually relapse. This has also been the attitude of many people in the professional medical community.

This book allowed living contributors to make their own decision about maintaining their anonymity as it relates to their own community. People were also free to choose anonymous attribution - usually their first name and last initial.

For deceased authors it was decided that, if that author, speaker, or presenter had been identified publically by last name as a member of one of the Twelve Step Programs, then they would be identified that way in this publication.

We determined we would not 'out' anyone who had not been identified through other sources.

Drunks: A Poem

A speaker brought this poem to an AA History event in Raleigh in early 2011, but did not know the author. After some research, the editors were able to locate the author and got his permission to include it in the Recovery Reader, with the understanding the book would remain available for free download and that the Print-on-Demand edition never be a source of profit for the Sponsor Magazine project. We are happy to present this powerful poem to readers of the Second Edition, published with the same agreement with the author or author's estates.

We died of pneumonia in furnished rooms
where they found us three days later
when somebody complained about the smell
we died against bridge abutments
and nobody knew if it was suicide
and we probably didn't know ourselves
except in the sense that it was always suicide
we died in hospitals
our stomachs huge, distended
and there was nothing they could do
we died in cells
never knowing whether we were guilty or not.

We went to priests
they gave us pledges
they told us to pray
they told us to go and sin no more,
   but go

we tried and we died

we died of overdoses
we died in bed
(but usually not the Big Bed)
we died in straitjackets
in the DTs seeing God knows what
creeping skittering slithering
shuffling things

And you know what the worst thing was?
The worst thing was that nobody ever believed
how hard we tried

We went to doctors and they gave us stuff to take
that would make us sick when we drank
on the principle of so crazy, it just might work, I guess
or they sent us places like Dropkick Murphy's
and when we got out we were hooked on paraldehyde
or maybe we lied to the doctors
and they told us don't drink so much
just drink like me
and we tried
and we died

we drowned in our own vomit
or choked on it
our broken jaws wired shut
we died playing Russian roulette
and everybody thought we'd lost
we died under the hooves of horses
under the wheels of vehicles
under the knives and bootheels of our brother drunks
we died in shame

And you know what was even worse?
was that we couldn't believe it ourselves
that we had tried
and we died believing that didn't know
what it *meant* to try

When we were desperate or hopeful or
deluded or embattled enough to ask for help
we went to people with letters after their names
and prayed that they might have read the right books
that had the right words in them
never suspecting the terrifying truth
that the right words, as simple as they were
had not been written yet

We died falling off girders on high buildings
because of course ironworkers drink
of course they do
we died with a shotgun in our mouth
or jumping off a bridge
and everybody knew it *was* suicide
we died under the Southeast Expressway
with our hands tied behind us
and a bullet in the back of our head
because this time the people that we disappointed
were the *wrong* people
we died in convulsions, or of "insult to the brain"
incontinent, and in disgrace, abandoned
if we were women, we died degraded,
because women have so much more to live up to
we tried and we died and nobody cried

And the very worst thing
was that for every one of us who died
there were another hundred of us, or another thousand
who wished that we *would* die

who went to sleep praying we would not have to wake up
because what we were enduring was intolerable
and we knew in our hearts
it wasn't ever gonna change

One day in a hospital room in New York City
one of us had what the books call
a "transforming spiritual experience"
and he said to himself

I've got it
(no you haven't you've only got part of it)

and I have to share it
(now you've ALMOST got it)

and he tried to give it away
but we couldn't hear it
the transmission line wasn't open yet
we tried to hear it
we tried and we died

we died of one last cigarette
the comfort of its glowing in the dark
we passed out and the bed caught fire
they said we suffocated before our body burned
they said we never felt a thing
that was the *best* way maybe that we died
except sometimes we took our family with us

And the man in New York was so sure he had it
he tried to love us into sobriety
but that didn't work either,
love confuses drunks
still he tried and still we died
one after another we got his hopes up

and we broke his heart, because
that's what we do

And the very worst thing of all the worst things
was that every time we thought we knew
what the worst thing was,
something happened that was even worse

Until a day came in a hotel lobby
and it wasn't in Rome, or Jerusalem, or Mecca
or even Dublin, or South Boston
it was in Akron, Ohio, for Christ's sake

a day came when the man said
I have to find a drunk
because I need him as much as he needs me

(NOW
you've got it)

and the transmission line
after all those years
was open
the transmission line was open

And now we don't go to priests
and we don't go to doctors
and people with letters after their names
we come to people who have been there
we come to each other
and we try
and we don't have to die

—Jack McC
standupoet.net

Newcomers

You will need to determine if this is something to simply hand to your prospect, or if it is information you would like to dole out as needed.

But the intent is to share with Newcomers.

sponsormagazine.info

A Message to Newcomers

We all come to our Fellowship from many places – towns, cities, villages, and farms. We come from Park Avenue or a park bench, from Yale or jail.

We are not united by our success, or fame, or wealth, or shame – we are united by the shared experience of having been lost, fearful, abandoned and alone.

We are united by our failure.

Together we have found the answer to our common problem and we have found a shared solution. We have found community with new brothers and sisters, new people to serve as families while we learn the new life and begin to repair, or lessen, the damage we have done in the throes of our pain and our common disease.

But this is good news. You have made it to the doors of Alcoholics Anonymous - you will learn the nature of our 'disease'. You will find the reason why you were unable to stop when you decided to stop. No matter how sacred a vow you may have made, no matter what pain you may have seen yourself cause to those you love, you still could not stop.

Most of us did stop - temporarily. Maybe for a day, or a few months, but there was always another failure and more self hate as a result of that failure

When AA began in 1935, almost no one belived that an alcoholic could be cured (and we have much the same attitude with addicts today). They arrived at churches and medical facilities and madhouses and prisons as a result of their steady decline. Famlies prayed and spent fortunes for cures, sanitariums and the help of legal and medical professionals. Sincere promises to stop drinking were made to themselves and others, and those promises were subsequently broken.

We know the secret that no one without the problem knows:

The reason we always went back to drinking was because it worked. In the opening to our Big Book - the book Alcoholics Anonymous - Dr. Silkworth of Townes Hospital said, "Essentially alcoholics drink because they like the effect."

What is the effect?

Alcohol is a depressant. It works on the same part of the brain as do opiates and THC (the active drug in marijuana). This is the lobe of the brain where humans make long term decisions. We depress our feelings. We lose our ability to plan for careers, happy families and a long life. But we also lose our fear, our guilt, our shame and dread for what may come next.

And we also lose our ability to feel love, to be a true friend, and/or to live up to the teachings we have been given and claim to believe.

We know things the people who never had the problem do not know. We know the sense of doom, and the sincere belief that things can only get worse. We know how the alcohol or drugs that once worked, stopped working. We know the terror of watching our lives spiral down.

We make several promises to you, the first of which is - You never have to pick up a drink again. You never have to pick up a drug again. You will find a way of living one day at a time that will free you from the burden of the past (but not the consequences of your actions). You will learn to deal with any problem - health, the death of a loved one, financial, legal, sexual and criminal - with people who have been through those struggles. We will show you what we have done.

One of our first promises is the title of one of the early chapters in the Big Book of Alcoholics Anonymous - "There Is A Solution." There is, and there is a world-wide community of people in our fellowship who will share that solution with you.

Another promise is – you never have to go through your crisis alone again. Unless you choose to. You can choose to throw it all away – you can choose to start drinking again, start using again, you can choose to stop going to meetings and to exclude us from your life.

Just stop going to meetings, get drunk, and get high. If you survive, we will welcome you back in. We don't shoot our wounded.

If you have made it to Alcoholics Anonymous, or one of the dozens of other 12-Step Programs that now exist…

Welcome. Glad you're here.

sponsormagazine.info

What Others Say About Us

Alcoholics Anonymous has only existed since 1935 but there is a large number of people who oppose us. Some of them have become very vocal and very visible.

You will need to make up your own mind.

Some say we are a cult. If so, we are a terrible cult - we don't tell you what religion to believe in, what deity to believe in... we don't even get to take your money1. You can leave and will be welcomed back…if you make it back.

Some say that the AA process does not work and they give statistics to prove their point. We have to question how they get their statistics from a society that is anonymous, where no one registers or reports (although some have to get sheets signed for courts, schools, bosses or other authorities who may require them to attend). No one reports how many people attend a meeting, or who is staying sober. But, still, in every local fellowship you will find people celebrating their first day or their first few months, or a few years, or several decades, of sobriety.

Some say we are a form of psychotherapy. We are not. If you are looking for therapy, go to therapy. We are a community of people who have shared certain experiences, who have found a way out of the lives that were destroying us, and want to share it.

Some people say we are just trying to get everyone converted to Christianity or some other specific religion. We have Protestants, Catholics, Evangelical and Orthodox Christians, and we have Jews, Muslims, Buddhists, Atheists and profoundly Anti-theists, all staying sober by making the phrase "A power greater than yourself" a new authority in their lives. What that power is, is up to you.

---

1 We do ask for contributions to cover costs in meeting, room rent, coffee, literature, under the "Seventh Tradition". .":Usually $1 or $2 per meeting, and if you don't have cash, no one is thrown out.

Some say that people in AA belive that only AA can help people get or stay sober. In fact, we hope you will find another method – people have simply gone back to church, made a commitment, gone to therapy, and been able to find long term sobriety; some people who go to therapy and deal with their personal demons are able to get and stay sober; some are able to just make a solemn vow to stop drinking and doing drugs and they succeed.

They used to call AA "the last house on the block. The place where you come after all the other methods have failed."

We are the people who have tried the other methods and they did not work – for us. We have tried all of the alternatives and have failed.

In the Big Book it says...

"Rarely have we seen a person fail who has thoroughly followed our path."

Page 58

But we have seen people who had failed to find and maintain long term sobriety succeed.

We invite you to begin and will share our experience with you.

Twenty and Four Questions

This list was prepared by psychiatrists of Johns Hopkins University and has been very valuable in helping the drinker decide for himself whether or not he is an alcoholic. It was first used as part of AA 12-Step work in Akron, OH.

Answer these questions as honestly as possible. Do not read ahead.

1. *Do you lose time from work due to drinking?*
2. *Is drinking making your home life unhappy?*
3. *Do you drink because you are shy with other people?*
4. *Is drinking affecting your reputation?*
5. *Have you gotten into financial difficulties as a result of drinking?*
6. *Have you ever stolen, pawned property, or "borrowed" to get money for alcoholic beverages?*
7. *Do you turn to lower companions and an inferior environment when drinking?*
8. *Does your drinking make you careless of your family's welfare?*
9. *Has your ambition decreased since drinking?*
10. *Do you crave a drink at a definite time daily?*
11. *Do you want a drink the next morning?*
12. *Does drinking cause you to have difficulty in sleeping?*
13. *Has your efficiency decreased since drinking?*
14. *Is drinking jeopardizing your job or business?*
15. *Do you drink to escape from worries or troubles?*
16. *Do you drink alone?*

17. *Have you ever had a complete loss of memory as a result of drinking?*

18. *Has your physician ever treated you for drinking?*

19. *Do you drink to build up your self-confidence?*

20. *Have you ever been to a hospital or institution on account of drinking?*

If you answered YES to one of the questions, that is a definite warning that you May be an alcoholic.

If you answered YES to two of the questions, the chances are that you Are an alcoholic.

If you answered YES to three or more of the questions, it indicates you are Definitely an alcoholic and in need of help.

ANOTHER WAY TO ASK THE TWENTY QUESTIONS

Read them again, but change the word 'drinking' to 'thinking'. Does that still apply?

The Four Questions

Only you can decide whether or not you are an alcoholic, although some professionals may offer very strong opinions on the subject.

There are four questions for you to answer to determine if you are an alcoholic:

1. *When you take a drink, can you control how many drinks you will have?*

2. *When you take a drink, can you control how long the spree will last?*

3. *When you take a drink, can you control what you will do while drunk?*

4. *Has the question of whether or not you are an alcoholic come up more than once?*

For most alcoholics the answer to the first three questions will be "no," and the answer to #4 will be "yes."

If you now know that you are an alcoholic, or even find that you simply have "the desire to stop drinking," you qualify as a member of AA.

What is the Cost?

One saying that has been popular in AA for many years has been:

"We are offering you our Program of Recovery and it doesn't cost you a dime!"

We do suggest you get a copy of the book Alcoholics Anonymous, which we affectionately call "The Big Book," but people have gotten sober working the Steps through their Sponsor's copy of the Big Book.

We pass the basket to cover the cost of coffee, renting the room and supplying the free pamphlets. Some meetings still include covering the cost of a free copy of the Big Book to a newcomer and if you can't afford a copy of the book in the beginning, almost all groups will make easy payment arrangements.

But what about the costs? You can actually figure out what it has cost you to sit in one of the chairs of our meetings.

First do some simple arithmetic. How much did it cost to buy what you needed to get drunk or high on a daily basis.

- How many years did you drink and/or use?

- Multiply the daily cost by 365.25 (the number of days in a year).

- Then multiply the annual cost by the number of years you were drinking and/or using.

You may have wanted to be the "big shot" by buying alcohol or drugs for others, so you need to add the costs of being 'host' and paying for the drinks or drugs to those you wanted to impress. Being the host provided a heady drug-like reaction by making you popular because of what you spent.

But that isn't the end of your calculations.

- How many times did you miss work because of being too drugged out to do the work, and how many times did you show up and not do the work you were being paid to do?

The former is direct loss.

The latter is theft - taking money under false pretenses.

- How much of your own possessions did you sell for much less than they were worth because you wanted money *Now*? Subtract the amount you received from the value of what you sold.

- How many 'loans' did you get and never paid back? You might want to look at your willingness to get those loans, knowing you had no intention of repaying the person or institution providing the loan.

Then there is the more direct form of theft. Did you ever take money or goods from someone and sell them? Try to create a list of these thefts to arrive at a total, then add it to your list of costs.

- Did you ever steal from a purse or pick someone's pocket?

- Did you ever rob someone face to face, with threats of violence or with a weapon?

- Did you ever steal goods or money by sneaking into a place where you were not supposed to be, such as breaking into a car or burglarizing a home or business?

Now, take the total of:

- The amount you spent on drugs or alcohol you used or provided.

- The total of unpaid loans.

- The amount of money which you either missed out on by not being fit to go to work, or by showing up and not doing the work for which you were paid.

- The total cash lost by 'short-selling' your own possessions.

- All cash received from the sale of items you stole and sold.

- All the money (and goods) you received by robbery, either by threats of violence or with a weapon or by burglary.

What is the total of cash involved?

We are not done. There are other costs that are not as simple to find.

- What is the cost of damage to your relatives?

- What about the damage you did to your parents?

- Your spouse?

- Your children?

- What friendships were soured by your betrayal or by the drain you put on those who called you 'friend'?

- What were the consequences of holding a series of jobs instead of the career you planned?

- Were you the owner of a business that failed because of your growing alcoholism or addiction?

- Did you have employees who suffered because of your disease?

Can you put a separate value to each of those?

This is not an Inventory.

This is simple accounting - what did it cost for you to come to meetings and sit in those chairs in all those basements, backrooms and rented spaces?

And after all you paid out and lost, you don't even get to take the chair home. It is usually not a nice chair, but it belongs to someone else. You leave it for the next meeting and the next alcoholic trying to do the work of the Steps.

For some this may be the beginning of an honest review of their personal record of loss and damage. We offer a system of 'amends' - the word means 'to repair or make better' - which is the beginning of improving a life that was a history of wrecking our own lives and the lives of people around us.

Coming to meetings, working with a Sponsor, working the Steps - these are all available without charge, but we do expect you to do the Work to get the Result. The Big Book gives promises. There are far more promises than those from Step Nine, which are read at the beginning of some meetings.

One of the first promises is the title of Chapter Two:

"There is a Solution"

The Words We Use

We of AA have many words that seem to mean something different within our society of people in Recovery. They are not secret - they refer to the many tools that help us.

The Steps

The key to our Recovery Program is found in "The Twelve Steps." Based on six steps from a previous Christian fellowship, the Steps were written in 1938 as part of the manuscript for the book Alcoholics Anonymous, called "The Big Book" in AA.

It contains the instructions for confronting your problem(s) - alcoholism, drug addiction or others which are the focus of dozens of newer 12-Step Programs - and then applying The Steps to achieve and sustain 'Recovery'.

Recovery

Recovery is our general reference for living life free from alcohol (or drugs or other substances or behaviors). This includes the process of confronting the problem, taking the actions (usually based on the 12-Steps or the actions required by those Steps) to repair (or make better) the things we ruined because of the disease – helping us to live life as a responsible, spiritually guided, adult human being.

Meetings

Regular meetings of AA are regular gatherings of people in Recovery, held by Groups. The Group may host one meeting per week or many. Publications are available with a list of days, times, and locations of meetings in your local area. These lists usually are also available online. Attend several different meetings and several different types (Open, Discussion, Speaker, Book Study, etc.) to find the one you want to make your Home Group, and then attend the meeting(s) for that Group regularly.

You will usually attend more than one meeting per week and are free to attend any of the meetings for which you qualify. You will find that attending meetings in other cities, states or countries can be a wonderful experience.

Groups

A Group consists of recovering alcoholics, usually the members who make the meetings possible. They gather one or more times each week to share their experience, strength, and hope.

Joining a Home Group helps end your alcoholic isolation and helps build the foundation for the work ahead.

Fellowship

The Fellowship consists of others who share our path to Recovery. The Fellowship is expressed in Meetings; through Literature; through using the Phone between meetings; through the Steps; and the sharing of our experience, strength, and hope outside the meetings.

The value of the Fellowship becomes more important when members share with you how to get through a crisis you are confronting, based on their experience with the same situation.

The Phone

We use the telephone as our "meeting between meetings." Regular contact with other people is a lifeline when new situations require us to deal differently with life on life's terms. We call our Sponsors and call other people we have met in the meetings. We encourage you to collect phone numbers. And don't just collect them - call them!

Service

We do Service to share our experience, strength, and hope; to make our meetings possible; to see how our experience can benefit others; and to give back to the Fellowship for what was given to us so freely. We become trusted servants - we do not govern.

Literature

There are many books on the subject of alcoholism and Recovery, but usually we are referring to two specific books, published for and by the members of the AA Program. These two books are: *Alcoholics Anonymous* (The Big Book) and *The Twelve Steps and Twelve Traditions* (The 12 & 12).

These two books give the specific steps of our Program, which we have found necessary to attain and maintain our sobriety. Many other 12-Step Programs have their own versions of these books.

There are many pamphlets available at most meetings or service offices. These address specific problems or address specific groups within the fellowship.

The books are available at our cost and the pamphlets are free.

Sponsor

A Sponsor is a person with substantial sobriety who is willing to share their experience, strength, and hope with you - to help you apply the 12 Steps to your life, to exercise the tools we offer. They share with you their personal experience in working the Steps. Sponsors are not therapists, counselors, bankers, or authorities. Sponsors are not perfect and may suggest other people in Recovery who may be able to help you with a specific problem.

Sponsors are just individual alcoholics working Recovery One Day at a Time.

Find someone who has Recovery as you want it and ask them what they did to get it.

Temporary Sponsor

A Temporary Sponsor is someone willing to answer your questions. They may only be a little bit ahead of you on the path of Recovery. A Temporary Sponsor will help you for the first month or two while you look for your permanent Sponsor.

Steps

The Twelve Steps enable you to deal with life without the crutches of alcohol and drugs. The Steps are written in order and must be worked in that order to be most effective. We work the Steps with a Sponsor and with the support of other members of the program who are ahead of us in the process - and we help those who come after us with what we have actually done.

The authority of AA comes from Page 20 of the Big Book - "We will tell you what we have done." (Not theory or ideas or opinions we have heard, but our personal experience.)

Singleness of Purpose

AA has a set of guidelines for meetings, one of which calls for a "Singleness of Purpose." In the days when that was written there were two Twelve Step Programs; Alcoholics Anonymous and Al Anon.

In the decades since that time more than 60 public Twelve Step Programs have been developed that cover a wide variety of substances and behaviors. Each maintains its own 'singleness of purpose' to identify who may, or may not, attend their meetings. Usually it is defined as those who want to stop the substance abuse or behavior that threatens to ruin their lives.

We do have some basic guidelines:

Go to Meetings

Go to meetings. Meetings are where you will make contact with the fellowship, find out what we mean by the Big Book and other references, get phone numbers, and discover how you fit into the AA fellowship.

90 in 90

There is an unofficial suggestion of committing to attend 90 meetings in 90 days. Part of the reason is that commitment gives you a real chance to understand what we have to offer, to learn of the different types of meetings available to you, and get valuable time detoxifying your body. And, at the end of 90 days, you may be able to have a clear enough mind to honestly answer the question: "Am I an Alcoholic?"

Don't Drink Between Meetings

Do NOT pick up a drink (or a drug) between meetings. If you do not take a drink, you cannot get drunk. If you think you might drink put it off for 15 minutes, then another 15 minutes, and so on until you can get to a meeting. Use the phone to call someone before you take a drink - after you take a drink there is nothing they can do to help. Some people got sober, and stayed sober, after their first meeting. Many people did not – but they kept going to meetings until they were able to reach Day 1. People who have been around for many years tell us "It is easier to stay sober than to get sober!"

"Clean and Sober"

This phrase is often used to distinguish between alcohol and drugs as they relate to Recovery.

However, when you look at the definition of 'sober' we find:

[soh-ber] adjective, soberer, soberest.

    1. not intoxicated or drunk.

    2. habitually temperate, especially in the use of liquor.

    3. quiet or sedate in demeanor, as persons.

    4. marked by seriousness, gravity, solemnity, etc., as of demeanor, speech, etc.: a sober occasion.

    5. subdued in tone, as color; not gay or showy, as clothes.

    6. free from excess, extravagance, or exaggeration: sober facts.

    7. showing self-control: sober restraint.

Only two of the definitions deal with alcohol. The rest have to do with a way of thinking, approaching or carrying oneself.

It is the belief of most of the authors in these pages that 'sober' is the way of life learned when we have successfully excluded our triggering substances, behaviors and thinking from our daily lives.

To stop, we stop. What we stop is indulging in the substances and/or behaviors that have ruined our health, our standing, our relationships and our negative effect on those around us. And when we have stopped, we begin to learn new ways to behave and think - the ways taught by the Steps and practiced by those within our fellowship.

The programs teach us how to live after we have stopped drinking.

Almost everyone coming into the substance-oriented Twelve Step Programs now knows about drugs, or has had a personal experience with them. The Twelve Steps are used in other programs and the same process of stopping the abuse, and then working the steps is utilized to live a new life. A life that is focused on healthy behavior and a spiritual foundation that shifts our focus from being self-serving and selfish to a new life of usefulness and service.

'Clean' refers to removing the substance from our body and our lives;

'Sober' refers to a way of living, which takes a while to learn and a lifetime to practice.

Alcohol has been around for thousands of years. Alcoholism goes back as far.

When we planted the first crops, those crops were always grain - wheat, maize, oats, rye, millet and rice. We grew grain to brew beer and to bake bread. Anthropologists have not been able to tell us which came first.

From the beginning there were certain people who could not handle alcohol. Where others drank without damaging their lives or bodies, our alcoholic forerunners exhibited the same self-destructive cycle known today.

When we added fruit to our agricultural development we made wine, and more people were found to be unable to avoid the alcoholic problems so well-known today. Adding distilled spirits into the mix brought an increase in human losses due to gin, whiskey and vodka.

We do not need to go into further detail, since most of the people reading this book know the extent of the damage done through personal experience, or their association with someone who has suffered the adverse effects alcohol can have.

Drugs, such as marijuana, opium, ket, coca leaves and others, have also been around for thousands of years, but did not result in modern addiction until the early 19th Century with the British Empire's opium trade with China, and the Dutch use of cocaine among slaves in the Carribean region.

Get a Big Book

The Big Book is the book of Alcoholics Anonymous. Copies are available for sale at almost every meeting. You can also get copies in used bookstores, or even the public library. We recommend you become familiar with the first 181 pages (164 basic pages plus Dr. Bob's story at the beginning of personal stories).

If you are a member of another Twelve Step program, they may suggest you buy their primary book of direction for that fellowship, such as the book Narcotics Anonymous for the Narcotics Anonymous fellowship.

Go to Several Book Study Meetings

At Big Book Studies a portion of the book is read and the group discusses its meaning. The Program is found in the Big Book and these study meetings will help you far more than reading the book by yourself.

Get a Home Group

When you have been to some meetings, it is suggested that you find a Home Group. That is a group you attend regularly where you get to know people (and to be known). And get busy in your home group - help set up the room, make coffee, set up literature, greet people at the door. Play a role in making the meeting possible. It is called "Service."

Get phone numbers. Some people will offer you their phone numbers - use them. There is nothing magical about having a list of numbers in your pocket. Call someone to ask what meetings they would recommend; call them when they've said something that specifically addresses a problem you are having; call them before you take a drink. Use the phone numbers you get!

Get a Sponsor

A Sponsor is someone who is ahead of you in the Program. Your Sponsor will get to know your story, they will share their story with you, and your Sponsor will show you how to work the Steps.

Do the Steps

This means that you must get together with a Book Study or Step Study group to decode the secret meaning of the literature2. We recommend you also sit down with your Sponsor, usually at the same day and time every week, to go through the Big Book and follow the directions.

When the Book asks a question, answer it.

When the Book says pray, pray (or do your own equiavalent).

When the Book says write, write.

When the Book says share, share.

When the Book says go do, go do. (But check with your Sponsor first.)

When the Book says to check yourself , check yourself.

Be sure to remember, a) the Steps are in order for a reason, do them in order; and b) the Steps are not done once and then you are done. Each step is necessary for the Step that follows.

Also, you accumulate the Steps. When you start Fourth Step, be sure you have Steps 1, 2 and 3 with you as you set pen to paper. When you get to the Ninth Step, be sure you have Steps 1–8 with you when you discuss your Amends

---

2 Most people do not realize there are two parts to the Big Book. There is the white part - that's the paper. You don't need what's in the paper. The black part is the ink - and that is where we have hidden all the important information. There is no third part.

with your Sponsor, or whoever you are doing your Steps with. When you are ready to begin the daily exercise of Steps Ten, Eleven, and Twelve, the previous nine Steps need to go with you, every step of the way.

The Steps teach us a way of life that other people seem to achieve without effort. For us, it is an effort.

But it is worth the effort.

Do Service

The meetings exist because people volunteer to set up the tables, make coffee, set out the literature, greet people at the door, or clean up after the meeting. This kind of service can help you to feel a part of the meeting and gives you the opportunity to talk with people casually.

Repeat on a daily basis

The Insanity of Alcoholism

The Insanity of Alcoholism is NOT the goofy behavior that people exhibit when they are drunk. Everyone who ingests enough alcohol will act goofy.

The Insanity of Alcoholism is the alcoholic's persistent return to alcohol in the face of overwhelming evidence that it is destroying his or her life.

There are some in our fellowship of Alcoholics Anonymous who have serious mental problems, but most of us joke about how "insane" or "crazy" or "goofy" we are or have been. When what we really are talking about is our emotional immaturity, our impulsiveness, our lack of self-discipline – our character defects if you will. Most of us would have a hard time describing many of our thoughts and actions as being insane. In fact, in some areas of life, we may exhibit a high degree of sanity.

However, there is something about the way we perceive the world around us that has always caused us a great deal of discomfort in simply living our lives.

Our general discomfort with living has much to do with the way we perceive the effects of alcohol. Our falling short of what is called "well-adjusted" is definitely a part of our makeup as an alcoholic. However, that alone does not separate us much from the general population. It is our physical as well as our mental response to alcohol that is INSANE, and that is what separates the alcoholic from the non-alcoholic.

There are two problems alcoholics have with alcohol: 1)the obsession of the mind, and 2) the compulsion of the body, an incomprehensible craving.

Somewhere along the line, early or late, we develop an obsession with the idea that alcohol eases our minds and solves our problems. Then, our physical response to alcohol manifests in what the "Big Book of Alcoholics Anonymous" calls an allergy. Our alcoholic bodies process the alcohol in a manner that causes us to crave more. The alcoholic insanity of our minds tells us that it is a good idea to drink to relieve our stress and to have fun. Once we start, our alcoholic bodies tell us we must drink more to satisfy the craving.

As every alcoholic should know, that is where the well-known cycle begins, and continues over and over again, leading to death, incarceration, or "wet brain" insanity. What Dr. Silkworth called the "phenomenon of craving," manifesting as an "allergy," is so overpowering that all else comes in second to our primary concern of getting the next drink, even life itself takes second place.

That, my friends, is the "insanity of alcholism."

It is only relieved and arrested by total abstinence, and as we have found, by the thorough application of the 12 Steps of AA in our lives and in all of our affairs to achieve a psychic change, a "spiritual awakening," leading to growth and maturity, and a firm grasp of the reality of life and the world about us.

A young man (with tears in his eyes) at his first AA meeting said:

"I'm here because I just want to live ...

that's it ... I just want to live."

It is as Simple as that!!!

Love and Peace,
Barefoot Bob H.

STEP 5.
The summit attained.
Jolly companions
A confirmed drunkard.

STEP 4.
Drunk
and
riotous.

STEP 6.
Poverty
and
Disease.

STEP 3.
A glass
too
much.

STEP 7.
Forsaken
by
Friends

STEP 2.
A glass to
keep the
cold out.

STEP 8.
Desperation
and
crime.

STEP 1.
A glass
With
a friend.

STEP 9.
Death
by
suicide.

19th Century Engraving of the common attitude toward drinkers at the time.

The Steps and Program

What They Are—What They Are Not

AA (the affectionate nickname for the fellowship of Alcoholics Anonymous) is something different. If you think you know what it is, it will disappoint you and you will go away looking for what you expected to find. You will miss what it is and, if you are an alcoholic of our type and moving along that doomed path, what it is may save your life.

People come to AA and try to tell themselves they already know what it is. When AA turns out to be something other than what they expected before they arrived, they miss the message and the hope, and go away disappointed.

Some people think AA is a church. It isn't. AA is a lousy church. We say that you have to have a power greater than yourself, which most of us call God, but we do not tell you what to believe. If you want church, go to church. That's where they do "church" right.

They think AA is therapy. AA is lousy therapy. If you want therapy, go to therapy. That's where they do "therapy" right. Many of us have used therapy as part of our program, but AA is not therapy.

They think AA is social services. Some AAs have been known to share cigarettes, rides, or have allowed a newcomer to sleep on the couch, but AA is lousy social services. Go to social services for that - they do it better.

The Preamble

"Alcoholics Anonymous is a fellowship of men and women who share their experience, strength and hope with each other that they may solve their common problem and help others to recover from alcoholism.

"The only requirement for membership is a desire to stop drinking. There are no dues or fees for AA membership; we are self-supporting through our own

contributions. AA is not allied with any sect, denomination, politics, organization or institution; does not wish to engage in any controversy; neither endorses nor opposes any causes. Our primary purpose is to stay sober and help other alcoholics to achieve sobriety."

The Big Book

The Big Book is the book "Alcoholics Anonymous," first published in 1939, written primarily by Bill Wilson and edited through discussion between the two AA groups (approximately 100 alcoholics) with additional input from family and various professionals. The book was written to carry the system of 12-Steps for Recovery - Recovery from the hopeless condition of alcoholism. It marked the first time a system was in place that could be worked if the instructions were followed. "Do the Work and you get the Result."

The Twelve Steps

The Twelve Steps are a set of principles, spiritual in nature ... Although based on the work outlined by the Oxford Group, a previous fellowship, the Steps were actually written down for the first time in 1938 during the writing of the Big Book.

The Program

The Program is the system of Recovery. Like all programs it is "a set of instructions to be followed in order." This means that jumping out of sequence makes it impossible to work the Program effectively. The Program is referred to a couple of times in the Big Book as "a design for living" that really works. It is based on the Twelve Steps, which are to be used as tools in our daily life

The Fellowship

The Fellowship is the collection of individuals, groups, and service structure that allows the regular meetings to exist and allows newcomers to find those meetings. The Fellowship is where we find the experience, strength, and hope of our members, whether in a discussion meeting, from the podium at a speakers meeting, or across two cups of coffee in a late-night diner.

The Literature

The Literature refers to those pieces of "conference approved" books, pamphlets, and multi-media presentations that have gone through the process of review and revision by the fellowship through the World Service Organization (WSO). The purpose of "conference approved" literature is to ensure that the content is a result of our shared experience in Recovery – not just an opinion from one person.

Conference approved literature includes:

Alcoholics Anonymous – The Big Book

Twelve Steps and Twelve Traditions – The 12 & 12

Dr. Bob and the Good Old Timers – AA History, the Akron viewpoint from Dr. Bob

Pass It On – AA History, the New York viewpoint from Bill W.

AA Comes of Age – AA organizational history starting with the 1955 World Service Conference.

Living Sober – Daily Guide for living the AA way.

Came to Believe – Exploration of 2nd and 3rd Step topics.

Language of the Heart – Bill Wilson's articles from the Grapevine

Experience, Strength & Hope – a collection of all of the individual stories of Recovery from all four editions of the Big Book

Daily Reflections – A book of reflections by AA members for AA members

Grapevine – AA's magazine

There are other "conference approved" books from WSO, plus several dozen pamphlets addressing individual topics of interest to those in Recovery.

The Twelve Traditions

The Twelve Traditions are a series of suggested guidelines to ensure the survival of AA and the independence of the individual and groups that compose AA. They are based on our first few decades of trial and error and do not hold the power of law over members or groups. They serve as guides based on our previous experience, strength, and hope as a Fellowship.

The Twelve Concepts

While the Steps and Traditions are commonly discussed in many meetings, there is a third document that is used in guiding the conduct of AA service boards or committees. The concepts are not a secret, but people usually do not encounter them until they have established their own Recovery for a couple of years and are ready to get involved with Service in a more structured setting.

The concepts are usually read at the beginning of meetings for local Intergroups, District Committees, Area Conferences and WSO functions.

More on the Steps

Alcoholics Anonymous is a Program3 of Action, and the Twelve Steps are the Actions that we have followed to attain and maintain Sobriety.

Working the Steps gives us the simple and direct actions necessary to help us from picking up a drink or any other mind-altering substance outside of direct medical supervision.

Working the Steps helps us find the way to deal with the guilt, shame, remorse, and fear that arises when we have stopped medicating ourselves with alcohol (and often with other substances and behaviors).

Working the Steps helps us learn to face and heal our pasts giving us time in the present to enjoy our lives, to become positive contributing members of our families and communities, and to live without the Fear that formerly drove our lives.

Working these Steps leads us to a Spiritual Awakening.

It is not required that the desire for Sobriety exists for us to begin working the Steps. That can come later.

How could you want Sobriety? How can you want something that was not part of your life before? How many people do you party with who were sober? If you had a period of sobriety from one of the many methods available but went

---

3 A Program is "A set of instructions, to be followed in order." This is true of computer programs, football programs, band programs, etc.

back to drinking, how much of your experience was a real commitment to being Sober?

You do not have to want Sobriety to begin. You only need to know Step Zero. At this point it is only necessary that you know your life cannot continue on as it has. You do not need to know the new way yet, but only be convinced that the old way must stop, no matter what!

At this point most alcoholics begin a long struggle to stop on their own – and to stay stopped. In the Big Book this is well described in the chapter "More About Alcoholism":

> *"Here are some of the methods we have tried:*
>
> *"Drinking beer only, limiting the number of drinks, never drinking alone, never drinking in the morning, drinking only at home, never having it in the house, never drinking during business hours, drinking only at parties, switching from scotch to brandy, drinking only natural wines, agreeing to resign if ever drunk on the job, taking a trip, not taking a trip, swearing off forever (with and without a solemn oath), taking more physical exercise, reading inspirational books, going to health farms and sanitariums, accepting voluntary commitment to asylums; we could increase the list ad infinitum."*
>
> *- Page 31, Alcoholics Anonymous*

Since the time when that was written, we have added professional treatment centers, drugs to keep you "sober," therapies, workshops, books, classes, tapes, CDs, websites, and support groups — along with those who oppose one or more of these approaches.

The program of Alcoholics Anonymous addresses these other methods in two of its traditions:

> *Tradition Nine: AA, as such, ought never be organized; but we may create service boards or committees directly responsible to those they serve.*
>
> *Tradition Ten: Alcoholics Anonymous has no opinion on outside issues; hence the AA name ought never be drawn into public controversy.*

Throughout AA literature they acknowledge that the Twelve Steps are not the only way to achieve and maintain Sobriety. For some people those other techniques have worked.

Some problem drinkers have simply set their minds to achieve Sobriety, fought the battle alone, and won. Others have gone back to church, stopped drinking, and lived new, sober, and successful lives. Some have gone to therapy, found sobriety, and lived healthy, successful lives.

But people in AA know the other side of that reality — we have seen people who have come, achieved success to the point of achieving years of Recovery, only to allow their old ways of thinking drag them back down to insanity, institutions, and death.

And death is not the worst thing that can happen when someone goes back to drinking.

When Step Zero has been achieved, years of struggle can end in disaster.

At that point, you have the choice to try another method, or (if you feel your problem and your life is as we describe it, you may then choose to join us and work the Steps.

Why Work the Steps?

"Working the Steps" means following the directions given in the book Alcoholics Anonymous, which presented the Steps that are now used by more than sixty Twelve Step fellowships.

Step One is difficult. It is a merciless admission that goes against everything an alcoholic has believed about his or her mastery of life.

Many people fight admitting that they are in the grip of a disease and mental compulsion that they cannot consciously master. Despite all evidence they have before them, the true alcoholic believes that with more strength, with more will, with more determination, they will one day be able to control their drinking and return to drinking without the problems and consequences.

"Many pursue this delusion to the gates of insanity or death!"   *Page 30*

Until they admit to their innermost selves that if they take a single drink, they cannot guarantee how long they will drink, how much they will drink, what they will do while drunk, or where they will be when they wake up.

"Lack of power, that is our dilemma."   *Page 45*

The powerless of this dilemma makes Step One require a great deal of work, made more difficult by the fact that we do not have the authority to declare any man or woman to be an alcoholic.

> *"We do not like to pronounce any individual as alcoholic, but you can quickly diagnose yourself, step over to the nearest barroom and try some controlled drinking. Try to drink and stop abruptly. Try it more than once. It will not take long for you to decide, if you are honest with yourself about it. It may be worth a bad case of jitters if you get a full knowledge of your condition."*

Page 31

The First Step requires something simple yet very difficult — the new man or woman must determine for himself or herself if the conditions of Step One are true. This means you must become honest enough to admit that these conditions are already true.

Step Zero

For most of us, Step Zero has been taken by screaming something like: "This must STOP!"

Step Zero is that point where you understand that your Problem, as shown through excessive drinking and/or drugging, has got to stop. This is not a Step from the Big Book, but everyone we have encountered who has succeeded with finding and maintaining Sobriety reports that they reached this point.

Throughout AA literature they acknowledge that the Twelve Steps are not the only way to achieve and maintain Sobriety. For some people those other techniques have worked.

Some problem drinkers have simply set their minds to Sobriety, fought the battle alone, and won. Others have gone back to church, stopped drinking, and lived new, sober, and successful lives. Some have gone to therapy, found sobriety, and lived healthy, successful lives.

But people in AA know the other side of that reality — we have seen people who have come, achieved success to the point of taking years of Recovery, only to allow their old ways of thinking drag them back down to insanity, institutions, and death.

And death is not the worst thing that can happen when anyone goes back to drinking.

When Step Zero has been achieved, years of struggle can end in disaster.

Have you reached Step Zero?

Have you tried everything within your power to get sober and to stay sober?

Is your life, with or without alcohol, unmanageable? This means the results of your best thoughts, plans, efforts, and actions have been tried and the results have been completely unmanageable by you.

We do know that people who find AA (and not everyone knows about Alcoholics Anonymous) who stay and who actually do The Work of the Twelve Steps, do recover.

Even if they don't believe it will work.

Even if they don't like it.

Even if they don't understand it.

Even if they are uncomfortable doing The Work.

Even if they are not religious.

Even if they don't find the spirituality others would approve of.

Even if they use the AA Group itself as their Higher Power.

Even if they suffer great reversals in health, love, and finances.

Even if they find great success in health, love, and finances.

Even if they have no idea of what a "spiritual life" might be.

Even if they lived what they thought was a deeply "spiritual life" but returned to drinking and the dark despair that comes with relapse.

Even if they believe there is no hope.

The Twelve Steps do not require that you believe Recovery is even possible when you come through the door.

You only need to know that you cannot continue the way of life you have led before.

You might come in because of a threat from a spouse, or a judge, or a doctor, or an employer.

It doesn't matter.

Show up. Come to see if what we have can help you. Come to see if you are really an alcoholic — or not.

If you decide you are an alcoholic and have seen people with the kind of Recovery you would like to have, do the Steps.

Do The Work, even if you don't think it will work for you. The Twelve Steps work.

Period.

sponsormagazine.info

Issues Other Than Alcohol

A Short History of Drug Abuse

For most of US History, alcohol has been legal. In some communities, and briefly on the national level, it was made illegal, but that never resulted in a lack of alcohol.

From the beginnings of the drug trade in the 19th Century, drugs were not regulated, forbidden, or illegal. They were looked down upon, like alcohol, and identified their own class of addicts as alcohol attracted its alcoholics.

It was the use and abuse of alcohol and drugs that identified the problem they created.

While alcohol and drugs were legal, both were highly profitable industries that defended themselves from legislation. Prohibition drove the problem of alcohol into criminal hands. Alcohol became more profitable when controlled by the underworld. Drugs too went from legal industries to criminalization, and profiteering by the underworld, and some of the newer drugs were created for legitimate reasons, but found their way into underworld channels.

The first pain killer was alcohol and it remained the only option for many lifetimes. When morphine entered the country, it was a hit for medical therapies and was highly addictive. During the Civil War soldiers of the North and South became so hooked on morphine, it was identified as "The Soldier's Disease."

In the magazines of the day, ads could be found that offered the cure for Alcoholism, the cure for Morphine addiction, (the cure for morphine addiction was…heroin). There were advertisements for brewery equipment, needles, and mail order drug sales, often on the same page.

Cocaine was introduced in the south and on plantations in Latin America, to get slaves to work faster – and was accompanied with a series of drug laws that can only be described as racist.

Public outcry demanded that all drugs be banned, but the lobbies for two of the drugs were too strong to permit such legislation. Those two drugs are still in use today: nicotine and caffeine.

By the 1930s, everything except nicotine and caffeine became underworld commodities, and moonshiners continued to produce alcoholic beverages after prohibition when the taxes were felt to be unfair.

After World War II, a whole new galaxy of drugs began to appear, only to be banned one at a time in later legislation, either locally or federally. The use of tranquilizers, diet pills, recreational formulations, hallucinogens, and "designer drugs" began and continues to rise to this day.

12-Step programs make it clear that it is not the substance that creates the alcoholic or the addict.

"Therefore, the main problem of the alcoholic centers in his mind, rather than in his body..."
                                                                                    Page 22

Exploration of this statement in relation to the changes in our society, in medicine and psychiatry, since the days when the Big Book was written, brings new questions related to prescriptions and mental health.

A Short History of Mental Illness

Like alcoholism and drug addiction, there is nothing new about Mental Illness except for the name.

For centuries, people with a wide array of problems that now come under the umbrella of "mental illness" were known under other names. They were "mad," "inverted," "selfish," or (most unfortunately) "demon possessed."

Untreated and without hope, these people were shunned or isolated, at best. Professional remedies consisted of exile, expulsion, imprisonment, confinement, experimentation, and attempts to heal the coditions with methods we now call torture, or even sanctioned murder.

Treatment models began to appear in the 19th Century and continue to evolve. For example the "belladonna" treatment for alcoholics, subjected sufferers to an array of revolutionary treatments with limited success, if any at all. Water treatments, electric shock, "magnetic" treatment, lights, salves, aromas, symbols, diets, restraints, magnets, radio waves, radiation, and bizarre concoctions passed into and out of favor.

The evolution of psychiatry as "the talking cure" seemed successful for the depressed, neurotic, or those driven into "crazy" behaviors as a response to events in their lives, but not until the latter part of the 20th Century did a pharmacological component enter the treatment.

Certain conditions, it appeared, were the result of actual chemical imbalances in the body of the afflicted. Lithium salts produce positive results in manic-depressives (now called bi-polar), but other drugs were developed that produced varying degrees of success in the patients identified as mentally or emotionally ill.

While a good argument can be made that the professional community began prescribing these drugs to quiet a patient's symptoms (and complaints) without affecting real change, others report that the judicious use of psychologically prescribed drugs could elevate the psychotic to the point where they could enjoy the same substance or behavior free life as any other candidate for membership in AA.

If they had the desire to stop drinking (which assumes they had experienced a problem with alcohol) they could get sober and work the Steps as equals.

"The capacity to be honest," which had been impossible to produce before, was appearing in men and women who would have previously been considered unreachable.

Individuals in AA, who have no training in medical or psychiatric matters, who would never presume to prescribe for polio, toothache, cancer, or other medical problems, sometimes feel fully qualified to pronouce judgement on anyone in treatment. We have heard many stories of people in treatment for mental illness with a grumble of "you're not really sober if you take that dope from the doctor." Time and again, newcomers who want to be 'good AAs' have gone off their medications based on such advice, had psychotic breaks and if they were lucky enough to make it back to sobriety, were subjected to the same judgement by amateurs who feel qualified to speak despite their complete ignorance of the medical realities for that person.

Someone who has no training or degree may drive a newcomer away with their judgements. This person is simply indulging in his or her own inflated Ego. If they are not a psychiatrist, they have an 'opinion' - which costs nothing and may not be correct for this newcomer.

Again -

"Therefore, the main problem of the alcoholic centers in his mind, rather than in his body..."   *Page 22*

Necessary Medications

In the beginning of Chapter Five, the Big Book refers to those

"... who suffer from grave emotional and mental disorders, but many of them do recover if they have the capacity to be honest."

In the progress of psychiatry, pharmacology, and various therapies, those with the grave emotional and mental disorders of Bill W.'s day can be elevated to the same starting point as any other alcoholic through judicious use of appropriate medications. For decades, individual members of AA have demonized anyone in such circumstances with the taunt, "if you're taking pills, you aren't really sober."

Over the years, unknown numbers of alcoholics, really wanted to be sober, have listened to the reprimand, thrown away their prescribed medications, and were quickly lost in drunkenness or various forms of social and literal suicide.

One member in a local fellowship who picked up a 20-year chip after almost 20 years of trying to get one year of sobriety, told the gathering at his Home Group: "I listened to people who told me that if I didn't stop using my meds, I wasn't sober, and I wanted to be sober more than anything. So I threw away my meds and wound up psychotic, drunk, and in jail or a hospital – or both. Without my meds, I cannot get to the starting point of being honest."

Guidelines for Prescriptions

Over the years, a few guidelines have evolved regarding how to deal with the prescriptions required by those in medical treatment for mental or emotional problems. These guidelines may or may not be acceptable to people within Alcoholics Anonymous.

1. *The patient does not choose the substance.*

2. *The patient does not choose the amount.*

3. *The prescription must be written by a doctor who has seen the patient and knows the specifics of his/her case.*

4. *The patient describes to the doctor his/her condition, sobriety needs, and concerns regarding prescriptions.*

5. *The patient always asks if he/she can take less than the prescribed amount. (Never more.)*

6. *Having expressed those concerns with the doctor, the patient takes the prescription as prescribed.*

7. *Taking one milligram (1 mg) over the prescribed dosage is using and the sobriety date must change.*

Patients may want a second opinion on their treatment, which should be discussed with his/her Sponsor, before changing physicians. The Sponsor can be of no use if the person attempting to find lasting sobriety is not open and honest with that Sponsor.

Over the years a series of guidelines have evolved to guide a sober member's relationship to prescriptions that are judged necessary to maintaining Recovery, specifically realated to chemical imbalances related to mental health:

Everyone in AA has opinions, but it is unfair to risk another's sobriety or life based on mere opinion.

Identification in Meetings

The Third Tradition states the only qualification for membership is that a person attending must have "the desire to stop drinking," but not to the exclusion of all other Recovery needs.

One member expressed the idea best with a simple statement: "I have other substances in my story, but in an AA meeting, I do not share my war story from those substances. I share my Recovery. I never want to be responsible for a newcomer leaving their first AA meeting thinking 'I don't belong in AA, I never used _____.'"

That does not mean that one is supposed to be a 'pure' alcoholic, which almost seems to be a contradiction in terms.

The strict identifcation of your own needs in Recovery does come into play with "closed meetings". "Open" meetings may be attended by anyone, whether they qualify as an alcoholic or not. "Closed" meetings require that ONLY people who qualifiy as an alcoholic may attend.

By tradition, every AA meeting has the right to set up their meeting as they see fit and some meetings are strict about being an alcoholic.

But it has never been said that if you are an alcoholic, you must be 'just' an alcoholic.

In his story, Bill W. writes of the use of heavy sedatives, Dr. Bob was given a "goofball" on the morning of his first day of sobriety, and several authors whose stories have appeared in the back of the four editions of the Big Book have shared that drugs have also played a part in their stories, and their personal recoveries.

Dozens of other 12-Steps programs began to appear as we recognized that abusers of other substances and behaviors could benefit from this program of vigorous action and spiritual awakening. Al-Anon became an official new program, closely followed by Narcotics Anonymous (NA).

When one identifies with Alcoholics Anonymous, it does not mean that Recovery is not needed for the abuse of other substances and/or behaviors. Many of us need to keep in mind several definitions of 'sobriety' as we go about our daily lives.

We have watched people claim they are 'still sober' who have stopped drinking, but continued to use various narcotics outside of a qualified doctor's care.

Qualification in Meetings

The intent of making members "qualify" in meetings (to identify as an alcoholic, or an addict, or other identifications for other Programs) is to provide a common focus. We form a fellowship of people attending the meeting, particularly in a "closed" meeting, who share the same alcoholic reality – that no newcomer leaves their first meeting hearing about the well-established or most recent trends in drug abuse and psychiatric problems, and then tells him or herself, "I do not belong in Alcoholics Anonymous. I didn't use drugs like that. I didn't do those things."

In the many other 12-Step fellowships, there is a similar 'primary purpose' of identifying one's own qualification for belonging which provides clarity of those meetings. But qualification is an important part of the First Step by admitting that we are an alcoholic (or the qualifier for the other fellowship you are attending).

admit [ad-mit] verb (used with object), admitted, admitting.

> *1. to allow to enter; grant or afford entrance to: to admit a student to college.*
>
> *2. to give right or means of entrance to: This ticket admits two people.*
>
> *3. to permit to exercise a certain function or privilege: admitted to the bar.*
>
> *4. to allow or concede as valid: to admit the force of an argument.*
>
> *Synonym - receive. 6. own, avow. See "acknowledge."*

In the beginning, newcomers are easily thrown off focus by outside issues, including drugs. The alcoholic, who is also a drug addict or addicted to some other substance or behavior, needs to respect the AA Newcomer who does not have these other addictions. Their story may include drugs, but in meetings we are supposed to share our struggle in Recovery rather than reinforce our wretched past.

The Third Tradition does not require that a member identify himself or herself in any way; that identification is a local custom. In most areas, they identify themselves by name and some way of saying that they are alcoholic. In other areas, they simply say their name and omit any identification.

This does not mean a member may not suffer additional problems, addressed by active participation in other fellowships – it is simply a clarification of their participation in that meeting's singleness of purpose.

After the end of World War II, when the Second Edition of our Big Book was prepared, the world had changed. Illegal drugs and the abuse of prescription drugs had flourished as never before in history. Designer drugs appeared to open new markets or escape existing laws. However, the intent remains the same, the compulsion remains the same, and (we hope) the dedication to the Twelve Steps and Recovery remains the same.

Bill Wilson wrote several times that the real goal of AA was emotional sobriety, the ability to deal with life on life's terms without mind altering drugs. It was his intent, as he reportedly said several times, to allow the alcoholic to attain a level of maturity and responsibility to permit them to function in the world exactly as a non-alcoholic, healthy person. People would not need to consider their alcoholic past in their dealings. The recovering alcoholic was to be held to the same standard as a non-alcoholic – through the Steps they would be elevated to common expectation of any healthy, functioning member of society.

The member who claims "sobriety," but still indulges in drugs, crime, abusive behavior or who judges other people's behavior is unclear of what we mean by "sobriety." As always, a dictionary definition is a good place to begin:

so·bri·e·ty [suh-brahy-i-tee, soh-] –noun
 1. *the state or quality of being sober.*
 2. *temperance or moderation, especially, (but not only) in the use of alcoholic beverages.*
 3. *seriousness, gravity, or solemnity: an event marked by sobriety.*

If the problem "centers primarily in the alcoholics mind" and we have identified "the" result of these Steps to be a Spiritual Awakening, then the repair of the problem and monitoring the result becomes our functioning definition of "sober."

In each program, we celebrate the time free from the substance or behavior that got us into the door.

When attending a closed AA meeting, we respect that door when asked to identify ourselves. We may qualify for membership in other 12-Step programs, but within AA, we are a recovering "alcoholic."

A list of other 12-Step programs, which may be needed in addition to AA, is provided at the end of this book.

What Does "Going to Any Lengths" Mean?

I have been asked this question again and again. I've also brought this subject up to just about every person I have ever worked with through the Steps. What follows is generally my response, taken from two sources. The only thing that I would want to add to this is living the Oxford Group's Four Absolutes of Honesty, Unselfishness, Purity, and Love (which can be found in their reverse negative form in the Big Book at the Fourth Step, Tenth Step, and Eleventh Step). – Barefoot Bob

The following Ten Points are a summary of the lifesaving directions given in the "How It Works" section of Chapter Five of the book Alcoholics Anonymous. These ten points have always been a failsafe guide for people who want to practice the Twelve Steps and they are to be considered as part of your daily Program.

– *Completely give yourself to this simple Program.*

– *Practice rigorous honesty.*

– *Be willing to go to any lengths to recover.*

– *Be fearless and thorough in your practice of the principles.*

– *Realize that there is no easier, softer way.*

– *Let go of your old ideas absolutely.*

– *Recognize that half measures will not work.*

– *Ask God's protection and care with complete abandon.*

– *Be willing to grow along spiritual lines.*

– *Accept the following pertinent ideas as proved by AA experience:*

   a) that you cannot manage your own life;

b) that probably no human power can restore you to sanity;

c) that God can and will if sought.

The following is taken from parts of Chapter One "Bill's Story" in the Big Book:

Page 8 (First Step)

No words can tell of the loneliness and despair I found in that bitter morass of self-pity. Quicksand stretched around me in all directions. I had met my match. I had been overwhelmed. Alcohol was my master.

Page 12 (Second Step)

My friend suggested what then seemed a novel idea. He said, "Why don't you choose your own conception of God?"

That statement hit me hard. It melted the icy intellectual mountain in whose shadow I had lived and shivered many years. I stood in the sunlight at last.

It was only a matter of being willing to believe in a Power greater than myself. Nothing more was required of me to make my beginning. I saw that growth could start from that point. Upon a foundation of complete willingness I might build what I saw in my friend. Would I have it? Of course I would!

Thus was I convinced that God is concerned with us humans when we want Him enough. At long last I saw, I felt, I believed. Scales of pride and prejudice fell from my eyes. A new world came into view.

PAGES 13–16 (Steps 3 through 12)

There I humbly offered myself to God, as I then I understood Him, to do with me as He would. I placed myself unreservedly under His care and direction. I admitted for the first time that of myself I was nothing; that without Him I was lost. I ruthlessly faced my sins and became willing to have my new-found Friend take them away, root and branch. I have not had a drink since.

My schoolmate visited me, and I fully acquainted him with my problems and deficiencies. We made a list of people I had hurt or toward whom I felt resentment. I expressed my entire willingness to approach these individuals, admitting my wrong. Never was I to be critical of them. I was to right all such matters to the utmost of my ability.

I was to test my thinking by the new God-consciousness within. Common sense would thus become uncommon sense. I was to sit quietly when in doubt, asking only for direction and strength to meet my problems as He would have me. Never was I to pray for myself, except as my requests bore on my usefulness to others. Then only might I expect to receive. But that would be in great measure.

My friend promised when these things were done I would enter upon a new relationship with my Creator; that I would have the elements of a way of living which answered all my problems. Belief in the power of God, plus enough willingness, honesty and Humility to establish and maintain the new order of things, were the essential requirements.

Simple, but not easy; a price had to be paid. It meant destruction of self-centeredness. I must turn in all things to the Father of Light who presides over us all.

While I lay in the hospital the thought came that there were thousands of hopeless alcoholics who might be glad to have what had been so freely given me. Perhaps I could help some of them. They in turn might work with others.

My friend had emphasized the absolute necessity of demonstrating these principles in all my affairs. Particularly was it imperative to work with others as he had worked with me. Faith without works was dead, he said. And how appallingly true for the alcoholic! For if an alcoholic failed to perfect and enlarge his spiritual life through work and self-sacrifice for others, he could not survive the certain trials and low spots ahead. If he did not work, he would surely drink again, and if he drank, he would surely die. Then faith would be dead indeed. With us it is just like that.

My wife and I abandoned ourselves with enthusiasm to the idea of helping other alcoholics to find a solution to their problems. It was fortunate, for my old business associates remained skeptical for a year and a half, during which I found little work. I was not too well at the time, and was plagued by waves of self-pity and resentment. This sometimes nearly drove me back to drink, but I soon found that when all other measures failed, work with another alcoholic would save the day. Many times I have gone to my old hospital in despair. On talking to a man there, I would be amazingly lifted up and set on my feet. It is a design for living that works in rough going.

We commenced to make many fast friends and a fellowship has grown up among us of which it is a wonderful thing to feel a part. The joy of living we really have, even under pressure and difficulty. I have seen hundreds of families set their feet in the path that really goes somewhere; have seen the most impossible domestic situations righted; feuds and bitterness of all sorts wiped out. I have seen men come out of asylums and resume a vital place in the lives of their families and communities. Business and professional men have regained their standing. There is scarcely any form of trouble and misery which has not been overcome among us. In one western city and its environs there are one thousand of us and our families. We meet frequently so that newcomers may find the fellowship they seek. At these informal gatherings one may often see from 50 to 200 persons. We are growing in numbers and power.

There is, however, a vast amount of fun about it all. I suppose some would be shocked at our seeming worldliness and levity. But just underneath there is deadly earnestness. Faith has to work twenty-four hours a day in and through us, or we perish.

Most of us feel we need look no further for Utopia. We have it with us right here and now. Each day my friend's simple talk in our kitchen multiplies itself in a widening circle of peace on earth and good will to men.

– Bill Wilson, 1954

Understanding Anonymity

AA Co-Founder - Dr. "Bob" Smith

So many in Alcoholics Anonymous, both old-timers and newcomers alike, do not have an understanding of the 11th and 12th Traditions relating to Anonymity; the relationship of Anonymity to the Spiritual Ideals contained in the 12 Steps of AA; or the principles and ideals of Trust, Honesty, Hope, Faith, Courage, Integrity, Willingness, Humility, Brotherly Love, Justice, Perseverance, Spirituality, and Service to One Another.

To the extent that my Sponsors explained it to me, and from what I have read from the history of AA, I will try to put this vital issue into some kind of proper perspective.

These selections from AA literature clarify the 11th Tradition and its intent.

In some sections of AA, anonymity is carried to the point of real absurdity. Members are on such a poor basis of communication that they don't even know each other's last names or where each lives. *As Bill Sees It, page 241*

Dr. Bob said there were two ways to break the Anonymity Tradition:

(1) by giving your name at the public level of press or radio;

(2) by being so anonymous that you can't be reached by other drunks.

Dr. Bob and the Good Old Timers
Page 264

The 11th Tradition states, in the short form, "Eleven – Our public relations policy is based on attraction rather than promotion; we need always maintain personal anonymity at the level of press, radio and films." (And we might also add TV at this level for further restriction.)

The 12th Tradition states, in the short form, "Twelve – Anonymity is the spiritual foundation of all our traditions, ever reminding us to place principles before personalities." (Even before my own personality.)

Dr. Bob stated that within the group, every member should know the first name, last name, address and phone number of all the members in the group. If these are not known, then we as a group are operating above the level of anonymity intended – We are not able to be of Service to One Another in time of need.

Did you ever try to look up someone in the phone book without knowing their last name? Or did you ever go into a hospital or jail to try to visit or carry a meeting to a sick or incarcerated member, and stand there with your mouth hanging open, when asked, "What is their name?"

"Sorry about that but we have our policies and procedures Sorry we can't help you."

Let us see what the long form of the 11th and 12th Traditions say about understanding Anonymity and the Principles we ought to live by.

11. *– Our relations with the general public should be characterized by personal anonymity. We think A. A. ought to avoid sensational advertising. Our names and pictures as AA members ought not be broadcast, filmed or publicly printed. Our public relations should be guided by the principle of attraction rather than promotion. There is never need to praise ourselves. We feel it better to let our friends recommend us.*

12. *– And finally, we of Alcoholics Anonymous believe that the principle of anonymity has an immense spiritual significance. It reminds us that we are to place principles before personalities; that we are actually to practice a genuine*

Humility. This to the end that our great blessings may never spoil us; that we shall forever live in thankful contemplation of Him who presides over us all.

Ahh yes. We are to be anonymous relative to the "General Public," as members of Alcoholics Anonymous. We ought not be publicly identified as members of Alcoholics Anonymous in the press, on the radio, or in films, videos, and TV, or any media which is disseminated to the General Public. It is a Humility thing; we have no need to say "How great we are!" We think that in this respect the Humility of AA will attract more suffering alcoholics to the program than any amount of advertising or promotion. It is a matter of Trust.

"Since our Tradition on anonymity designates the exact level where the line should be drawn, it must be obvious to everyone who can read and understand the English language that to maintain anonymity at any other level is definitely a violation of this Tradition. The AA who hides his identity from his fellow AA by using only a given name violates the Tradition just as much as the AA who permits his name to appear in the press in connection with matters pertaining to AA.

"The former is maintaining his anonymity ABOVE the level of press, radio, and films, and the latter is maintaining his anonymity BELOW the level of press, radio, and films - whereas the Tradition states that we should maintain our anonymity AT the level of press, radio, and films."   Dr. Bob's comment

Our Egos are trying to get attention. We lose our Humility and spoil the great blessing we have been given. The truth is that any one of us may fail to stay sober as a result of our Ego and failure to practice the steps in all our affairs. We should be ever mindful that no action we take as individual members should affect AA as a whole. Our very lives depend upon the survival of AA and our Unity. Without AA, all we have left is drunkenness and the slide into oblivion.

The principle of Trust is first and foremost, the foundation of all spiritual principles and ideals. We should never break another member's anonymity to anyone outside the AA group. To do so would break Trust, and without Trust, all the other principles are Impossible.

Has any alcoholic ever been able to be Honest, or practice any of the other principles and ideals, with something or someone he didn't trust?

Of course not.

We may break our own anonymity in the process of trying to help another, but we must never break the anonymity of another.

Looking at the First Three Steps

Having covered the information in pages xxiii through page 63 of the Big Book, Alcoholics Anonymous, we asked ourselves the following questions when taking the first three Steps.

First Step
We admitted we were powerless over alcohol that our lives had become unmanageable.

If, when I honestly want to, can I quit entirely (because of the mental obsession), or if when drinking, do I have little control over the amount I take (because of the physical allergy)?

If you've answered "no" to the first part and "yes" to the second, you're probably alcoholic. If that be the case, you may be suffering from an illness which only a spiritual experience will conquer. (page 30)

Drunk or sober (suffering from "untreated alcoholism"), do I have trouble with personal relationships? Can I control my emotional natures? Am I a prey to misery and depression? Can I make a living (a happy and contented life)? Do I have a feeling of uselessness? Am I full of fear? Am I unhappy? Do I find that I can't seem to be of real help to other people? (page 52)

Do I fully concede to my innermost self that I am alcoholic? (page 44)

Second Step
Came to believe that a Power greater than ourselves could restore us to sanity.

Do I now believe, or am I even willing to believe, that there is a Power greater than myself? (page 47)

Do I have a conception of that Power which makes sense to me? (page 46)

When we became alcoholics, crushed by a self-imposed crisis we could not postpone or evade, we had to fearlessly face the proposition that either God is everything or else He is nothing. God either is or He isn't. What is my choice to be? (page 53)

Because so much of the Program revolves around your Spiritual Life, we have created a whole section devoted the the Question of Spirit.

Third Step
Made a decision to turn our will and our lives over to the care of God as we understood Him.

Third Step Decision

> *"Next, we decided that hereafter in this drama of life, God was going to be our Director. He is the Principal; we are His agents. He is the Father, and we are His children."* Page 62

To affirm this decision, we say the Third Step Prayer:

> *"God, I offer myself to Thee—to build with me and to do with me as Thou wilt. Relieve me of the bondage of self, that I may better do Thy will. Take away my difficulties, that victory over them may bear witness to those I would help of Thy Power, Thy Love, and Thy Way of life. May I do Thy will always!"* Page 63

"Third Step Prayer" from the Big Book is a suggestion. Some people with serious sobriety, serious clean time, may have presented it to you as a ritual.

The Prayer they present is not a magic do for you because you said the magic words.

You must say the Prayer, but in your own words. Remember, in the following paragraph the book says:

> *"The wording was, of course, quite optional so long as we expressed the idea, voicing it without reservation. This was only a beginning, though if honestly and humbly made, an effect, sometimes a very great one, was felt at once."* Page 63

Now, with all of this said, we need to get to the meat of the Third Step. As you may have heard "making a decision" means nothing until it is followed with the commitment to take actions.

If, however, you find it hard to relate to the words as written in the Big Book, if you do not use "Thee" and "Thine" as part of your normal language, you can take the Prayer and restate it in your own words so that you can say a heartfelt Prayer of surrender and willingness to proceed with your Recovery.

In the Third Step we decided to turn our thoughts and actions over to the care of God. The way we carry out that decision is by taking the actions of Steps 4 through 9. We found in Chapter 4, "We Agnostics," that God dwells deep down within us. We've been blocked from God's Power because of our own self-will – our character defects and shortcomings (i.e. selfishness, dishonesty, resentment, fear, guilt, shame, remorse, anger, etc.). The first step of getting us "unblocked" is Fourth Step: Made a searching and fearless moral Inventory of ourselves.

A COMPLETE GUIDE TO WORKING THE STEPS IS FOUND IN THE SECTION "STEPS AND TRADITIONS", LATER IN THIS BOOK

Recovery Reader, Second Edition

Spirituality

"Having had a spiritual awakening as the result of these Steps..."

Twelfth Step

The Spiritual Awakening is the only result of the Twelve Step program of Recovery. The restoration of health, happiness, belonging, character, and material possessions are reflections of our acceptance of this life-changing gift.

This is the most personal aspect of Recovery. Each member of Recovery has a slightly different personal way of describing it, living it, and sharing it, but they all reflect "THE Result."

These articles are offered to help achieve and sustain this personal experience and surrender to our Spiritual way of life.

God As You Understand God

Sponsormagazine.ino

Religion and Alcoholism

Every culture has had something to say about alcoholism. For Christians and Jews, it can be found in the Old Testament, Proverbs 23:29-35, they say:

29) Who hath woe? Who hath sorrow? Who hath contentions? Who hath babbling? Who hath wounds without cause? Who hath redness of eyes?

30) They that tarry long at the wine; they that go to seek mixed wine.

31) Look not thou upon the wine when it is red, when it giveth his color in the cup, when it moveth itself aright.

32) At the last it biteth like a serpent, and stingeth like an adder.

33) Thine eyes shall behold strange women, and thine heart shall utter perverse things.

34) Yea, thou shalt be as he that lieth down in the midst of the sea, or as he that lieth upon the top of a mast.

35) They have stricken me, shalt thou say, and I was not sick; they have beaten me, and I felt it not; when shall I awake? I will seek it yet again.

In Buddhism there are the Five Precepts by which you are supposed to live:
- Avoid Killing,
- Avoid Lying,
- Avoid Stealing,
- Avoid Sexual Misconduct, and
- Avoid Intoxication

Islam teaches that believers are to abstain from alcohol in all its forms. (The word "alcohol" is from Arabic.)

The Native American/First Nations have borne the hardest hit from alcoholism from the very beginning. While Central and South American pre-

Columbian civilizations had alcohol in various forms, the North American tribes did not have long term exposure to alcohol and its effects.

The first guides to Recovery in this country came with a spiritual way of life advocated by tribes in the early 18th Century. But even with this early start, one out of every six deaths on Reservations and one in every ten deaths in Native communities is attributed directly to alcohol or alcoholism4.

The earliest efforts at a spiritual approach to freedom from alcoholism in the New World was in the early 17th Century through Native American abstinent societies. Native Americans from North America did not have exposure prior to it being brought by Europeans, and they had no defense against alcoholism. In 2008 Federal Centers for Disease Control and Prevention reported 11.1% of deaths due to alcoholism in the Native American Community, versus 3.3% among the non-Native population.

Indigenous people from South and Central America did brew and use alcohol and had some established ability to deal with alcohol when it was introduced from colonial forces, but they also have a disproportionate number of deaths and health issues related to alcohol.

The Twelve Step programs made a breakthrough from the Protestant Christian-only beginnings by adopting "God as you understand God." Members with long term sobriety will tell you that they have seen the result of the Twelve Steps benefit anyone willing to make the surrender of Ego, which Recovery requires. The results have been seen in many schools of Christianity (Catholic, Orthodox. Protestant, Evangelical, etc.), Jews, Moslems, Hindus, Buddhists, Tribal members, Atheists and more.

It even works for the most strident anti-theist, if that person is willing to make the surrender of Ego by following the directions given in the book. Many people report that all they needed to begin was the use of the fellowship as a "power greater than themself" and Good Orderly Direction (or the collective consciousness of the geshtalt in the Group of Drunks).

There is no reason the Program cannot work for you.

---

4 http://www.ibtimes.com/native-americans-tragedy-alcoholism-214046

Stop Playing God

Sometimes at an AA meeting you will hear "Let something with the ability to do what you cannot do be your Higher Power."

In my case, I was told, "That tree out there can stand in one place for sixty years. You can't do that. Make that tree your Higher Power."

I did not take well to that. "What the hell good will it do to have a tree as my Higher Power?" I asked, playing right into his hands.

He grinned. He grinned that big, old, evil AA Sponsor grin and said, "That way we git the whole idea of a 'Higher Power' out of the hands of the asshole who has had it so far!"

And then I realized he meant me!

It was not their plan to have me make a tree, or a lightbulb, or a doorknob, my higher power. It was for me to give up the idea that "I" could be my own Higher Power.

You may be tempted to make your significant other your Higher Power. Or your financial security may feel like your Higher Power.

I was told I had to let go of the illusion I was a Higher Power.

"But I never thought I was God," the newcomer will protest.

Really?

Every time you decided how things should have been, or played the "If Only..." game to have things work out the way you wanted them to be, you were pushing God out in favor of your desire and judgement.

"If only he hadn't found out..."

"If only she didn't get pregnant..."

"If only my parents had more money..."

"If only that cop hadn't been there..."

Sound familiar?

We had to give up playing God – it didn't work.

Prof. Ernie Kurtz wrote the first significant work on AA History and called the book "Not God." It was a simple statement of who they were in the beginning. The ones who started Alcoholics Anonymous were "Not God."

We have to learn that we aren't either.

Approaches to a Higher Power

Some people have a serious problem with religion or what has previously been presented to them as "God."

They stress that the newcomer must first admit they cannot continue the way they have been going. They say that most of us have "The Drunk's Prayer," regardless of whatever faith they might express. it is commonly repeated as:

"God, I can't live like this. Please help me."

The key difference between AA and the other religious approaches to Recovery was that AA said the alcoholic, the addict and the people qualifying for other Twelve Step programs must first get through the door and admit their need to change before they can be made to jump through the hoop of religion.

Some people have been able to turn to religion and be given relief from their problem with alcohol or drugs. Some people have also turned to psychology and achieved a lifetime without alcohol.

But these solutions have not worked for "alcoholics of our type." There are several types of drinkers, but we who identify as alcoholic have a particular combination of enjoying the effect of the drink (or drug), we build up a resistance and require larger doses, we obsess on the next drink or dose. We become fearful when it looks as if our supply will be cut off.

Fear, in fact, drives most of an alcoholic's behavior and it is a matter of control for the alcoholic to cling to the belief that his or her answer to their problems will come from an act of self will, some untapped inner strength, or some new medical treatment. The issue of spirituality, of God or religion might be good for other people, but almost all alcoholics convince themselves that it is not something they need.

Spirituality is not based on dogma. It is a willingness to discover where they fit into the universe – to find the place where they belong, their "proper size."

The idea of Willing Submission, whether someone else agrees with their conception of a Higher Power or not, is a common part of most religions. In Christianity, Judaism, Hinduism, Sikh and Buddhism, it is accepted that you must surrender your will to what each religion teaches is true. The word "Islam" means "surrender."

The structure of the Steps requires a progression of honesty and action.

Honesty and Action

First you must admit to having the problem that is trying to kill you. That is the beginning: Honesty, and it leads to the Drunk's Prayer.

Second you must change your thinking to accept that, no matter how far down you have gone, there is a 'power' that can restore you to a sane and useful life.

A decision is neither honest or dishonest, but making the decision is Action.

Taking an Inventory (Step Four) is an Action, but it requires the Honesty of Steps One, Two and Three to achieve the 'fearless and searching' qualification to be Honest again.

To share the Inventory, to expose the secrets, admit to the guilt, confess the wrongs, and take the risk of revealing those truths to another human being is a key Action. And it only works if you're honest.

Admitting that you have defects and shortcomings and identifying what they are is Honesty. Becoming willing to have them removed is an Action. It is an internal action, whether anyone sees it or not.

Asking is an Action, but have you been Humble? If you are not Honestly Humble, you cannot expect the next actions to be meaningful. Being Humble requires that you accept that the response you receive by asking to have defects and shortcomings removed is not up to you. It is up to whatever Higher Power you accepted in the Second Step – or that has evolved since that bit of Honesty.

Making the list of people you have harmed is more Honesty, and Action, which does not have any effect if you are not Honest.

Making Amends is more Action, but it must be an Honest desire that you want to repair, or make better, the damage you have done (the definition of Amend) and that the willingness of others to accept your effort is not up to you.

Continuing to Practice These Principles is more Action, with the willingness to be Honest - every day, all day.

Prayer and Meditation require Honesty to make the effort to express what you Honestly feel (Prayer) and to make the effort to get quiet and Meditate on the next change you make to keep what you have found (and maybe get a little better).

Carrying the Message is Action, and if you try to carry something you haven't got, you aren't being Honest.

When in doubt, get busy, get Honest and – if it is the right thing to do – take Action.

Suggestions

There is another suggestion. Completely unofficial, of course. The person objecting to the "God" aspect begins their Prayer as:

"God, in whom I do not know if I will ever believe…" and then says the Prayer.

In the Twelve Steps and Twelve Traditions, the Serenity Prayer ends with "Thy will, not mine, be done."

Your definition of "thy" is based on your personal conception of God, the Power Greater Than Yourself.

The Drunk's Prayer

The Drunk's Prayer is

"God, I can't live like this. Please help me."

G.O.D.

It is sometimes suggested that a newcomer use the group as a Higher Power because the men and women in that group can do what the newcomer can't: stay sober. They come to understand "God" as "Good Orderly Direction" or "Group of Drunks."

Doorknobs, Trees & Light Bulbs

Some old-timers say the struggling newcomer should accept some inanimate object as their Higher Power. "That tree can stand in one spot for sixty years - you can't do that. Make that tree your Higher Power…" Or a light bulb. Or a doorknob.

Anything other than the alcoholic! The idea is not to worship that item but to stop worshiping your own brain as the force that rules reality. As one old-timer said, "It gets your life out of the hands of the idiot who's had it so far!"

Prayers from the Big Book

"I earnestly advise every alcoholic to read this book through, and though perhaps he came to scoff, he may remain to pray."
William D. Silkworth, MD - Page xxx

"God is everything or He is nothing. God either is or He isn't. What was our choice to be?"
Page 53

"We asked His protection and care with complete abandon."
Page 59

Third Step

God, I offer myself to Thee – to build with me and do with me as Thou wilt. Relieve me of the bondage of self, that I may better do Thy will. Take away my difficulties, that victory over them may bear witness to those I would help of Thy Power, Thy Love and Thy Way of Life. May I do Thy will always!
Page 63

Fourth Step

RESENTMENT

We asked God to help us show them the same tolerance, pity, and patience that we would cheerfully grant a sick friend. When a person offended we said to ourselves, "This is a sick man. How can I be helpful to him? God save me from being angry. Thy will be done."
Page 67

FEAR

We ask Him to remove our fear and direct our attention to what He would have us be.
Page 68

SEX

We ask God to mold our ideals and help us live up to them.
Page 69

In Meditation, we ask God what we do about each specific matter.   *Page 69*

To sum up about sex: We pray for the right ideal, for guidance in each questionable situation, for sanity and for strength to do the right thing.

Page 70

Fifth Step

We thank God from the bottom of our heart that we know Him better. *Page 75*

We ask if we have omitted anything.   *Page 75*

Sixth Step

If we still cling to something we will not let go, we ask God to help us be willing.   *Page 76*

Seventh Step

My Creator, I am now willing that You should have all of me, good and bad. I pray that You now remove from me every single defect of character which stands in the way of my usefulness to You and my fellows. Grant me strength, as I go out from here, to do Your bidding. Amen.   *Page 76*

Eighth Step

If we haven't the will to do this, we ask until it comes.   *Page 76*

Ninth Step

LEGAL MATTERS

We ask that we be given strength and direction to do the right thing, no matter what the personal consequences might be.   *Page 79*

OTHERS AFFECTED

If we have obtained permission, have consulted with others, asked God to help.

Page 80

INFIDELITY

Each might pray about it, having the other one's happiness uppermost in mind.

Page 82

FAMILY

So we clean house with the family, asking each morning in Meditation that our Creator show us the way of patience, tolerance, kindliness and love.

Page 83

Tenth Step

Continue to watch for selfishness, dishonesty, resentment and fear. When these crop up, we ask God at once to remove them.　　　　*Page 84*

Everyday is a day when we must carry the vision of God's will into all our activities. "How can I best serve Thee – Thy will (not mine) be done."

Page 85

Eleventh Step

NIGHT

After mediation on the day just completed, "We ask God's forgiveness and inquire what corrective measures should be taken."　　　*Page 86*

MORNING

Before we begin our day, "We ask God to direct our thinking, especially asking that it be divorced from self-pity... dishonest or self-seeking motives."

Page 86

In thinking about our day, "We ask God for inspiration, an intuitive thought or decision."　　　　*Page 87*

After meditation, "We ask God to show us all through the day what our next step is to be, that we be given whatever we need to take care of such problems. We especially ask for freedom from self-will, and are careful to make no requests for ourselves only. We may ask for ourselves, however, if others will be helped. We are careful never to pray for our own selfish ends."　　*Page 86*

ALL DAY

As we go through the day we pause, when agitated or doubtful, and "We ask for the right thought or action."　　　　*Page 87 - 88*

Twelfth Step

Ask Him in your morning Meditation what you can do each day for the man who is still sick. The answers will come IF your own house is in order.

Page 164

Your job now is to be at the place where you may be of maximum helpfulness to others, so never hesitate to go anywhere if you can be helpful. You should not hesitate to visit the most sordid spot on earth on such an errand. Keep on the firing line of life with these motives and God will keep you unharmed.

Page 102

But Remember...

The wording was, of course, quite optional so long as we expressed the idea, voicing it without reservation. *Page 63*

When ready, we say something like this... *Page 76*

Prayers recited like magic incantations can have little effect. We must pray from our heart, with all the honesty and willingness to mean exactly what we say.

It works, if we work it.

We will die, if we don't.

Problems with Prayer

OVERCOMING THE INTELLECTUALIZATION OF PRAYER

Many people arrive in AA with a bias against the custom of saying Prayers, or at least the Prayers common in the Program and Meetings.

For the Christian Objection

Many Christians take the injunction against memorized or dictated Prayers seriously. This is found in the New Testament in Mark 6:4 and 6:5

> *"And when thou prayest, thou shalt not be as the hypocrites are: for they love to pray standing in the synagogues and in the corners of the streets, that they may be seen of men. Verily I say unto you, they have their reward.*

> *"But thou, when thou prayest, enter into thy closet, and when thou hast shut thy door, pray to thy Father which is in secret; and thy Father which seeth in secret shall reward thee openly."*

When the groups perform the "Serenity Prayer," "The Lord's Prayer," or the "St. Francis Prayer," many are simply showing the willingness to participate in the ritual of opening or closing a meeting.

It is not Prayer – it is ritual and extends the comfort of a predictability to approach the serious work of Recovery.

They do not know they are not praying, but many use this avenue to find their way to faith while confronting the pain and crisis created by alcoholism.

Most meetings allow for personal Prayer in silence, but your participation is an act of willing submission to the process of Spiritual Awakening, which is the only result of the Twelfth Step and the effect for which we work, regardless of your specific beliefs of a Spiritual life.

For the Non-Christian Objection

Alcoholics began as part of a Christian organization, the Oxford Group. When asked to provide a "Christmas Message" for the Grapevine in 1953, Bill Wilson responded by saying:

> *"The more I thought it over the more I got buffaloed. I said, 'Gee, this society of ours has moved into every quarter of the Earth. Here a great many of us are Christians. A good many are not. We have Jews who look to Jehovah. Out on the plains we have Indians who look to the Great Spirit. And now that we have established beachheads in the Pacific Islands, in Asia, in India, in South Africa... We know that we have brothers and sisters who look to Allah, and some to Buddha.'*

> *"And I thought to myself, 'How can anybody possibly talk about Christmas to all these?'*

> *"Then came this thought, 'Well, by whatever name we call it, we of AA have Christmas every day. In the sense that we give and in the sense that we receive.'*

> *"Yes. The kind of giving that demands no reward. The kind of loving that bears no price tag."*
> *Bill Wilson, 1953*
> *At his 18th Anniversary*

When AA separated from the Oxford Group, the invitation to Recovery took the form of a Higher Power, "a God of your understanding," which can be the God of your own faith.

Some people think the AA program is trying to convert everyone to a specific religion. Religion is not the job of AA – faith is the job of the person in Recovery and is between them and their personal Higher Power.

For the Non-Believer Objection

Contrary to propaganda spread about Alcoholics Anonymous as a religious front, those who do not believe, or actively do not believe, are welcome and invited into the rooms.

We would not be in AA if we had not already experienced enough of a change to know that our ideas had proved false and did not keep us sober. On page 52 of the Big Book, after outlining the various forms of suffering that our unmanageable lives had presented to us we asked:

"Was not a basic solution of these bedevilments more important than whether we should see newsreels of lunar flight? Of course it was."   Page 52

Many Christians object to the Prayers, as well, because their faith tells them to pray from the heart, not based on set, scripted Prayers.

Prayers are a custom going back to the time of AA's formation as part of the Oxford Group. To say the words of the Prayer is not praying, any more than saying the Pledge of Allegiance was pledging to the flag or the country. As a child, I was required to say the Pledge of Allegiance because that was the way my school day started.

There are also many people for whom the Prayer and the Pledge are genuinely who they are or what they believe.

For those of us who have long worshipped at the altar of the Human Brain, intellectual pride can be sufficient to keep us drunk. We have seen non-believers stay sober based on their personal knowledge that they are not the greatest power of the Universe, particularly when they had spent so much of their lives acting as if they were.

Saying the Prayer is not intellectual hypocrisy, it is the concession that staying sober is more important than intellectual pride; that finding the new life is more important than "being right."

Those who do not have a faith, or are very actively against the very concept of any religion, may have a more difficult job attaining and sustaining long-term Sobriety. Our Egos may push us to stop drinking for months, or even years, but we can be guaranteed that life will provide some punches that will require more than our solitary mental prowess can muster.

Many people that come to AA use the rooms (the body of people who stay sober) as their Power Greater than Themselves. They could do together what they failed to do alone and they were a visible resource for those who could not, or would not, concede the core of "spiritual."

Turning back to our favorite reference, dictionary.com, we find several entries for "spiritual:"

spir·it·u·al [spir-i-choo-uhl] – adjective

   1. of, pertaining to, or consisting of spirit; incorporeal.

2. *of or pertaining to the spirit or soul, as distinguished from the physical nature: a spiritual approach to life.*

3. *closely akin in interests, attitude, outlook, etc.: the professor's spiritual heir in linguistics.*

4. *of or pertaining to spirits or to spiritualists; supernatural or spiritualistic.*

5. *characterized by or suggesting predominance of the spirit; ethereal or delicately refined: She is more of a spiritual type than her rowdy brother.*

6. *of or pertaining to the spirit as the seat of the moral or religious nature.*

7. *of or pertaining to sacred things or matters; religious; devotional; sacred.*

8. *of or belonging to the church; ecclesiastical: lords spiritual and temporal.*

9. *of or relating to the mind or intellect.*

—noun

10. *a spiritual or religious song: authentic folk spirituals.*

11. *spirituals, affairs of the church.*

12. *a spiritual thing or matter.*

For our purpose, many meanings of the word can apply, but it is the first definition that we feel best serves the understanding of "spirit" as presented through the Program.

"1. of, pertaining to, or consisting of spirit; incorporeal."

A feature of AA Recovery that has proved to be a serious obstacle for intellectuals in the Program has been the necessary concession that there are things in our life that are not subject to discussion under the laws of physics and our understanding of the material world.

We find a level of coincidence far beyond statistical norms, which guide us to the next correction phase of our life and Recovery that becomes increasingly difficult to accept as random chance.

We find that when we do the Program the way the Program says to do it, we find periods of unexplained comfort, serenity, and sometimes happiness. Areas that used to be a problem, which left us feeling lost or hopeless, are slowly made clear and we can move forward, even when we do not fully understand the reason for the change. Problems that once blocked us are solved, set aside or accepted.

Over time, we realize our ability to understand our own reality is limited. The human brain cannot adequately classify or reduce reality to understandable terms.

Religious people have a way that works for them, regardless of our judgment of their beliefs. For them, "God did it." is a perfectly acceptable answer.

Perhaps we can end the intellectual war by simply admitting "it happened" and remain open to learning, experiencing, and possibly, understanding more as time goes on.

There is a limit to understanding as it affects the real world. If you fall off a high building, understanding gravity does not change the rate at which you fall.

Many things simply are. They exist and can have effects on our lives, emotions, and our place in the world, without supplying an answer for our ever-questioning brain.

Intellectual alcoholics love to judge things as "good" or "bad," but in Recovery we are bombarded with realities that defy our judgment – so we are faced with a dilemma.

Do we accept a reality we cannot understand, which gives us health, joy, and belonging, or do we insist on rejecting the reality of Recovery to the small part we can classify, thus remaining isolated, risking Recovery in favor of an imagined superiority?

When you stand in the room and say the words to the Prayer, or simply stand with the other people in the group as they say the Prayer, you are really in a room of AA, really with people who have shared the pain of your experience and who are willing to share their Recovery with you.

Why fight?

> *"First, Alcoholics Anonymous does not demand that you believe anything. All of its Twelve Steps are but suggestions. Second, to get sober and to stay sober, you don't have to swallow all of Step Two right now. Looking back, I find that I took it piecemeal myself. Third, all you really need is a truly open mind.*

Just resign from the debating society and quit bothering yourself with such deep questions as whether it was the hen or the egg that came first. Again I say, all you need is the open mind."

Twelve Steps and Twelve Traditions

Page 26

The Peace Prayer of St. Francis

BY DR. CHRISTIAN RENOUX
ASSOCIATE PROFESSOR, UNIVERSITY OF ORLEANS, FRANCE

The preceding translations were drawn from over 20 sources of the Aramaic Prayer found through internet searches, some of them of more academic repute than others. By reading several different versions of a translation, you can get an idea of the real meaning within the original document and choose the version most resonant with your understanding.

Original Text of the Peace Prayer

Belle prière à faire pendant la Messe
Seigneur, faites de moi un instrument de votre paix.
Là où il y a de la haine, que je mette l'amour.
Là où il y a l'offense, que je mette le pardon.
Là où il y a la discorde, que je mette l'union.
Là où il y a l'erreur, que je mette la vérité.
Là où il y a le doute, que je mette la foi.
Là où il y a le désespoir, que je mette l'espérance.
Là où il y a les ténèbres, que je mette votre lumière.
Là où il y a la tristesse, que je mette la joie.
Ô Maître, que je ne cherche pas tant à être consolé qu'à consoler,
à être compris qu'à comprendre,
à être aimé qu'à aimer,

car c'est en donnant qu'on reçoit,

c'est en s'oubliant qu'on trouve,

c'est en pardonnant qu'on est pardonné,

c'est en mourant qu'on ressuscite à l'éternelle vie.
                              Source: La Clochette, n° 12, déc. 1912, p. 285.

The English version

Lord, make me an instrument of Your peace;

Where there is hatred, let me sow love;

Where there is injury, pardon;

Where there is doubt, faith;

Where there is despair, hope;

Where there is darkness, light;

And where there is sadness, joy.

O Divine Master,

Grant that I may not so much seek

To be consoled as to console;

To be understood, as to understand;

To be loved, as to love;

For it is in giving that we receive,

It is in pardoning that we are pardoned,

And it is in dying that we are born to Eternal Life.

Amen.

Origin of This Prayer

The first appearance of the Peace Prayer occurred in France in 1912 in a small spiritual magazine called La Clochette (The Little Bell). It was published in Paris by a Catholic association known as La Ligue de la Sainte-Messe (The Holy Mass League), founded in 1901 by a French priest, Father Esther Bouquerel (1855-1923). The Prayer bore the title of 'Belle prière à faire pendant la messe' (A Beautiful Prayer to Say During the Mass), and was published anonymously. The author could possibly have been Father Bouquerel himself, but the identity of the author remains a mystery.

The Prayer was sent in French to Pope Benedict XV in 1915 by the French Marquis Stanislas de La Rochethulon. This was soon followed by its 1916 appearance, in Italian, in L'Osservatore Romano [the Vatican's daily newspaper]. Around 1920, the Prayer was printed by a French Franciscan priest on the back of an image of St. Francis with the title 'Prière pour la paix' (Prayer for Peace) but without being attributed to the Saint. Between the two world wars, the Prayer circulated in Europe and was translated into English. It was attributed for the first time to Saint Francis in 1927 by a French Protestant Movement, Les Chevaliers du Prince de la Paix (The Knights of the Prince of Peace), founded by Étienne Bach (1892-1986).

The first translation in English that we know of appeared in 1936 in Living Courageously, a book by Kirby Page (1890-1957), a Disciple of Christ minister, pacifist, social evangelist, writer, and editor of The World Tomorrow (New York City). Page clearly attributed the text to St. Francis of Assisi. During World War II and immediately after, this Prayer for peace began circulating widely as the Prayer of St. Francis, especially through Francis Cardinal Spellman's books, and over the years has gained a worldwide popularity with people of all faiths.

For more information, see the book by Dr. Christian Renoux, La prière pour la paix attribuée à saint François: une énigme à résoudre, Paris, Editions franciscaines, 2001, 210 p.: 12.81 euros + shipping (ISBN: 2-85020-096-4). – Order From: Éditions franciscaines, 9, rue Marie-Rose F-75014 Paris.

Note: Dr. Christian Renoux, is continuing his research on the propagation of this Prayer, and is looking for new information about its publication in English between 1925 and 1945, and in all other languages between 1912 and today. Our thanks to Dr. Renoux for his permission to publish the Original Text of this very popular Prayer and the history of its origin.

The Lord's Prayer
An Interpretation from the Aramaic

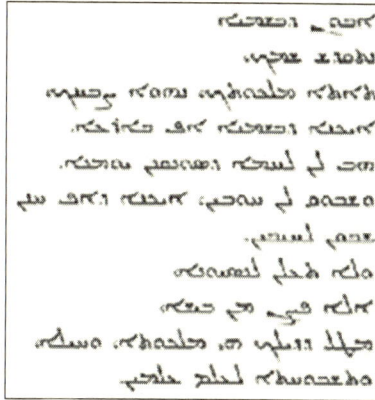

Although we know the Prayer was written in Greek (a trader's dialect called "Kohlne"), the words were first spoken in the era's native language of Aramaic.

Aramaic has its own structure, grammar, and cultural references; there are no words for colors, but comparisons to things of that color. There is no word for daily; the two syllable word for God-the-Father is a source of intense debate as to the complexity of the meaning. Over twenty translations can be found on the web.

In Aramaic, ideas can merge or interact with the words before or after to deepen the meaning. This also means you can argue different interpretations according to the meaning of the word you are using.

This author is not a Christian. When asked why I say the Lord's Prayer at the end of the meeting, it is because of what the Prayer says!

TRANSLATION KEY

In Parentheses – (King James Standard)
Italic Bold – Aramaic

- *Bulleted – Translation(s) directly from Aramaic*

(Our Father)
Ahwûn

- My Source/Creator
- O cosmic Birther, from whom the breath of life comes
- Radiance that Saturates the universe

(Who art in Heaven)
D'bwaschmâja

- That fills/saturates the universe, above and below
- That who fills all realms of sound, light, and vibration
- That who is all of substance and vibration

(Hallowed be Thy Name)
Nethkâdasch schmachv

- Your name is already sacred
- May Your Light / Truth be experienced in my utmost holiest
- allow me to see / know / believe

(Thy Kingdom Come)
Têtê malkuthach

- Your Heavenly Domain approaches
- Your Justice approaches
- Your Will is already being done in Heaven

(Thy Will be done on Earth as it is In Heaven)
Nehwê tzevjânach aikâna d'bwaschmâja af b'arha

- Let your Will be true on earth (that is material and dense) just as it is in the universe (all that vibrates)

- Your Will is already being done within the Earth as it is already being done in the heavens

(Give us this day Our Daily Bread5)
Hawvlân lachma. d'sûnkanân yaomâna

- Give us wisdom (understanding, assistance) according to our need
- Sustain/Nourish me

(And forgive us our debts as we forgive our debtors)
Waschboklân chaubên wachtahên aikâna daf chnân schwoken l'chaijabên

- Forgive me and my wrongs to the extent I am able to give forgiveness to others.

(And Lead us Not into Temptation)
Wela tachlân l'nesjuna

- Let us not be lost in superficial things (materialism, common temptations)
- Free me from desire or free me from lies/illusion
- Please do not put me to the test
- Detach the fetters of faults that bind us, just as we let go the guilt we hold of others
- Allow me the same forgiveness to others as you are already showing to me

(But deliver us from Evil)
Ela patzân min bischa

- But let us be freed from that which keeps us off from our true purpose
- Be my direction / purpose

---

5 There is no reference of time in Aramaic, so daily is not a concept - it is always "today."

(For Thine is the kingdom and the power)
Metol dilachie malkutha wahaila wateschbuchta

- From You comes the all-working will, the vital strength to act
- You are the source of the song that is life

(and the Glory Forever and Ever)
L'ahlâm almîn

- Sealed in trust, faith and truth
- I confirm with my entire being
- As you are truly the only God and deserving of all my worship

(Amen)
Amêin

The word Amen (Tiberian Hebrew "Amein" pronounced ah-MAIN, Arabic "Amin" pronounced AH-men) translates as "So may it be" or "Truly" and is a declaration of affirmation found in the Hebrew Bible, the New Testament, and the Qur'an. It also has come to mean "As it is," "Verily," "I agree," "Let it be," or "Well said."

It was used by the Jewish congregation to affirm the words said by the leader of the worship. It was later adopted by the Christians from the Jews as the concluding formula for a Prayer. In Islam it is the standard ending of recitation of sutras (chapters or divisions).

The preceding translations were drawn from over 20 sources of the Aramaic Prayer found through internet searches, some of them of more academic repute than others. By reading several different versions of a translation, you can get an idea of the real meaning within the original document and choose the version most resonant with your understanding.

Three & Seven: The Full Prayer?

There is no "Amen" at the end of the Prayer in the Third Step. The Prayer in the Seventh Step picks up exactly where the first Prayer leaves off.

Between the "two Prayers" we do our Fourth and Fifth steps in order to break the cycle of secrecy and self-hate that has run our lives to the point where we have placed an appropriate focus on ourselves and the personal defects we must surrender in order to improve our own lives and the lives of those around us.

As always, the Prayers are suggested and it is often more effective to re-word the Prayer into your own words, but if all you can do is say the words on paper, try to mean them with your heart.

Prayer of Steps 3 and 7

> *(3) God, I offer myself to Thee - to build with me and do with me as Thou wilt. Relieve me of the bondage of self, that I may better do Thy will. Take away my difficulties, that victory over them may bear witness to those I would help of Thy Power, Thy Love and Thy Way of Life. May I do Thy will always!*
>
> *(7) My Creator, I am now willing that you should have all of me, good and bad. I pray that you now remove from me every single defect of character which stands in the way of my usefulness to you and my fellows. Grant me strength, as I go out from here, to do your bidding. Amen*

But over the years people have raised questions.

Were they intended to be a single Prayer? Probably not. The first half (the part from the Third Step Prayer) is written in Middle English, while the last half (from the Seventh Step Prayer) is written in Modern English. The difference is immediately noticable.

Again, the wording of both Prayers are a matter of personal choice and expression.

If you have a problem, consider the intent of the Prayer(s) and say them in the way that will have meaning to you.

Believer, Seeker, Agnostic, Atheist, Anti-Theist

WHO'S WHO AND WHAT'S THE DIFFERENCE

Language evolves. Over time, a word will gain a meaning in popular use long before it is adopted by academics.

Several words in common use around AA create a good deal of confusion. This article defines the four most common words related to individual spiritual outlooks and proposes a new word to offer some clarity to the discussion.

When someone who does not hold a belief attempts to explain the belief, the result is filtered through the speaker's own belief system. A Believer defining an Agnostic is much the same as a banker explaining communism. Someone who does not understand a position will re-define it to suit his or her own purposes, and most often to make the other side look foolish or wrong.

The purpose of this article is to introduce new positions in the area of personal belief. Atheists and Agnostics have too often been described by Believers, and are sometimes perceived as arrogant and condescending.

Believers have been described by Anti-Theists, which could be called the arrogant describing the blind. All assert that their own positions are what should be true for others. This mistake ignores the fact that the very personal failures that brought us into Recovery, and most of our other failures as well, have been the result of our brain and its judgments. We are tempted to re-define others within our own terms and then respond to what is actually our own internal creation - instead of simply dealing with the other person where he or she is.

Our growth is dependent on a belief in "a power greater than ourselves." This belief evolved in 12-Step groups beyond the initial religious limitations of the Protestant and primarily male Christian group where it began. When the focus was changed from the Christian God to "a Higher Power," it became possible for newcomers to address their immediate challenge – alcoholism, drugs, behaviors, etc. – without having to jump through the hoop created by the belief of those with longer Recovery that "You must start where I have arrived after much work." It made it possible for newcomers without a religious background to partake of the blessings of Recovery without any additional requirements imposed by religious dogma.

Recovery is often not a return to a previous state, but delivery to a completely new experience of being part of a greater reality, a larger community, and the embrace of a non-physical reality we all share.

When I speak of "non-physical" reality, it is an attempt to frame all five of these positions within the context of emotion, compassion, and the expression of our highest natures. Love is irrational, but love is experienced.

The compassion and impulse of an individual to charge into a burning building to save a stranger at the risk of his or her own survival, is irrational. To some extent, the willingness to sacrifice for our own children actually works against personal benefit and sometimes our very survival.

But all of these are real, despite the lack of rational motive. The "Higher Power" is open to personal interpretation. Believers tend to pre-determine that it must mean a deity or separate intelligence and define all other views from that viewpoint. Agnostics tend to pre-determine that any teachings or discussion can only arrive at the point where the mystery outweighs the beliefs of the teaching. The Atheist maintains that it can all be accepted without a defined intelligence above the human level and that any human attempt to describe that reality must fail to provide a complete comprehension. The most strident Anti-theist would be hard-pressed to argue that they are greater than a hurricane or a wild fire, but hold that all actions and processes must be subject to rational analysis. The seeker keeps looking for the answers and may or may not arrive at one of the other positions.

Each is ultimately doomed to frustration when they have not made someone else conform to their own position within the continuum of faith.

Believer

This word is commonly understood to mean anyone who subscribes to a set of beliefs. This can involve any of the world's religions or a newly-devised faith. The key is the commitment of the individual to a defined belief system and its attendant rituals, doctrines, and practices.

At the core of the Believer is a conviction in a defined deity or God (by whatever name) and the traditions, scripture, and practices of a specific religion.

People involved in a formal religious life – Christians, Muslims, Jews, Hindus, etc. – are classified as Believers.

Seeker

A Seeker is someone who has not yet settled on a specific set of beliefs, but who does have faith that there is a belief appropriate for them. Seekers tend to try a variety of existing beliefs and conduct research to locate a system in which they can believe.

Such beliefs may not be part of a specific or recognized religion, faith, holy text, or doctrine. It can be a personal mix of beliefs that are expanded or reduced as the Seeker sees fit.

Many Seekers continue to search for new ideas after they appear to have settled on a given set of beliefs, and some even cycle continuously from one belief system to another.

Agnostic

The word 'agnostic' creates confusion because it is usually defined by someone other than the Agnostic himself. The definition that commonly arises in such cases comes from "gnosis" (NOS-iss) which means "knowledge."

In the Greek language, the prefix a- before a word adds the meaning "without." "Agnostic" (AG-noss-tick) thus means "without knowledge."

Most Agnostics will tell you that they believe the reality of a "God", of whatever definition, is beyond the intellectual ability of the human mind to comprehend. However, sayings like "any God small enough for me to understand is not big enough to do the job" or "I cannot hold the ocean of God in my teacup of a brain" are used to explain their thoughts. It does not matter how other people define God, it will be God as you understand God.

Agnostics function based on ethics, codes, behaviors, practices, and customs that do not involve a deity while also not necessarily ruling out the existence of one.

Atheist

The word "atheist" is derived from the Greek word "theos," meaning "deity" or "God," and serving as the foundation of words like "theology" (the study of religion). "Atheist" therefore means "without a deity" or "without God."

Technically, an Atheist believes there is no deity to be worshiped. Most scientists or people who believe in science's explanations would qualify as atheistic, although many hold sets of beliefs (are Believers) without seeing conflicts between religious doctrine and scientific theory.

The Buddhist religion can be considered both agnostic and atheistic; it is not a religion in the Believer's sense discussed earlier. It is more an 'approach' or philosophy to a spiritual life. You can find devout members of several formal religions who also maintain various Buddhist practices, such as Buddhist and Christian, Buddhist and Shinto, Buddhist and Confucian. People can subscribe to a set of practices, morals, and beliefs - with or without a supreme deity - according to their personal practice.

More confusion can be created because Buddhism is very flexible and does not disbelieve other faiths - – Buddhism has retained local belief systems (demons, Goddesses, etc.) while adapting to new cultures which causes outside observers to think that Buddhists in Europe or North America hold the same belief in these deities held by Buddhists in Nepal or Southeast Asia.

This is not necessarily the case.

Anti-Theist

This is not a recognized word and is being proposed to define an observable set of beliefs. With the Greek base "theos" and the prefix "anti-" meaning "against" or "in opposition to," this new word is intended to mean a belief that not only maintains there is no deity or God, but actively opposes or works against the belief in such a deity by others.

Anti-theism is sometimes referred to as "Militant Atheism" in the press and has become the most publicly known face of Atheists, particularly the branch known as the "New Atheists." Anti-theists often adopt the same intolerant attitudes as militant Believers, seeking to change the personal beliefs of others to conform to what they believe.

Anti-theist, as a word, is proposed to separate the personal non-deity belief system from the more strident approach of controlling the personal beliefs of others.

Even the most virulent Anti-theist can proceed in Recovery by simply admitting to the rational fact that there are forces greater than himself or herself. They do not walk out during the hurricane to tell it to stop; they do not run under the falling tree to prove they are more powerful. Rational thought can place them in their proper place in natural existence, even without acknowledging any sort of supernatural "intelligence."

Our False God

The real purpose of this essay is to open up the concept of Willing Submission – to remove our brain as the object of worship.

People take thoughts emerging from their own brains as divine revelation, regardless of the amount of evidence of the failure of that brain to come up with a simple plan for successful daily living.

People express their belief in the brain with daily language and attitudes related to their own or someone else's intelligence. "He's so smart....;" "She's a genius...;" or "They're dumber than a bag of hammers...;" are some examples. All are said with a level of emotional attachment to the value of a "good brain" or the deficit of a "small brain."

This use of language reveals a new idea in our new idea of a 'Higher Power' - the magnificent Human Mind.

Many of those possessing the greatest brains have been unable to live successfully, whether they turned to the problem of alcohol, addictive substances, or behavior. Many intelligent people that enter Recovery will 'think' their way back into the saloons and behaviors that defeated them.

And fail.

Many newcomers less intellectually inclined, or "stupid" people, have simply done what the steps and the Big Book say, end their relationship with their addiction, and begin to live functional, reasonably happy lives.

Which confuses the over-intelligent.

You may have heard an old AA saying:

There is no one too stupid to 'get' the AA program, but there are a lot of people way too smart.

Willing Submission

The concept of Willing Submission is common to all of the major faiths. You submit to the Deity, the doctrine, the teachings, the morals, or other definition of how a person should live in their daily life.

The word "Islam" translates as "the Surrender."

Buddhism requires a surrender of the Ego to end suffering.

Christianity teaches Willing Submission and obedience to the manifestations of authority inherent to that particular belief system – the church, Bible, pastor, teacher, husband, etc.

Willing Submission creates the possibility of living without giving in to lusts, cravings, desires, delusions and distortions. No one performs perfect submission, but the effort to attain that state provides a foundation for better, more responsible behavior. Daily effort is required to guard against the subtle rise of the once conquered Ego

A Believer or Agnostic may follow the required submission to the code of behaviors dictated by their faith, seeing them as Divine Law or requirements of the faith. An Atheist or Anti-theist may admit they live under the "Laws of Nature" or the "Laws of Physics" and it will be sufficient to move them forward in Recovery – or they may have to admit that the idea of 'Ego deflation' works where great thoughts had failed.

Determine the definition of your own spirituality, your relationship to the non-physical realities of love, emotion, and compassion. Follow the dictates of the moral code to which you subscribe, whether you feel they are divinely commanded or rationally extracted.

Take the time to express your truth – your fear or appreciation or desire for direction – and it will not matter if you call it "Prayer" or "Deep Thought." Sit quietly and experience calm and it does not matter if you call it "Meditation" or "Contemplation."

It need matter only to you, and you can allow others to wrestle with the question of where they fit in the continium of spiritual reality. Each must accept that their own mighty brain is not the object of worship, but that the reality of the world as an expression of God's Creation or Natural Forces is greater than their limited brain will ever fully comprehend.

Atheism, Moral Psychology, and the Deus Non Vocatus in Early Alcoholics Anonymous

A NON-THEISTIC / ATHEISTIC WAY OF WORKING
THE TWELVE STEPS: WILLIAM E. SWEGAN6
BY GLENN F. CHESNUT
© 2014 by the Author, All Rights Reserved. Used by Permission.

William E. Swegan (Sgt. Bill), in The Psychology of Alcoholism, Chapter 18, "Recovery through the Twelve Steps," explains how some early AA's (like himself in the 1940s and 50s) successfully worked the steps from the standpoint of a truly dedicated ethical humanism.

Second Step. "Came to believe that a Power greater than ourselves could restore us to sanity."

Bill Swegan's Higher Power here is the laws of nature, the healing forces within nature which can return our minds to sanity and reason, and the very rationalistic idea of the power of truth and honesty which gives us the power of understanding other people with more compassion for their differing points of view.

"I cannot fight universal laws and principles and succeed. The basis of these principles is all-powerful, and everything in the universe is subject to them. Some who come into the twelve step program object that if something cannot be touched or felt, it cannot exist. The law of gravity also cannot be touched or felt. But no human being can throw a baseball up into the air so hard that it will float up there in the air and never come spinning back down. As a baseball player, I had to learn how to throw a baseball with the right velocity to make it come

---

[6] Copyright by Author, Glenn F. Chestnut, All Rights Reserved. Used by permission.

down at the right place and the right level, and this required learning to work with the Law of Gravity instead of thinking I could just ignore that rule of nature. We are surrounded by powers and forces greater than ourselves at all times."

The power we are searching for here cannot be touched or felt directly, but it is a Healing Power which is capable of restoring our sanity, which we can see at work in the lives of those who have already been working the twelve step program. It is the power of truth and honesty itself, but it is also the power of compassion and understanding.

If this step is carried out properly, those who work it first begin to incorporate within their internal makeup the positive feeling that they are not alone any more. Fear then begins to subside.

Third Step. "Made a decision to turn our will and our lives over to the care of God as we understood Him."

"We must notice the phrase 'as we understood Him,' which means that if traditional religious language makes no sense to me, I am free to think of this Healing Power of truth, honesty, compassion, and personal transformation in ways that do make sense to me. Even now, well over fifty years after I first got sober, I do not feel comfortable with heavily religious language, because I still do not understand it (even though I gladly allow those in the program who do understand it to talk about their Higher Power in that way)."

You will notice that when I first came into the A.A. program, my own spirituality centered around the spirit of helping and caring for others and saving human lives, which I used to replace my old spirit of egocentrism, anger, and selfishness. That simple decision (another key word which appears in this step) allowed me to get sober and stay sober, and begin living harmoniously with the universal principles of nature."

Fifth Step. "Admitted to God, to ourselves , and to another human being the exact nature of our wrongs."

In his discussion of this step, Bill Swegan completely omits any reference to God, and it is also not described by him as a "confession" in the more religious sense of that word. Instead, his principal emphasis is upon restoring positive communications with other members of our families, especially when we are feeling extremely guilty about the harm we did to them while we were drinking.

"It is an arduous task indeed to establish positive communications with another person when I have in fact been feeling guilty about the harm I caused that other person. But defective communications cause continual frustrations, and are the source of continuing conflicts, particularly in the immediate family. It is traumatic for alcoholics to talk over some of the events in which they have been involved with their own families. Some alcoholics seek a 'geographical cure' by walking out and fleeing from their families, rather than attempting a positive resolution of the differences which exist in their homes. The hurt done by fleeing becomes more acute, the closer the ties are in the family."

Sixth Step. "Were entirely ready to have God remove all these defects of character."

On the surface, Bill Swegan sounds more religious here than in his discussion of any of the other steps, but we need to remember that when he speaks of "coming to terms with the power of God, as we understand Him," he means the laws of nature, the healing forces of nature, and the very rationalistic idea of the power of truth and honesty to restore our minds to sanity and reason.

Seventh Step. "Humbly asked Him to remove our shortcomings."

In Bill Swegan's discussion here, he does not talk about asking God for anything.

What he does do is recommend that we practice Humility, which he describes in rationalistic terms as "the willingness to learn."

Eleventh Step. "Sought through Prayer and Meditation to improve our conscious contact with God as we understood Him, praying only for knowledge of His will for us and the power to carry that out."

The key phrase here is Bill's statement that "It seems easier for alcoholics and addicts to fight God than to fight their illness."

His central message here is that we need to quit fussing about religion all the time, and start working on fixing what is wrong with our alcoholic minds, which is what is causing us all our real troubles.

Bill's Higher Power here is not a personal God figure, but a set of "spiritual concepts," that is (for him at any rate) the laws of nature, the principles of reason, and so on. We need to meditate and think about the importance of learning to trust that there are logical solutions to all of our truly important problems.

But even more important, "faith and trust in oneself is...essential to progress in the program." As an alcoholic, I have all too often come to believe that my life is doomed, that I will never find happiness or any kind of a good life, and that it is pointless to try to act logically and responsibly because "the world is against me" or "God is against me" -- when the REAL PROBLEM is that I have lost faith and trust in myself. All too many alcoholics feel "programmed for failure," and plagued by continual self-sabotage, where every time they come to the brink of success, they are driven by some sick need to destroy everything.

So one of the most important keys to Recovery for most alcoholics is to give them hope and restore their self-confidence. For Bill, effective daily meditation needs to include things like self-affirmations and continual re-affirmations that it is all right for me to be successful and to feel good about myself.

Conclusion

Nothing in all of this is incompatible with belief in a loving personal God who always takes care of me and will never let me or my family come to any hurt or harm, and Bill Swegan never attacks people who want to believe that.

But he does insist that I do not have to believe that in order to work the program successfully, get sober, and find true serenity and a good life.

When his mother died when he was a small child, when the bombs were dropping on him and his best friends at Pearl Harbor on December 7, 1941, and at a number of other times in his life, Bill Swegan did not believe that it was rational or realistic to believe in a supernatural power who would guarantee that he and his loved ones would never die or be injured. He had learned better than that, first hand.

And Bill's private observation to me was that people who claim to believe in a personal God and talk about that all the time but who refuse to do a real Fourth Step or do the other things he is talking about here, never in fact end up feeling good or achieving any real serenity. They seem to spend all of their time obsessed with fear and resentment, and attacking other people and attempting to start needless quarrels with everyone around them.

sponsormagazine.info

Alternatives to "God"

Individual members may have issues with any of the religious origins and customs within Alcoholics Anonymous. These may be because their pride turns any such discussion into an intellectual exercise, or an argument the newcomer can manipulate. They may come from a neurotic need to defy all authority and authority figures, real or imagined.

These issues with religious origins or customs may be because of previous experiences with individuals or groups who have used the traditional meanings to gain their own means, do damage or simply use a religious guise for some personal abuse.

The Group Itself

Many newcomers who have such problems may be relieved that such objections were easily overcome by those who came before by turning God into an acronym. It has meant "Good Orderly Direction" for some. For others it was the "Group of Drunks" - the members in AA who had stayed sober when the newcomer could not. This substitution is mentioned on Page 107 of the book Twelve Steps and Twelve Traditions.

"God" Like "Mother"

Some people have suggested that other people's idea of God is none of our business. Even if we use the same word, we may not mean exactly the same thing.

They suggest we use the word "God" the same way we use the word "Mother." Everyone has their own idea of who the word "Mother" represents. For many it means the woman who gave birth, but for a growing number it means the woman who played the same role as the woman who gave birth would have traditionlly filled. It may be a grandmother, or an aunt, or an adoptive mother, or simply someone who was in your life to serve the function.

Similarly, when we say "Mother" we have a face that comes to mind and most other people have a different face than the one we see. Brothers and sisters may see the same face, but even they may see the face a little differently.

If our own mother-figure was a flawed human being, we need to be able to see that Mother-we-wanted or -needed whenever we hear the word.

The "God as we understand God" needs to be just that personal.

sponsormagazine.info

Meditation for Beginners

There are only
Two ways to fail.
To not complete, or
To not begin.
                    -- Buddhist saying

This is not an official or authorized document. It is a reflection on the various ways to practice developing a quiet mind for spiritual growth and inner peace.

Meditation is not something you do.

Meditation is the things you do not do.

Meditation is not magic.

Meditation is tuning into yourself like a radio where the radio no longer picks up the desired station.

Meditation is not scientific.

Meditation is finding an inner calm and spiritual guidance.

There is no official form of Meditation.

Some Meditation practices are complex and based on a single, approved form of spirituality.

Beginners' Meditations must be simple.

Religions and beliefs have a tradition of Meditation as part of its practice.

Catholics have the rosary.

Protestants have group prayers and weekly schedules.

Monks and nuns of all faiths have beads and chants.

Hindus have the centering techniques of Yoga.

Moslems have the trance dancing dervishes.

Native Americans have traditions of vision quests and spending time in quiet contemplation.

Atheists have their personal routines or areas of thought.

They all work.

Find the style and method that works best for you.

Do Not Try to Find God While Meditating.

Think of being young and going to a store. It may be the grocery store with your mother, an aunt, or some other grown-up. It may have been to a department store, the fair, a school event, or a festival.

If you get separated from the adult, the worst thing you can do is to go looking for them.

You might miss each other if both of you are moving.

Sit still and wait for them to find you.

And they will find you.

While you are waiting, you can be calm and secure in the knowledge that they are searching for you and you are making yourself findable.

You are lost – not God, no matter how you understand God.

If you become still and stay right here, right now, you give yourself the chance to be found.

You make yourself "findable."

And you can find peace, no matter what is going on in your life.

Ways to Meditate

Meditation requires a dedicated time spent with your chosen practice and repetition. A simple timer can set limits on the time spent meditating – a watch alarm, a kitchen timer, etc.

You can meditate alone or with others – both ways have value.

Meditation can be doing nothing or doing something.

Meditation can be made more meaningful by contemplation of an image, or a verse, or a saying; or by sitting looking inward at a memory of such an idea.

Meditation can be an effortless stepping away from stress and worry.

Meditation can be found in a favorite incense, the fragrance a certain flower, or appreciating the aroma of your favorite cup of coffee. Or you may surrender the idea of having a 'favorite' odor and simply accept where you are and how it is right now.

Meditation can be listening to a particular type of music, or singing. It can be people nearby talking or what you might think of as silent.

Meditation can be watching a favorite image, scene, or the abstract movement in a stream of water, or people walking by, or clouds, or the motion in a lava lamp.

Meditation can be performing a task; gardening, knitting, dancing, drawing, working a potter's wheel, building a wall, cooking, running, or riding a bicycle.

You can meditate being still or moving. Some people meditate best sitting in a natural setting with no agenda; others find a strict liturgy leads to mental and emotional liberation. Some meditate better by walking a familiar path, or a path on which they have never been.

None of these are required, but you can choose parts of any of them to improve your personal Meditation.

Many people have been meditating for years and not even known it. They have something they do that provides repetition and makes them comfortable exactly where they are, doing what they are doing.

They often look forward to it, not understanding why it gives them such a sense of peace.

You will discover the form that gives you the best calm. Begin with a few suggestions, and even when you find your favorite way to meditate, try other ways as well.

You can always discover a new answer that does not make the old answer wrong, but enriches you by giving you more than one channel.

A Simple Beginning

There is no required decoration, device, furniture, or approved chant for Meditation – but someone you know may have a suggestion from their own experience.

Find a spot to be comfortable, or at least more comfortable than you are normally. At times, this may not be completely comfortable, particularly in the beginning. Someone may suggest a position, a posture, or something else they use for their own Meditation.

Determine a way to limit your beginning Meditation – a timer, a specific length of music, or other indicator. Later, you may want to sit and meditate for as long as you feel focused and relaxed.

You may start in a quiet setting; a room, a spot outdoors where you will not be disturbed, or even sitting in a car. Later, you will be able to meditate anywhere, regardless of noise or distraction.

You may start with a familiar movement; walking, running, gardening, knitting, cooking, singing, reading, or whatever gives you the most quiet.

Don't expect anything. If you do expect something, don't criticize yourself or try to make yourself wrong for having the expectation. Simply notice it and understand you are trying something new and may have no experience in how to 'not expect.' You aren't meditating to criticize yourself.

You can sit, or begin the motion as you feel most comfortable. In the beginning, it is usually suggested that you not lay down to relax. You could easily go to sleep and it is not the purpose of Meditation to bring on sleep.

Start with one thing - something simple:

a smell,

a sound,

a motion,

a passage or verse for contemplation.

If moving, how long do you want to be doing your movement (not where you will go or the product of your action)?

The Meditation

Don't worry about the past or project into the future.

Concentrate on the moment you are in – right now, right here.

Notice your breathing.

Notice the sounds around you.

Notice what you see, or close your eyes.

Notice the smells.

Notice the tastes.

Notice the feel of air brushing against your skin or the cloth against your skin.

But try to not "think" about any of them. Avoid thinking if they are good or bad, pleasant or annoying, useful or beautiful – just notice them, as they are.

If you should accidentally start thinking, that is not bad. Just notice that you are thinking about something and try to get your attention back to the experience of being aware of this exact moment.

Maybe you will have someone come to you and want to talk while you are being quiet. That means that as part of your "now" you have someone who wants to talk to you. It may be about something for their own benefit, but you have someone who wants to talk to you.

Was that always true?

Successful Meditation

With successful Meditation you simplify your life to the exact moment where you are.

You will find a new starting point in "here" and "now."

You will discover that every moment in your life has had a "here" and "now," but you missed them because of thoughts of "there" and "then."

You will find a new ability to recognize new answers, the ability to change directions with less stress, and the serenity that comes from without.

You will notice the lost opportunities of the past without criticism or judgment. Simply notice the difference between a life lived in the "there" and "then," and a new life lived in the "here" and "now."

If you remember the idea of being lost in a store, you will discover how to meditate to make yourself "findable" to your own Higher Power, or God as you understand God.

"We will understand the word
serenity, and we will know peace..."
Page 84

Steps & Traditions

The Steps are shared by almost all of the existing 12-Step Recovery Fellowships. They help us to make the changes needed to deal with the pain that brings new people in, they help us repair the lives that have been damaged (not just our own), and build a new life that is based on healthy, meaningful, and fulfilling principles.

We have gathered tips to "work" the steps going back to the 1940s from a large body of authors, speakers, and Sponsors. As they sometimes say "Take what you need and leave the rest."

The Traditions are not as widely accepted, but were written to show us where we had failed. We have failed newcomers, failed our fellowship and failed each other – particularly when alcoholics in Recovery decide they are going to "fix" it.

We hope this short presentation on the Steps & Traditions will help new people, and those with long term sobriety, obtain a better understanding of their origins and purpose.

An Overview of the Steps

Alcoholics Anonymous is a program of action, and the Twelve Steps are the Program we have followed to attain and maintain Sobriety.

Through the Steps we are given the simple and direct action necessary to help us not pick up a drink or any other mind-altering substance outside of direct medical supervision.

Through the Steps we find the way to deal with the guilt, shame, remorse, and fear that rises when we have stopped medicating ourselves with alcohol (and often with other substances and behaviors).

Through the Steps we learn to face and heal our pasts to give us time in the present to enjoy our lives, to become contributing members of our families and communities, and to live without the Fear that formerly drove our lives.

Through these Steps we achieve a Spiritual Awakening.

It is not required to have the desire for Sobriety to begin working the Steps. That can come later.

How could you want Sobriety? How can you want something that was not part of your life before? How many people do you party with who were sober? If you had a period of sobriety from one of the many methods available, or even from a previous exposure to the Twelve Steps, but went back to drinking, how much of your experience was a real connection to be Sober?

You do not have to want Sobriety to begin. You only need to know Step Zero. At this point it is only necessary that you know your life cannot continue on as it has. You do not need to know the new way yet, but only be convinced that the old way must stop, no matter what!

At this point most alcoholics begin a long struggle to stop on their own – and to stay stopped. In the Big Book this is well described in the chapter "More about Alcoholism:"

"Here are some of the methods we have tried:

"Drinking beer only, limiting the number of drinks, never drinking alone, never drinking in the morning, drinking only at home, never having it in the house, never drinking during business hours, drinking only at parties, switching from scotch to brandy, drinking only natural wines, agreeing to resign if ever drunk on the job, taking a trip, not taking a trip, swearing off forever (with and without a solemn oath), taking more physical exercise, reading inspirational books, going to health farms and sanitariums, accepting voluntary commitment to asylums we could increase the list ad infinitum."

Page 31

Since that was written, we have added professional treatment centers, drugs to keep you "sober," therapies, workshops, books, classes, tapes, CDs, websites, and support groups — along with those who oppose one or more of these approaches.

The program of Alcoholics Anonymous addresses these other methods in two of their traditions:

Tradition Nine: AA, as such, ought never be organized; but we may create service boards or committees directly responsible to those they serve.

Tradition Ten: Alcoholics Anonymous has no opinion on outside issues; hence the AA name ought never be drawn into public controversy.

Throughout AA literature it is acknowledged that the Twelve Steps are not the only way to achieve and maintain sobriety. For some people those other techniques have worked.

Some problem drinkers have simply set their minds to sobriety, fought the battle alone, and won. Others have gone back to church, stopped drinking, and lived new, sober, and successful lives. Some have gone to therapy, found sobriety, and lived healthy, successful lives.

But people in AA know the other side of that reality — we have seen people who have come, achieved success to the point of accruing years of Recovery, only to allow their old ways of thinking drag them back down to insanity, institutions, and death.

And death is not the worst thing that can happen when someone goes back to drinking.

When Step Zero has been achieved, years of struggle can end in disaster.

At that point, you have the choice to try another method, or (if you feel your problem and your life is as we describe it) you may then choose to join us and work the Steps.

Steps: Step Zero to Step One

For most of us, Step Zero has been some form of screaming: "This must STOP!"

This book assumes you have already passed through Step Zero and Step One. If you have not yet explored the First Step, set this book aside until you have completed Step One and are convinced that you are an alcoholic.

Step Zero is that point where you understand that your Problem, as shown through excessive drinking and/or drugging, has got to stop. This is not a Step from the Big Book, but everyone we have encountered who has succeeded with finding and maintaining Sobriety reports that they reached this point.

Why Work the Steps?

Step One is difficult. It is a merciless admission that goes against everything an alcoholic has believed about his or her mastery of life.

Many people fight admitting that they are in the grip of a disease and mental compulsion that they cannot consciously master. Despite all evidence they have before them, the true alcoholic believes that with more strength, with more will, with more determination, they will one day be able to control their drinking and return to drinking without the problems and consequences.

"Many pursue this delusion to the gates of insanity or death!"

- Page 30

Until they admit to their innermost selves that if they take a single drink, they cannot guarantee how long they will drink, how much they will drink, what they will do while drunk, or where they will come to when they wake up.

"Lack of power, that is our dilemma."

- Page 45

The powerlessness of this dilemma makes Step One require a great deal of work, made more difficult by the fact that we do not have the authority to declare any man or woman to be an alcoholic.

*"We do not like to pronounce any individual as alcoholic, but you can quickly
diagnose yourself, step over to the nearest barroom and try some controlled
drinking. Try to drink and stop abruptly. Try it more than once. It will not
take long for you to decide, if you are honest with yourself about it. It may be
worth a bad case of jitters if you get a full knowledge of your condition."*

Page 31

The First Step requires something simple and very difficult — the new man
or woman must admit to themselves if the conditions of Step One are true. This
means you must become honest enough to admit that these conditions are
already true.

Have you reached Step Zero?

Have you tried everything within your power to get sober and to stay sober?

Is your life, with or without alcohol, unmanageable? This means the results of
your best thoughts, plans, efforts, and actions have been tried and the results have
been completely unmanageable by you.

We do know that people who find AA (and not everyone knows about
Alcoholics Anonymous) who stay and who actually do The Work of the Twelve
steps, do recover.

Even if they don't believe it will work.

Even if they don't like it.

Even if they don't understand it.

Even if they are uncomfortable doing The Work.

Even if they are not religious.

Even if they don't find the spirituality others would approve of.

Even if they use the AA Group itself as their Higher Power.

Even if they suffer great reversals in health, love, and finances.

Even if they find great success in health, love, and finances.

Even if they have no idea of what a "spiritual life" might be.

Even if you lived what you thought was a deeply "spiritual life" but returned
to drinking and the dark despair that comes with relapse.

Even if you believe there is no hope.

The Twelve Steps do not require that you believe Recovery is even possible when you come through the door.

You only need to know that you cannot continue the way you are going.

You might come in because of a threat from a spouse, or a judge, or a doctor, or an employer.

It doesn't matter.

Show up. Come to see if what we have can help you. Come to see if you are really an alcoholic — or not.

If you decide you are an alcoholic and have seen people with Recovery the way you would like to have it, do the Steps.

Do The Work, even if you don't think it will work for you. The Twelve Steps work.

Period.

The Birth of the Twelve Steps

The Twelve Steps were not a part of the early process before the publication of the Big Book. The Oxford Group used a "six step" system that was not written down, but rephrased in various ways through the years.

In December, 1938, during one of the meetings about the development of the book in Bill's house on Clinton Street, Bill Wilson and Hank Parkhurst were becoming full of themselves – talking about putting "some of that spirituality stuff" into the book because it would help sales.

At that point, Bill's wife, Lois, who had been listening from the kitchen, erupted into the discussion. Lois stuck her finger into Bill's face and said, strongly, "If you keep talking like that, mister, you're going to forget the God who got you sober and you're going to drink!"

Overwhelmed with what that would mean, Lois burst into tears and ran upstairs, leaving Bill and Hank in an awkward silence. Hank excused himself and went home, leaving Bill to digest what had just happened.

Bill had been a member of the Oxford Group for several years, and the OG had a system of Prayer, followed by Meditation, called 'Quiet Time'. Bill retired to a small bed he had built under the stairs, a necessity because Bill was too tall to stretch out on a regular sized bed. He prayed and meditated on the problem before him.

After about an hour, he sat up, took the yellow pad and pencil from their regular position on the table next to his bed, and began to write.

He broke down the Oxford Group's Six Steps into smaller chunks and, when he was satisfied, he counted them and found he had broken those original Steps into Twelve. Twelve appealed to him as a Christian, and he shared them with the other members of his New York "Alcoholic Squad", as the members of the Oxford Group had come to call this little band of recovering alcoholics in their midst.

After that introduction, Hank's secretary Ruthie Hock typed up the Steps and sent a copy to the Akron group for discussion.

The Steps, as they appear today, are only a few words different from the original longhand list.

The Original Six Steps

The Twevle Steps were based on the Oxford Group's Six Steps, a tool for reordering your life under the Princples of their Fellowship. While they were widely known and accepted, there was no written 'source' for the steps and several people who reported on the Oxford Group Steps refer to them in three different ways in the published version of the Big Book, and in later talks rephrased the Six Steps differently every time they were raised.

In 1953 Bill Wilson was asked to write down the Oxford Group Steps and turned over this list.

If you have trouble reading Bill's writing, it says:

For Ed -

1. Admitted Hopeless

2. Got Honest with self

3. Got Honest with another

4. Made Amends

5. Helped others without demand

6. Prayed to god as you understood Him.

April 1953
Ever, Bill W.
Original AA Steps.

For God:
1. Admitted hopeless
2. Got honest with self
3. Got honest with another
4. Made amends
5. Helped others without demand
6. Prayed to God as you understand Him.

Ever
Bill W.
April 1943

Original Six Steps

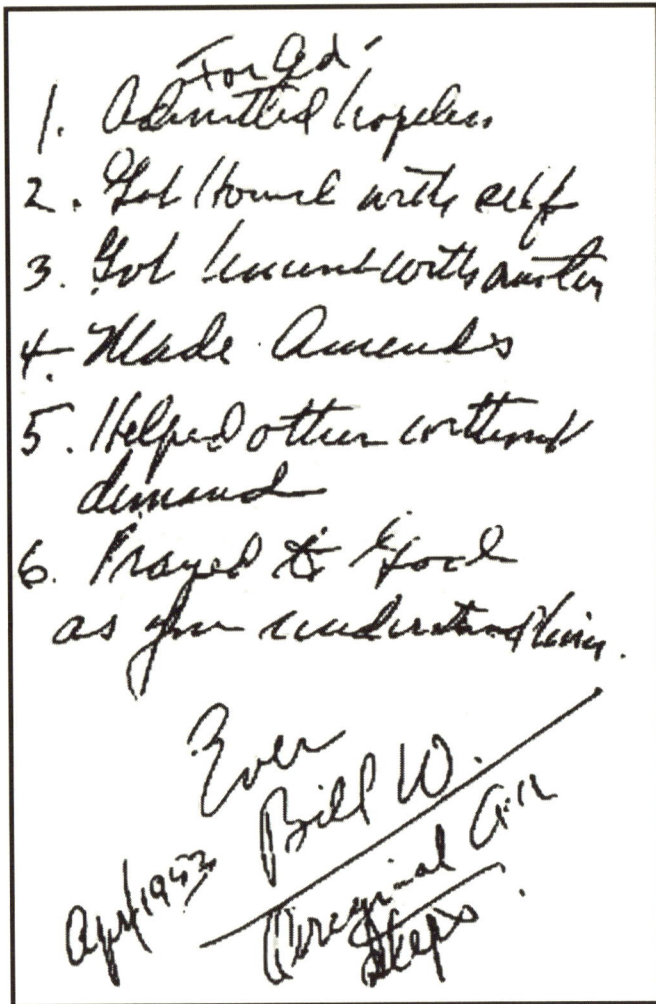

Bill Wilson's handwritten Six Steps

Looking at the First Three Steps

Having covered the information in pages xxiii through page 63 of the Big Book, Alcoholics Anonymous, we asked ourselves the following questions when taking the first three Steps.

Step One - *We admitted we were powerless over alcohol that our lives had become unmanageable.*

- If, when I honestly want to, can I quit entirely (because of the mental obsession), or if when drinking, do I have little control over the amount I take (because of the physical allergy)?

- If you've answered "no" to the first part and "yes" to the second, you're probably alcoholic. If that be the case, you may be suffering from an illness which only a spiritual experience will conquer. (page 30)

- Drunk or sober (suffering from "untreated alcoholism"), do I have trouble with personal relationships? Can I control my emotional natures? Am I a prey to misery and depression? Can I make a living (a happy and contented life)? Do I have a feeling of uselessness? Am I full of fear? Am I unhappy? Do I find that I can't seem to be of real help to other people? (page 52)

- Do I fully concede to my innermost self that I am alcoholic? (page 44)

Step Two - *Came to believe that a Power greater than ourselves could restore us to sanity.*

- Do I now believe, or am I even willing to believe, that there is a Power greater than myself? (page 47)

- Do I have a conception of that Power which makes sense to me? (page 46)

- When we became alcoholics, crushed by a self-imposed crisis we could not postpone or evade, we had to fearlessly face the proposition that either God is everything or else He is nothing. God either is or He isn't. What is my choice to be? (page 53)

Because so much of the Program revolves around our Spiritual Life, we have created a whole section devoted the the Question of Spirit.

Step Three - Made a decision to turn our will and our lives over to the care of God as we understood Him.

Third Step Decision

"Next, we decided that hereafter in this drama of life, God was going to be our Director. He is the Principal; we are His agents. He is the Father, and we are His children."   *Page 62*

To affirm this decision, we say the Third Step Prayer:

"God, I offer myself to Thee—to build with me and to do with me as Thou wilt. Relieve me of the bondage of self, that I may better do Thy will. Take away my difficulties, that victory over them may bear witness to those I would help of Thy Power, Thy Love, and Thy Way of life. May I do Thy will always!"
                                                            Page 63

"Third Step Prayer" from the Big Book is a suggestion. Some people with serious sobriety, serious clean time, may have presented it to you as a ritual.

The original form of the Seventh Step began, "Humbly, on our knees..." But the original authors removed that phrase based on the group conscience that resulted in the book we know.

The Prayer they present is not a magic do for you because you said the magic words.

You must say the Prayer, but in your own words.

"The wording was, of course, quite optional so long as we expressed the idea, voicing it without reservation. This was only a beginning, though if honestly and humbly made, an effect, sometimes a very great one, was felt at once."
                                                            Page 63

Now, with all of this said, we need to get to the meat of the Third Step. As you may have heard "making a decision" means nothing until it is followed with the commitment to take actions.

If, however, you find it hard to relate to the words as written in the Big Book, if you do not use "Thee" and "Thine" as part of your normal language, you can take the Prayer and restate it in your own words so that you can say a heartfelt Prayer of surrender and willingness in order to proceed with your Recovery.

In the Third Step we decided to turn our thoughts and actions over to the care of God. The way we carry out that decision is by taking the actions of Steps 4 through 9. We found in Chapter 4, "We Agnostics," that God dwells deep down within us. We've been blocked from God's Power because of our own self-will – our character defects and shortcomings (i.e. selfishness, dishonesty, resentment, fear, guilt, shame, remorse, anger, etc.) The first step of getting us "unblocked" is Step Four: Made a searching and fearless moral Inventory of ourselves.

Ken D., Los Angeles, CA • Joe A. Raleigh, NC • Cliff D., NYC
Fred S., Raleigh, NC and other anonymous authors

Simple Directions

A Fourth Step Inventory Guide

WARNING: TRAVEL BEYOND THIS POINT WITHOUT A SPONSOR IS NOT ADVISED.

Step Four – Made a searching and fearless moral Inventory of ourselves

This guide is not the idea of one person.

Scott L. offered his excellent presentation of the Inventory Process in four talks available for free from the xa-speakers.org website.

The "One Way Group" Inventory Guide, written by the late Ken D. of Los Angeles, in 1959 is offered to help jog your memory or point you to a thought that will improve your Inventory.

The Primary Purpose Group of Plano, TX makes excellent helpings of experience, strength and hope available through its recorded speakers and website material.

"Circuit speakers" at conventions of Alcoholics Anonymous have added their impact to the Inventory process. Speakers like Chuck C., Clancy I., Tom I., Chris and Myers R., Sandy B.

Additional material was made available on the internet through several excellent sources of documents, podcasts, workshop materials, speaker recordings and original essays which highlight more of our shared experience strength and hope.

A list of web sites is included in the back of this book and you are encouraged to explore these web sites, but not at the expense of postponing your Fourth Step.

Above all you will have the experience of your Sponsor to help you overcome your personal obstacles to the massive house-cleaning and correction that began when you accepted the truth of the First Step.

If your Sponsor says anything that conflicts with this guide go with what your Sponsor has to say for your personal program.

There is only one way to do the Inventory wrong, and that is to not do one!   –
Simple Directions

The AA Steps owe a great deal of their structure to the six steps of the original Oxford Group, a Christian fellowship dedicated to the ideal fellowship of the First Century church. When asked about The Oxford Group's "Six Steps," Bill W. wrote the following scrap to explain their process:

Our Steps 4 through 9 are a clarification of the Oxford Group's simple Step Four "Make Amends." The expansion was intended to break down the process to allow an alcoholic to do each part of the process and do it as thoroughly as possible.

If you have made it to Step Three, your Sponsor and your meetings will confirm that the next Step is to be taken immediately. In the Big Book, Alcoholics Anonymous, the direction begins in Chapter Five, at the bottom of page 63,

"Next we launched out on a course of vigorous action, the first step of which is a personal house-cleaning, which many of us had never attempted."

It is the intent of this guide to help make a searching and moral Inventory as guided by the book.

Steps One, Two and Three did not create the problem - they are the statements of the truth of your disease and your situation. They are the beginning of the leveling of pride and Ego, which we are told will become a lifelong process. In each of these steps you begin the difficult process of telling the truth.

You did not become an alcoholic because you admitted to Step One. You simply admitted what was already true.

You did not create a High Power through Step Two, you simply admitted to the truth that you are not God or the Higher Power of your personal understanding.

In Step Three you did not achieve anything beyond taking that deep breath to begin the work of Recovery.

"The Work" is often referenced in AA meetings, but sometimes people can go for years without knowing what "The Work" is. For simplicity, let us take a moment to define "The Work" for your own progress.

The Big Book is clearly divided between the basic text of the front (Cover through Page 164, or Page 181 to include Dr. Bob's Nightmare, depending on who you are talking to) and the stories in the back.

But on closer examination we find a second structure in the book. The area from the Cover through Page 52 are a summary for Step One - defining alcoholism and the alcoholic, with an introduction to the spiritual nature of our disease.

On Page 52, although discussion of the meat of Step Two has already begun, there is a paragraph that gives the summation of "our lives had become unmanageable." It is sometimes called The Bedevilments.

The previous pages discuss the changes seen in the 1930s as the result of technological progress. The authors and early members of our fellowship all came from a time when "man will never fly" had been changed to include regularly scheduled flights to China from San Francisco. They had seen horses and carriages give way to automobiles. They had seen communications move from newspapers and telegraphy to newsreels, movies, radio and telephones.

The paragraph on Page 52 raises a list called "The Bedevilments". It says:

> "We had to ask ourselves why we shouldn't apply to our human problems this same readiness to change the point of view. We were having trouble with personal relationships, we couldn't control our emotional natures, we were a prey to misery and depression, we couldn't make a living, we had a feeling of uselessness, we were full of fear, we were unhappy, we couldn't seem to be of real help to other people - was not a basic solution of these bedevilments more important than whether we should see newsreels of lunar flight? Of course it was."

At each of the statements it is best to pause, to ask if that part of the paragraph applies to you.

• Were you having trouble with personal relationships?

- Were you able to control your emotions?

- Were you prey to misery and depression?

- Could you make a living?

- Were you full of fear?

- Were you unhappy?

- Were you able to be of real help to other people?

- Do you see that your solution of these bedevilments is more important than other pursuits?

The Bedevilments on Page 52 are the end of Step One and the opening to the work of Step Two.

On page 88 you are at the end of Step Eleven.

Page 89, the chapter "Working With Others" is the beginning of Step Twelve, which continues through the rest of the book, including the stories in the back. Those stories are people sharing their Experience, Strength and Hope with you as their Twelve Step call on you.

The 36 pages from page 52 to page 88 contain Steps Two through Eleven. These pages, these Steps are "The Work."

Do the Work and you get the result!

You are the only one who can say if you are willing to move forward, but as with the rest of your work in the Twelve Steps, it is best to have an advisor, a "native guide" for the new territory – a Sponsor.

Understand that many of the men and women with double-digit sobriety report that they have not seen anyone start a Fourth Step and then hesitate before beginning their amends in Step Nine and stay sober!

The process requires completion. Alcoholics are great beginners, but not so good at finishing what they start. If you make the commitment, then take the action and the results will follow. Finish this process!

You will never feel finished. The book tells us this is "the beginning of a lifelong process," but it also tells us that this way of life is "a design for living that really works."

It is suggested that you follow the direction of your Sponsor. If you are not using a Sponsor, it is important that you have someone who can guide you - do not attempt this process on your own. You can never see your eye with that same eye. You must use a mirror, and your Sponsor is your mirror.

The pressure built by performing the Inventory can only be reduced through the thorough examination and organization of what comes out of it. Your Sponsor will help you organize and prioritize the results - what is revelation, what is Ego, what is fear, what is pride and what is an asset.

Through the Fifth Step you will come to see yourself, possibly for the first time.

In the Sixth Step you will realize what parts of you are either defective, or which are lacking, and become willing to have those defects and shortcomings removed.

In the Seventh Step you will take the same deep breath you took in Step Three to turn everything over to the Higher Power in which you have come to believe. You will not tell that Higher Power what is to be removed or to be kept - you ask to have everything that stands in the way of your service to others removed.

In Step Eight you will return to this Inventory - most people add to the list begun in Step Four - to determine how you and your disease have damaged the people, institutions and relationships around you. You will find that - if you are to stay sober - you are willing to do whatever is required to make those damages heal, or at least make it better.

And in Step Nine you will step back into the world to heal the damage of your past and establish a new foundation for life without the weight and, the guilt, the shame, the fear, and the selfishness of your past.

But none of this can begin without the thorough house-cleaning required on Pages 63 and 64 of the Big Book.

Prepare yourself for this process. Discuss your fears with your Sponsor. Gather your materials and begin.

Dr. Bob's Review

If you visit the home of Dr. Bob in Akron, one of the things you will find is a review of Steps One, Two and Three. It would be appropriate for you and your Sponsor to examine this document before you proceed to Step Four. If you cannot be content with the answers to this set of questions, you may need to go back to your earlier work before proceeding to Step Four.

Step One (Yes or No)

a *Have you learned and have you fully conceded to your innermost self that you are an alcoholic?*

b *Do you have any reservations or lingering ideas that one day you will be immune to or UNAFFECTED by drinking alcohol?*

Step Two (Yes or No)

a *Do you believe, or are you even willing to believe, that there is a power greater than you?*

Step Three (Yes or No)

a *Are you convinced about Steps One and Two?*

b *Are you convinced that any life run on self-will can hardly be a success?*

c *Are you convinced that your troubles are basically of your own making, and that they arise out of you and that you are an extreme example of self will run riot?*

d *Are you convinced that you must be rid of this selfishness?*

e *Are you convinced that your selfishness is killing you?*

f *Are you convinced that there is often no way of entirely getting rid of self without a Higher Power's aid?*

g *Are you convinced that you must have a Higher Power's help?*

h *Are you convinced that you have to quit playing the role of a Higher Power - that it never worked?*

i *Are you convinced that a Higher Power is going to be your Director, Principal, Father, and Employer?*

j *Are you convinced that you have thought well about taking this Step?*

k *Are you convinced that you can at last abandon yourself utterly to a Higher Power?*

Are You Ready for The Prayer?

*God I offer myself to Thee - to build with me and do with me as Thou wilt.
Relieve me of the bondage of self that I may better do Thy will. Take away my
difficulties, that victory over them may bear witness to those I would help of
Thy power, Thy love, and Thy way of life. May I do Thy will always!"*

Remember, the next paragraph on Page 63 says "The wording, of course, is
quite optional." It is important that you mean what you pray. If you can take the
words as presented and come to mean them, the Prayer as written can work for
you.

If, however, you find it hard to relate to the words as written, if you do not
use "Thee" and "Thine" as part of your normal language, you can take the Prayer
and re-state it in your own words so that you can say a heart-felt Prayer of
surrender and willingness to proceed with your Recovery.

An Important Note

The Big Book says at the end of Step Three (emphasis added):

*"NEXT we launch out on a course of VIGOROUS action, the first step of which
is a personal house-cleaning, which many of us had never attempted. Though
our decision (Step Three) was a vital and crucial step (so it's important), it
could have LITTLE PERMANENT EFFECT (it doesn't amount to much)
unless AT ONCE (immediately or now) followed by a STRENUOUS
EFFORT to face (where we face these things is in Steps 4 - 6), AND to be
rid of (where we get rid of these things is in Steps 7 - 9), the things in
ourselves which had been blocking us (we can't turn our will and our lives
over to the care of God until we get unblocked from doing so by immediately
and quickly working Steps Four through Nine. Our liquor was but a
symptom. So we had to get down to causes and conditions.* Page 76

Preparation

Before he died, Dr. Bob told Bill "Keep it Simple." You can follow that in
your Inventory.

The first thing you need to do is talk with your Sponsor. Does your Sponsor
agree that you are ready to take this next step? Go through this booklet with your
Sponsor to be sure that he, or she, agrees with the process it presents. Your
Sponsor may have used a different system and if anything is found in these pages

that is in conflict with your Sponsor - go with the direction your Sponsor gives you. Your Sponsor knows you better than the authors of this booklet!

Get a notebook to dedicate to your Inventory. It can be a simple spiral bound notebook, a composition book or other empty volume. You can usually find good ones in dollar stores, or you might have one left over from a previous "good intention" attempt at the Steps which is still blank and usable.

Keep two or three reliable pens or pencils with you. That way the excuses "my pen stopped working" or "my pencil broke" will not be valid.

Have your own copy of the Big Book and, if your Sponsor agrees, a copy of Twelve Steps and Twelve Traditions.

Your Sponsor may suggest a certain number of sessions per week - 20-60 minutes committed in advance. Your schedule may only allow one session per week, a certain number of times per week, or commit to time spent on your Inventory every day - make this decision with your Sponsor and then live up to your commitment to your Recovery.

Try to find a place where you can concentrate to work. It should be quiet - free of distractions but you will hear of people who worked on their Inventory while the kids were making noise elsewhere in the house, or they worked on their Inventory sitting in their car at a lake or wooded spot, or sitting in a coffee shop, or a public library or even when attending a special "writing" meeting occasionally offered by individual AA groups. You will find you can complete your Inventory if your commitment is to finish and is not dependant on some condition you set before you begin.

When you sit down to write, be comfortable and take a few moments to be quiet. Pray and meditate as you feel is appropriate - you may be able to find the quiet you need in a few moments, or you may need ten or twenty minutes of Prayer and Meditation to begin.

Don't try to decide in advance what you should or should not write down - if you think of it, write it down.

If you are writing an Inventory after a relapse, talk to your Sponsor. Most Sponsors tell a returning member of AA not to depend on the previous Inventory (or inventories). The issues raised on those previous inventories were not handled by someone who stayed sober.

Remember, we can write too little for our Inventory, but we can never write too much.

NOTE: Your Inventory is not a long narrative to explain everything. Your Sponsor may (or may not) approve of you writing such a narrative as part of your Recovery, but that is not your Inventory. The Inventory is clearly shown in the Big Book and this guide is to help you complete that process.

You may not like, agree with, understand, or want to do some of this work. We do not care what you like, agree with, understand or want to do ... we care what you do! What you like, agree with, understand or want to do is what brought you here.

This is the work you must do to stay sober. As the shoe company ad says --

"Just do it!"

Your Fourth Step Inventory Notebook

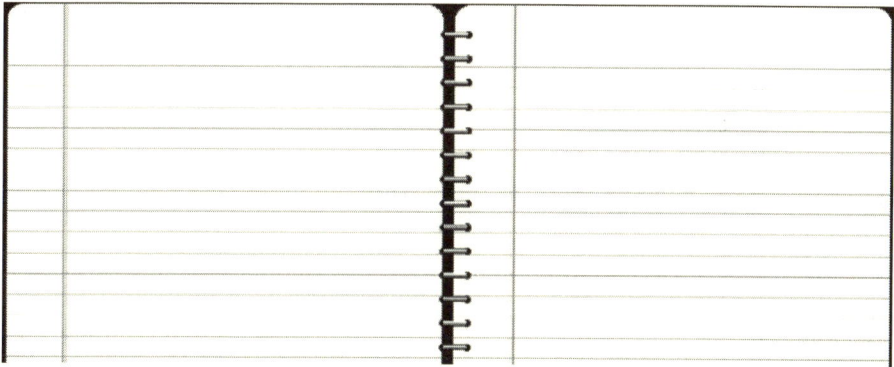

Three Benefits of the Inventory

Nothing will come up that you have never thought about before. Doing an Inventory will give you the experience of seeing all of these moments from your life, from your history of dysfunction and disease, in one place. The patterns of your behavior will become apparent.. You will see them in a new light and your worst aspects will become your greatest lessons.

Writing the Inventory in long hand, and not writing it on a computer or speaking it into a tape recorder, requires the rhythmic action of physically writing. And, if you are like most of us, you do not like your own handwriting. While some part of your brain is complaining about how you make O's or A's or I's or L's, the truth can get out without your brain censoring your words.

And finally, writing the Inventory stops your story from changing. Whether you know it or not, every time your have told part of your story it has changed – just a little. You were a little more holy, they became more evil.

Over time those tiny changes have shifted the story from what was true. The Inventory gives you a chance to find the Truth that has slipped away from you.

The Notebook

Get a simple notebook. At the time of this writing one of the most used products for school is a "spiral bound notebook". It is a pad of paper, usually punched with three holes to be held in a regular three-ring binder, but held together with a wound wire - the spiral binding.

You can use loose leaf notebook paper, or a bound "composition book," but whatever you use it should be intended to use like a book, turning from one page to another.

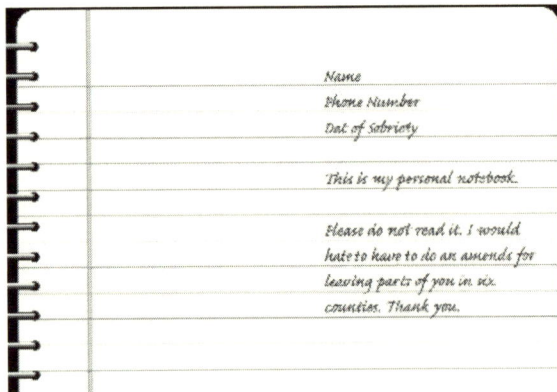

Name

Phone Number

Date of Sobriety

This is my personal notebook.

Please do not read it. I would hate to have to do an amends for leaving parts of you in six counties. Thank you.

Page One

Open the notebook and on the first page write your name, your contact info and whatever else your Sponsor feels you should put on that page. Sometimes that can include the date of sobriety, or a request that anyone finding your notebook not read it - almost everyone doing an Inventory chooses to keep their unfinished Inventory under lock and key.

COMMIT

With your sponsor, commit to exactly how much minimum time you are willing to devote to the writing of this inventory. This should take into account work time, family commitments and health, but you must commit to taking the time to do the work.

The Two Page Spread

When you open the notebook from the first page, you have a two page spread in front of you. Use that to your advantage.

On the right side, draw a line down the page, approximately in the middle.

You will do several sections of the Inventory, but under each section you will follow the same format. On each section you work down the column, not across.

Go to Page 65 of your Big Book to see the example given. This is a variation on that sample.

Name	Why on the list (19 words MAXIMUM)
Mr. Brown	His attention to my wife; told my wife about my mistress, Brown may get my job at the office.
Mrs. Jones	She's a nut - snubbed me. She committed her husband for drinking, he's my friend. She's a gossip.
Employer (Name)	Unreasonable - unjust - Overbearing. Threatens to fire me for drinking and padding my expense account.
Wife (Name)	Misunderstand and nags. Likes Brown. Wants house put in her name.
Mr. Mary (1st Grade)	Made fun of my voice in front of the class.
Becky	Laughed at me in front of my friends in cafeteria. Gave me the nickname "squirrely"
Cousin Ralph	Had better toys than me, wouldn't share them, or let me take any home.
Dr. Phiro	Told my parents about my test results before telling me,

Take that deep breath again, become calm and put your pencil to the paper...

Column One: Who

At the top of the left side page, on the left side of the red line draw down the page, write the word 'Name'.

Remember, work down the column, not across.

The insruction for this column is: "write a name, skip a line, write a name, skip a line, write a name..."

It does not matter how you feel about this person, institution or situation - write a name, skip a line, write a name, skip a line.

If you have someone special that you have a lot to write about - write a name, skip a line, write a name, skip a line, write a name. There is no 'special' entry.

That is not a suggestion - that is a direction. You will see why we do this in the next stage.

DO NOT decide what you do and do not have to put on your Inventory. DO NOT decide "I've already dealt with this (and don't have to do it)". If it comes up, put it down. It doesn't matter if it was when you were four, or last Saturday - put it down on paper. This paper. Right here, right now.

You are going to do several lists. You will list your resentments. You will list your fears. You will list your sexual misconduct. You will list assets. And more. You will use this same technique for every topic.

For this column, all you have to do is write a name, skip a line and write a name.

Some names may appear on more than one list.

When you can look at the list for 15 or 20 minutes and not come up with a new name, then you are ready to do the next column.

Name	Why on the list (19 words MAXIMUM)	Affects my ...
Mr. Brown	His attention to my wife; told my wife about my mistress; Brown may get my job at the office.	Sex relations, self-esteem (fear) Security
Mrs. Jones	She's a nut - snubbed me. She committed her husband for drinking, he's my friend. she's a gossip.	Personal relationships, self-esteem (fear)
Employer	Unreasonable - Unjust - Overbearing. Threatens to fire me for drinking and padding my expense account.	Self esteem (fear), security
(Name) Wife	Misunderstood and nags. Likes Brown. Wants house put in her name.	Pride - Personal sex relations Security (fear)
(Name) Mr. Mary	Made fun of my voice in front of the class.	Pride, self-esteem, relationships with classmates.
(1st Grade) Becky	Laughed at me in front of my friends in cafeteria. Gave me the nickname "squirrely"	Pride, self-esteem, relationship with my friends.
Cousin Ralph	Had better toys than me, wouldn't share them, or let me take any home.	Greed, Pride, Envy, felt I did not deserve nice toys.
Dr. Phizo	Told my parents about my test results before telling me,	Pride, fear, how my parents

Column Two: Why?

On the left hand page, at the top of the page on the right side of the red line write "Why on the list."

When you have your list of names, you will be tempted to write a long narrative of how they have wronged you. Your Sponsor may decide you should write such a narrative - but that is not your Inventory. That is a long narrative of how the world has wronged you - and it will not keep you sober!

For your Inventory you need to identify exactly why each of these names have appeared on your list, and do so in a clear and simple manner. Think of it as a report - "just the facts."

You may want to tell what someone else thought or wanted. Don't do it. You do not know what someone else thought or wanted - even if they told you, they might have been lying. You don't know.

Why they are on your list should be considered and the shortest possible statement will cut to the core of your reaction to them and what they did, or what you may think they did.

Look closely at the sample from Page 65 in the Big Book. The name with the longest reason for being on the list uses only 19 words. We are learning to discipline ourselves and this is an exercise in the indulgence of "explaining." When you write more about why they are on your list, you begin explaining why they are wrong and why you were right, or the other way around.

No more than 19 words per name in the corresponding second column.

That is not a suggestion, that is a rule. You write a maximum of 19 words per name.

You might want to write that rule on the top of this column, so you don't 'forget'. Understand, we usually want to explain it all - and explain it in a way that makes us look righteous and makes them look as bad as possible.

You also do not need to deal with what their motive may have been - you are the one here trying to put your life in order. They are not. We cannot do anything about them. You are here for your life, for your Recovery. We can only deal with you.

What matters is your perception and what you thought and did. Short and sweet.

Keep it simple.

The example from Page 65 has another feature we will use. The one who has the most written about why they are on the list gets just 19 words to explain why they were named.

If we are following the directions, you should be able to state, in 19 words or less, exactly why they are on your list.

When you write the reason for the name being on our list, you are to tell us what happened. This column is reporting - even the phrase like "she's a nut" might be allowed if that is why she is on your list, even if you aren't qualified to make a determination of another person's sanity.

Write no more than 19 words, no matter what. Do not explain, just say why they are on your list.

Don't rush it, but don't drag your feet.

Affects my ...	
Sex relations, self-esteem (fear)	
security	
Personal relationships, self-esteem (fear)	
self esteem (fear) , security	
Pride - Personal sex relations	
security (fear)	
Pride, self-esteem, relationships with classmates.	
Pride, self-esteem, relationship with my friends.	
Greed, Pride, Envy, felt I did not deserve nice toys.	
Pride, fear, how my parents	

Column three: What It Effects

HERE IS YOUR CHANCE TO TELL WHAT THAT PERSON, IDEA, INSTITUTION OR SITUATION THREATENED.

Was it your personal standing or position?

Your pride?

Your financial security?

Your self esteem?

The way it caused other people to view you?

Your sexual relationships?

Your business relationships or friendships?

Your legal position?

Your criminal activities?

Do you have something that was affected that is NOT listed in the examples?

Column Four

Column Four will take up the last column of your two-page spread. Leave this column blank until you get together with your Sponsor for your Fifth Step.

This is what we often refer to as "The exact nature of the problem."

Your Sponsor, or the person with whom you share your Inventory, can help you decide what to put down in that part of the page. This column will provide you with focus on where your behavior and attitudes need to change.

You will also find the beginnings of your Eighth Step list in your exploration of your Inventory and what it has revealed.

A great deal of it may be repetitive. You may find things like "Dishonesty," "Manipulation," "Lying," "Fear," or some other problem come up over and over again. Do not be surprised – you are not creating brand new defects but expressing the same defects over and over.

But this should be discussed with the person who hears your Fifth Step.

The Lists

We are told to Inventory our Resentments, which is how this section began. When you have completed the three columns for Resentment, turn to a fresh two page spread, draw your line down the middle of the right hand page and do your next areas.

There are two primary lists suggested.

Fears

We do not like to admit to fear unless we can use that admission to manipulate someone else's thoughts or feelings. With alcohol or drugs we avoided feelings and fear was one of the biggest to avoid.

Face your fear by listing, using the exact same method, each fear or incident of fear. Name, skip a line, name. Why that name is on your list and what was affected.

Sex

You are expected to list your resentments, your fears, and your sexual conduct. You will also deal with people you have harmed (Step Eight). Use the same format - write a name, skip a line, write a name (or some indicator), even if you can't think of the specific name of the person involved.

On page 70 the Big Book says,

> "To sum up about sex: We earnestly pray for the right ideal, for guidance in each questionable situation, for sanity, and for the strength to do the right thing. If sex is very troublesome, we throw ourselves the harder into helping others. We

think of their needs and work for them. This takes us out of ourselves. It quiets the imperious urge, when to yield would mean heartache."

Additional Topics

You and your sponsor may decide there are specific areas you need to Inventory in detail, such as stealing, criminal activity, secrets or other topics.

Something New

If you have an area you need to Inventory, some area you are afraid will drive you out to get drunk or get high, you can use the Inventory process to detail exactly what is there, and do a new Fifth Step to understand it, then develop a way to change yourself, confront the deficiencies within you that this Inventory reveals, and the see how you can work new Amends to discharge the shame, damage or other negative effects of this area.

Being honest with this level of Inventory can also help you carry your message to the people who are newer than you and may need to turn to you to find how to handle the same problem with their own Recovery.

The One Way Prompts

Later in this chapter you will find a list of suggestions from the One Way Group in Los Angeles from around 1960. After each list it ads "others not listed", so you can add more that may not have been recognized for inclusion.

The "Prompts" from the One Way Group may help you fill out your third column. Assets

When you have finished your Resentments, Fears and Sex lists,

Following the directions means following all of the directions. For your Inventory this will include your assets.

A business which takes no regular Inventory usually goes broke. Taking complete Inventory is a fact-finding and a fact-facing process. It is an effort to discover the truth about the stock-in- trade.   *Page 64*

The purpose of doing an Inventory of your assets is not to give you a chance to reduce the impact of your fears, your resentments, your sexual conduct or the people you have harmed.

In the same way people may use the "Seven Deadly Sins" as a guide to their defects, it may be appropriate to use the "Seven Heavenly Virtues" in relation to your assets. This is a simple list and may be outside your spiritual structure - it is intended as focus for your Inventory. All of the world's faiths and codes of ethics have similar lists of goals and positive attributes we try to achieve.

> *Chastity - This is not simply the maintaining of sexual virginity until marriage, but also your conduct in all areas of sex. Did you lie for sex, manipulate, cheat on your spouse or otherwise place your personal desire over your behavior.*

> *Temperance - This is not simply avoiding alcohol. This idea is the ability to be moderate in all areas - food, righteousness, pride, sex, possessions, etc. Were you temperate in any of the areas of your life?*

> *Charity - Did you care for others with your time, resources and affections, or did you give to get? Was your generosity based on helping the other person or institution, or on what benefit you would receive in pride, goods, services, recognition or reputation?*

> *Dilligence - Did you complete what you began? Did you complete work or projects only so far as your return was concerned? Do you have a long list of accomplishments or a trail of broken promises - of beginnings without completion?*

> *Patience - Could you wait for things to turn out or did you push, become frustrated, manipulate, demand? Was your patience complete or measured to the level of getting what you wanted?*

> *Kindness - Were you kind? To others? To strangers? To animals? To children - your own and others? Was your kindness followed with gossip or back-biting? Was it done to feel or show your superiority? Was the focus of your kindness on others or on yourself?*

> *Humility - Were you able to go unrecognized and be satisifed that the right thing was done? Did you want or demand that people recognize your actions and that credit was not assigned to someone other than you.*

Assets

Assets
Leadership
Friendship
Compassion
Love
Organization
Desire to learn
Nurturing

Did you have gifts? These would be abilities that just seemed to come easily to you in the way of talent, understanding or intuition. Did you share those gifts for the benefit of others or did you use them to manipulate events to your own ends?

If you were given the gift of leadership, did you use it to lead and benefit those who would follow, or did you use it to grab as much as you could or get other people to do what you wanted them to do?

If you could comfort, did you withhold that comfort until your target gave you what you wanted or provided something you could use to satisfy your own greed or desire before you would use your gift?

Did you have talents in areas that brought benefit or comfort to others? Music? Counseling? Cooking? Organizing? Did you use these talents for your own benefit or for the benefit of others?

Was your asset something that was a benefit to those around you or used as a weapon to control situations and people to feed your own desires?

Use a fresh page in your notebook and write a list of assets, gifts or talents or abilities you feel you have been given. What have you been given the talent to do.

As you did with your names, work down the column.

Beside each asset, write how you have used it.

The purpose of knowing your assets is to show where you have been given a gift, and where you have abused that gift in the course of your alcoholism.

If you identify an asset that you have used correctly - do not try to "fix" it! Be grateful and, when the time comes, be ready to turn that asset over to your Higher Power to allow it to benefit those you would help.

It is the nature of alcoholics in the throes of the disease to injure and abuse other people and to lessen and abuse themselves in the constant struggle for more of everything. We demanded more money, sex, power, prestige, possessions, or satisfaction but no matter how great our acquisitions, we were never satisfied.

We take more pride in our ability to be more defective than others and judge everything about ourselves as defective.

In the Ninth Step promises we are told:

"No matter how far down the scale we have gone, we will see how our experience can benefit others."

Judgement

One of the most important lessons we learn is that our judgement of others, or ourselves, has been damaged by our disease. What we consider our most wonderful feature may turn out to be damaging to other people. We find that our worst history becomes our greatest asset in helping others.

At this point we not only need to work at our willingness to have our defects removed and our shortcomings corrected, but become willing to use our assets as they were intended – for the benefit of others – or to let them go.

Accepting that we have assets, and that we have not used those assets properly, is a final phase in becoming willing to have the Higher Power we found in Steps Two and Three take over everything in our lives.

Our defects. Our shortcomings. Our assets.

Everything.

Inventory Prompts

These are prompts to help you think of topics during your Inventory. These are drawn from the One Way Group of Los Angeles, as recorded by Ken D., and applied through the Inventory Notebook sessions of Scott L., and several other Inventory guides available through the internet or discussed in the talks by speakers on http://www.xa-speakers.org.

People Prompts

[ ] Father (Step)
[ ] Mother (Step)
[ ] Sisters (Step)
[ ] Brothers (Step)
[ ] Grandmother
[ ] Grandfather
[ ] In-Laws
[ ] Husbands
[ ] Wives
[ ] Aunts

[ ] Uncles
[ ] Cousins
[ ] Clergy
[ ] Police
[ ] Lawyers
[ ] Judges
[ ] Doctors
[ ] Employers
[ ] Employees
[ ] Co-Workers

[ ] Creditors
[ ] Teachers
[ ] Friends
[ ] Acquaintances
[ ] Girl Friends
[ ] Boy Friends
[ ] Parole Officers
[ ] Probation Officers
[ ] AA Friends
Plus others not listed

Institutional Prompts / Marriage

[ ] Marriage
[ ] Bible
[ ] Church
[ ] Religion
[ ] Races
[ ] Law

[ ] Authority
[ ] Government
[ ] Education System
[ ] Correctional System
[ ] Mental Health System
[ ] Philosophy

[ ] Nationality

Plus others not listed

Principles Prompts

[ ] Retribution
[ ] Ten Commandments
[ ] Jesus Christ
[ ] Satan
[ ] Laws

[ ] Rules
[ ] Death
[ ] Life After Death
[ ] Heaven
[ ] Hell

[ ] Adultery
[ ] Golden Rule
[ ] Seven Deadly Sins
[ ] Social Responsibility
Plus others not listed

Fears Prompts

[ ] Dying
[ ] Insanity
[ ] Rejection
[ ] Loneliness
[ ] Diseases
[ ] Alcohol
[ ] Drugs
[ ] Relapse
[ ] Sex
[ ] Sin
[ ] Self-Expression
[ ] Authority
[ ] Heights
[ ] Unemployment
[ ] Employment
[ ] Parents
[ ] Losing a Spouse
[ ] Losing a Child
[ ] Animals
[ ] Insects
[ ] Police
[ ] Jail

[ ] Doctors
[ ] Stealing
[ ] Creditors
[ ] Being Found Out
[ ] Homosexuals &
    Lesbians
[ ] Failure
[ ] Success
[ ] Responsibility
[ ] Physical Pain
[ ] Fear
[ ] Drowning
[ ] Men
[ ] Women
[ ] Being Alone
[ ] People
[ ] Crying
[ ] Poverty
[ ] Races
[ ] The Unknown
[ ] Abandonment
[ ] Intimacy

[ ] Disapproval
[ ] Rejection
[ ] Confrontation
[ ] Sobriety
[ ] Hospitals
[ ] Responsibility
[ ] Feelings
[ ] Getting Old
[ ] Hurting Others
[ ] Violence
[ ] Writing Inventory
[ ] Being Alive
[ ] Government
[ ] Gangs
[ ] Gossip
[ ] Wealthy People
[ ] Guns
[ ] Change

Plus others not listed.

Sex Prompts

[ ] Abortion
[ ] Adultery
[ ] Animal Sex
[ ] Incest
[ ] Sadism (causing mental
    or physical pain to
    others)
[ ] Masochism (causing
    mental or physical
    pain to self)

[ ] Rape (statutory or
    forced)
[ ] Same Sex
[ ] Any Deviation from
    Normal
[ ] Molesting
[ ] Pornography
[ ] Prostitution
[ ] Fraud Sex (false
    promises)

[ ] Masturbation
[ ] Arson (re: desire)
[ ] Sexual Repression
[ ] Fetish
[ ] Transvestism

Plus others not listed.

The Sex Ideal

Dear God, please help me to see what You want for me regarding relationships with others and my sex life.

The original "Inventory Guide" was handed out in a 'vest pocket' format. It was typeset using the old -technology of "hot type" and printed by hand on similar vintage "proofing press," then folded, stapled and trimmed by hand. The materials from the "Inventory Helper" comes from that original hand-out.

The One Way Group Inventory Guide handout

INVENTORY GUIDE

HIT BOTTOM (Steps 1-2-3)

1. We admitted we were powerless over alcohol—that our lives had become unmanageable.
2. Came to believe that a power greater than ourselves could restore us to sanity.
3. Made a decision to turn our will and our lives over to the care of God as we understood him.

SURRENDER (Step 4)

4. Made a searching and fearless moral inventory of ourselves.

EGO TRANSFER (Step 5)

5. Admitted to God, to ourselves and to another human being the exact nature of our wrongs.

HUMILITY (Steps 6-7-8-9)

6. Became entirely ready to have God remove all these defects of character.

7. Humbly asked him to remove our shortcomings.
8. Made a list of all persons we had harmed and became willing to make amends to them all.
9. Made direct amends to such people wherever possible, except when to do so would injure them or others.

MAINTAIN HUMILITY (Steps 10-11-12)

10. Continued to take personal inventory and when we were wrong promptly admitted it.
11. Sought through prayer and meditation to improve our conscious contact with God as we understood him, praying only for knowledge of his will for us and the power to carry that out.
12. Having had a spiritual awakening as the result of these steps, we tried to carry this message to alcoholics and to practice these principles in all our affairs.

FOURTH STEP INVENTORY

IT IS ONLY BY THE ACT OF THOROUGHLY WRITING THIS FOURTH STEP INVENTORY THAT WE ARE ABLE TO UNLOCK THE MENTAL OBSESSION FROM THE SUBCONSCIOUS MIND, HEART, PERMANENTLY. ONE CAN WRITE TOO LITTLE—NEVER TOO MUCH.

PART 1
RESENTMENTS
Pages 64 thru 67
of
ALCOHOLICS ANONYMOUS

Write from 3 to 6 sentences about each of these negative emotions as they apply to your case against PEOPLE, INSTITUTIONS or PRINCIPLES.

IT IS ONLY BY THE ACT OF THOROUGHLY WRITING, FULL DISCUSSION WITH AN UNDERSTANDING PERSON AND FORGIVENESS THAT WE CAN EVER BE FULLY RID OF THESE DESTRUCTIVE RESENTMENTS.

ANGER	PRIDE
HATRED	INTOLERANCE
CRITICISM	LUST
JEALOUSY	INERTIA
ENVY	SELFISHNESS
GREED	SELF PITY

IN ALL CASES IT WILL BE VERY NECESSARY TO WRITE MANY OF THESE INVENTORIES IN ORDER TO BE FULLY RID OF RESENTMENTS.

EIGHTH STEP LIST
Page 76
of
ALCOHOLICS ANONYMOUS

The Eighth Step list is made at the same time that we make Step Four. This Eighth Step list is the second step that requires us to write. THE ACT OF WRITING THIS LIST PROVES OUR WILLINGNESS IN THE SUBCONSCIOUS MIND, HEART, TO MAKE AMENDS.

PART 2
FEAR
Page 68
of
ALCOHOLICS ANONYMOUS

Write from 3 to 6 sentences about each FEAR that you have ever experienced—especially those that you think no longer bother you. The following list is only a PARTIAL GUIDE and should serve to bring up many more personal fears.

FEARS CAN ONLY BE REMOVED BY THOROUGHLY WRITING THEM AND THEN THOROUGHLY DISCUSSING THEM WITH AN UNDERSTANDING PERSON. MANY INVENTORIES WILL BE NECESSARY IN ORDER TO THOROUGHLY DIG OUT THESE UNKNOWN FEARS.

1. death
2. insanity
3. religion
4. God
5. people
6. institutions
7. principles
8. insecurity

9. rejection	34. failure
10. disease	35. success
11. cancer	36. inferiority
12. venereal disease	37. desires
	38. accidents
13. tuberculosis	39. marriage
14. rheumatism	40. self appraisal
15. arthritis	41. self honesty
16. sex misconduct	42. impotence
	43. police
17. past crimes	44. suffocating
18. authority	45. ego deflation
19. discipline	46. ridicule
20. alcohol	47. responsibility
21. drugs	48. sarcasm
22. gambling	49. moral codes
23. obesity	50. heart trouble
24. obsessions	51. stealing
25. animals	52. disliked
26. insects	53. pain
27. spiders	54. self pride
28. snakes	55. spiritual pride
29. heighth	56. justice
30. dark	57. politics
31. water	58. other races
32. claustrophobia	59. jails
	60. asylums
33. public speaking	

PART 3
SEX (False Shame and Guilt)
Pages 68 thru 70
of
ALCOHOLICS ANONYMOUS

Write from 3 to 6 sentences about each of the sex experiences listed below. It is of equal importance to write of DESIRES as well as ACTUAL ACTS.

GREAT CARE SHOULD BE USED IN SELECTING A REAL UNDERSTANDING PERSON FOR THIS DISCUSSION. HE SHOULD REMOVE YOUR FALSE FEELING OF GUILT—NOT JUST STIR THEM UP.

TO REMOVE IMPOSSIBLE MORAL CODES THAT WE COULD NOT LIVE UP TO IS THE PRIMARY PURPOSE OF THIS INVENTORY. WE THEN BEGIN TO FORM OUR OWN SAFE AND SANE IDEAL FOR OUR FUTURE SEX LIVES.

1. Indecent Exposure
2. Abortion
3. Adultery
4. Animal Sex
5. Incest
6. Sadism (Mental or Physical pain on others)
7. Masochism (Mental or Physical pain on self)
8. Rape (Statutory or Forceful)
9. Sex relations with the opposite sex (Any deviation from normal)
10. Sex relations with the same sex
11. Molesting
12. Pornography (Literature or Photos)
13. Prostitution (Any association with)
14. Fraud Sex (False promises)
15. Masturbation
16. Racial Sex (People of different color or race)
17. Arson (Repressed sex desires)
18. Sex Repression (Repression of any desire)
19. Any sex act or desire not listed which is considered abnormal
20. Fetish (Especially for clothing of the opposite sex)

Step Five

"This is the step that separates the men from boys" (or the girls from women). Step Five breaks the pattern of secrets and isolation that have kept us drunk and held down by our disease."

Twelve Steps and Twelve Traditions, Page 63

Your Sponsor is one of the tools of the program and like any tool it will not help you if you do not use it appropriately. Your Sponsor will give you some directions on how your Fifth Step will be conducted - the place, time, duration and process.

Most Fifth Steps are done with the Sponsor and the person whose Fifth Step is being heard separated from distractions. You Sponsor may want you to go to a special location (your home, the Sponsor's home, a peaceful outdoor location, etc.) to get this personal time - the goal is to remove distractions so you can concentrate on the work of breaking the lifetime habit of keeping the secrets and hiding the truth from yourself and others.

This is when you will use column four on your Inventory. It is commonly called "What is Your Part?"

Before taking Step Five we are given some specific directions to review our work so far.

"If we have been thorough about our personal Inventory, we have written down a lot. We have listed and analyzed our resentments. We have begun to comprehend their futility and their fatality. We have commenced to see their terrible destructiveness. We have begun to learn tolerance, patience and good will toward all men, even our enemies, for we look on them as sick people. We have listed the people we have hurt by our conduct, and are willing to straighten out the past if we can. " *Page 70*

"When we decide who is to hear our story, we waste no time. We have a written Inventory and we are prepared for a long talk. We explain to our partner

what we are about to do and why we have to do it. We should realize that we are engaged upon a life-and-death errand. Most people approached in this way will be glad to help; they will be honored by our confidence."   *Page 75*

There is no "perfect" Fourth Step - the World Service Office is not reserving a special niche for your Inventory to show the world how an Inventory should be done. You do your Fourth the very best you can do it and - most often - will find that there is enough relief from the past to move forward with your Recovery.

There is only one way to do it wrong - to not do it.

Your Sponsor will probably ask questions to clarify some of the points you have written - it will be your opportunity to give more detail on the 19 words you were allowed for anything on your list.

You may be directed to write into the fourth column of the Inventory to identify the exact nature of the problem. What was your part in this entry on the Inventory? What does it tell you about yourself, your personal defects or shortcomings?

A Sponsor will usually tell you something of their own story to show how they have had to deal with items from their own Inventory. Your Sponsor will also guide you away from focus on how others have harmed you, but how you have participated in the process of stepping on their toes and causing them to retaliate. Sometimes a Sponsor will need to point out when you have been taking something as a personal injury that was simply a fact of life affecting others at the same time.

On page 46 of the Twelve and Twelve it says:

> *"The Sponsor probably points out that the newcomer has some assets which can be noted along with his liabilities. This tends to clear away morbidity and encourage balance. As soon as he begins to be more objective, the newcomer can fearlessly, rather than fearfully, look at his own defects."*

You do not need to understand the process - this is not about building your intellectual strength, but getting down to the basic, honest feelings that have been the foundation of your resentments, fears and relationships.

Let your Sponsor guide you and know that there is nothing on your list that does not have a name - and a name means someone else has done it, felt it or had to deal with it. You are not alone.

It is important that you not try to do a Fifth Step alone. You use an Inventory to focus on your own problems - not the defects of the names on your lists. It is for you, your discovery of your own defects and shortcomings, your own spiritual journey and cleaning your side of the street.

You will most likely think of more to go on an Inventory after you do your Fifth Step and it doesn't matter what you call the continuation of your Inventory. The Tenth Step says "Continued to take personal Inventory..." so you might want to look at additions as part of your Tenth Step or a new Fourth Step.

You may find there is a particular area of your life where you want to focus on a new Inventory - your marriage, secret crimes (such as stealing, hidden judgements, gossip, withholding care or money or connection with children or parents, etc.). Discuss these with your Sponsor to determine the best way to approach such new house-cleanings.

The only thing that matters is doing the work and putting pen to paper. Just do it. Your Fourth Step is a real milestone in your commitment and progress to your Recovery.

Step Six

The Big Book only gives one paragraph on Step Six and, while the Twelve Steps and Twelve Traditions gives further instructions, this Step requires you to review the first five Steps to find out what your Inventory has revealed - or confirmed - about your own problems.

> *"Returning home we find a place where we can be quiet for a hour, carefully reviewing what we have done. We thank God from the bottom of our heart that we know Him better. Taking this book down from our shelf we turn to the page which contains the twelve steps. Carefully reading the first five proposals we ask if we have omitted anything, for we are building an arch through which we shall walk a free man at last."*

> *"Is our work solid so far?"*

> *"Are the stones properly in place?"*

> *"Have we skimped on the cement put into the foundation?*

> *"Have we tried to make mortar without sand?"*　　　　　　Pages 87-88

The Big Book frequently uses terms "short-comings" and "defects." One way to look at these problems is to define them, even if Bill did not write the definitions in the Big Book, several other people have provided definitions over the years.

For our purpose, let us think of a "short-coming" as something you need to have but do not have enough of (such as honesty, integrity, tolerance, love, charity, forgiveness, etc.).

A "defect" can be thought of as something you have, but is either wrong, damaged, or being used to make it a weapon to cause damage to others.

Both of these problems need to be cleared, but first you must know what is true about yourself, even if it means losing some of the old comfort of your victim-hood, your righteousness, your belief that you were right or that you had the ability to define the world or other people.

The purpose is to see your own real problems - the thing that either led you to drink or to find comfort in alcoholic numbness and oblivion.

Hopefully in your Inventory you found a few things of value - the Big Book tells us to Inventory EVERYTHING, including our assets. Assets are not there for us to take comfort that we still have something worth keeping - assets are things we have the ability to do but which we may not have used properly or something that we do well that will be of use in our new purpose:

> *"Our real purpose is to fix ourselves to be of maximum service to God and the people about us."*   *Page 89*

The challenge of Step Six is to look at our own desire to hold onto a defect because of the benefit we receive from it – and we have manipulated well known human flaws, from Seven Deadly Sins to our own special flaws, to serve our desires and selfish goals.

Are you willing to live a life, striving to be an honest adult, unlike what you have done before you entered your Recovery?

Are you willing to stop gossip? This means to stop repeating things you did not experience, based on the hearsay of other people, or "improving" the story to make it clear to others what you want it to say?

Are you willing to stop lies? To stop "embellishing" your stories or withholding the truth to appear more virtuous, or to be loved, if lust isn't your primary focus?

If you give up greed, are you afraid you will lose motivation to make a living or not get things you think you deserve?

If you have been known for sloth, or procrastination, are you willing to do the work required, but which people do not expect you to perform?

If your wrath is removed, how will you feel with situations when you feel you have been wronged? Are you willing to live by the same rules you expect of the people around you?

Can you live without your "righteous indignation" when you are positive that the other side is wrong and that you may not win? Even at work? Even in politics? Even in questions of religion?

If you succeed in surrendering your pride, do you think you will never feel satisfaction over true accomplishments?

Step Six prepares you for the work of Step Seven, which requires that you be willing to have God take over everything in your life to heal your problems and make you the person you have the capacity to be.

The goal is to prepare you to be a whole, healthy, emotionally sober, happy human being.

Step Seven

Step Seven may not be what we expected when we began. It is not coming up with a list of things we want God to fix and then putting in our service order to have the changes made to our specifications.

On page 76 we are given what many people call the Seventh Step Prayer:

"When ready, we say something like this:

"My Creator, I am now willing that You should have all of me, good and bad. I pray that You now remove from me every single defect of character which stands in the way of my usefulness to You and my fellows. Grant me strength, as I go out from here, to do Your bidding. Amen."

But many people say that the Third Step Prayer does not end with "amen" and that the Seventh Step Prayer does. This is because they are thought of as one enveloping Prayer.

Together they read:

"God I offer myself to Thee - to build with me and do with me as Thou wilt. Relieve me of the bondage of self that I may better do Thy will. Take away my difficulties, that victory over them may bear witness to those I would help of Thy power, Thy love, and Thy way of life. May I do Thy will always! My Creator, I am now willing that You should have all of me, good and bad. I pray that You now remove from me every single defect of character which stands in the way of my usefulness to You and my fellows. Grant me strength, as I go out from here, to do Your bidding. Amen."

Even if you find other wording to be more appropriate, are you in full agreement with the terms of this Prayer?

Are you willing to turn everything over to God or a Higher Power of your understanding, holding nothing back?

Are you sure you have not deceived yourself by withholding some detail of your past, your desires, your plans or your expectations of how your life and Recovery are supposed to unfold?

This step is complete surrender. We were told:

"The results were nil until we let go absolutely." Page 58

In the beginning we said we were willing to go to any lengths for victory over alcoholism. These are the lengths to which we must go.

We try to clean house to the best of our ability, knowing that we will continue cleaning for as long as we live.

We strive to be honest in our dealings with those around us, with ourselves, with our past and with our Higher Power.

We work for progress, knowing we will never attain perfection.

Can you confirm to yourself that you have, to the best of your ability, done the work intended behind the Prayer?

If you believe you have done the best you can do to this point, knowing you may improve later, you are ready to move into the work of Steps Eight and Nine.

Step Seven With A Worksheet

One of our visitors asked us if we knew of a Step Seven worksheet. There are, of course, a plethora of such things, most of them for sale somewhere. One of our members was curious about creating something more of a Step Seven think-sheet. And he did. And it's free. And here it is.

Step Seven: - Humbly asked Him to remove our shortcomings.

What shortcomings?

The "exact nature of our wrongs" in Step Five is expressed in terms of "defects of character" in Step Six, and offered up to God for removal as "shortcomings" in Step Seven. Bill Wilson, when asked why he used three different sets of words to define character defects, said it was to avoid repetition. Therefore, he intended that there be no significant distinction. Some members waste time by differentiating the three expressions, which we term, simply, as character defects.

When Step Five is performed well, we leave with a list of our character defects. In Step Six, we progressively become willing to have these removed from us, and in Step Seven, we pray that they might be removed.

Make a grid similar to the one below and list your defects of character in it. If an example we have entered applies to you, let it remain. If not, replace it with one of yours that is not listed.

Some of these may be familiar to you.

Willingness for Removal

We have identified seven possible levels of your willingness to have each character defect removed. These are:

1 - Already removed

2 - Absolutely willing

3 - Almost willing

4 - Reluctant, but willing to be willing

5 - Give me more time

6 - I don't think I will ever be willing

7 - Never

Place one of these level indicators in the right column of the grid for each character defect. Add other defects as you learn them.

Character Defect List

1 is Low Willingness - 7 is High Willingness

Defect	Willingness to Have Removed
1. Abusiveness	1 2 3 4 5 6 7
2. Anger/Wrath	1 2 3 4 5 6 7
3. Dishonesty	1 2 3 4 5 6 7
4. Envy	1 2 3 4 5 6 7
5. Fear	1 2 3 4 5 6 7
6. Gluttony	1 2 3 4 5 6 7
7. Greed	1 2 3 4 5 6 7
8. Humility	1 2 3 4 5 6 7
9. Irresponsibility	1 2 3 4 5 6 7
10. Lust	1 2 3 4 5 6 7
11. Pride	1 2 3 4 5 6 7
12. Procrastination	1 2 3 4 5 6 7
13. Stinginess	1 2 3 4 5 6 7
14. Thoughtlessness	1 2 3 4 5 6 7

As you know from reading the 12&12, our stubborn insistence to "never" allow a defect to be removed must, itself, be removed.

If your willingness level for any item is not 1 or 2, you will want to repeat the exercise again later.

We are certain that God will not remove from alcoholics the defects of character that we do not admit we have. This fact explains one of the reasons we must take Steps 4 and 5. We also know that God may remove our defects only to the extent that we are willing for them to be removed. That is why we take Step Six. He does not intrude upon our private desires to cohabit with the trash in the garbage can.

Humility?

Are you Humble? Place a check mark next to each of the statements in the form which identifies your level of Humility?

Describe your level of Humility

__ I am so low, I cohabit with worms.

__ I deserve contempt and condemnation.

__ I am worthless.

__ I am filled with guilt, shame, remorse and self-loathing.

__ I feel like being totally honest.

__ I have little interest in impressing others.

__ I have nothing to hide from God.

__ I am coming to really know who I am.

Even though the dictionary says that Humility describes one of lower status, that is not the spiritual significance of Humility. Therefore, the first four statements above describe humiliation, not Humility.

The root is "hum," the same root as in humus and humor. For us, Humility means "down to earth." Humility means honest, real, and without phoniness. Our role model, Mother Teresa had it right when she said, "If you are truly Humble, nothing can touch you, neither disgrace nor praise, because you know who you are."

So, we enter into Step Seven with honesty, willing to stand naked, so to speak, before God, hiding nothing, and with no hidden motives.

More about God

In Step Seven, we ask God to do something – to remove our shortcomings. But not all conceptions of a Higher Power are likely to improve us. Some of the Higher Powers we have encountered are a tree, a moving van, a rock, the classic light bulb, and even the AA Group itself, which is suggested as a last resort starting point in AA literature. Amongst these, the only possible candidate for removing shortcomings might be the AA Group.

However, we think it is not prudent to go through your defects catalogue before your Group. You would be exposing yourself unnecessarily. You would get confused and incompatible reactions from them. At best, the Group, or even your Sponsor, might give you some insight into the nature of your wrongs and some remedial possibilities.

So, you might as well bite the bullet and open yourself up to the spiritual source, which we might as well call "God" for communication purposes. Here is an opportunity for you to identify further your own conception of God. This is not completely a true-false exercise. Some of your responses might require some contemplation. Thinking deeply on these questions is the benefit of doing it.

Your Own Conception of God

What is the name of your Higher Power?

Where is your Higher Power located?

What is the primary location of your Higher Power at the time you are meditating or praying?

Do you pray in a special posture? A special place? Why?

Is your motive underlying the Prayer as important as the thoughts and words of the Prayer itself?

Should your message be specific and precise, or is it OK to be vague in your requests to your Higher Power?

Place a checkmark next to the defects which God is likely to remove?

___ Defects of which you are not aware.

___ Defects that stand in the way of your usefulness to God.

___ Defects that stand in the way of your usefulness to others.

___ Defects that annoy you.

___ Defects that interfere with your happiness.

Once you have asked your Higher Power to remove your defects (shortcomings), will they be gone?

Does your Higher Power reward you when you comply with His will?

Does your Higher Power punish you when you do not comply with His will?

Is it necessary for you to attend or be a member of a church?

It is important to note that we ask only for the removal of defects of character which stand in the way of our usefulness to God and our fellows. What about the ones that are painful to us? We do not hand a list to God of our understanding and demand that the defects we choose be removed.

In the Seventh Step we give up our judgements - of others and of ourselves, but more importantly we give up our right to decide what we deserve or do not deserve – remember what brought us to this place.

We should never pray for what we deserve - most of us would not survive receiving it.

Inventory Summary

Use this list as a quick review of the process outlined in this booklet.

Use Your Sponsor

- If your Sponsor wants to do anything differently, go with your Sponsor's direction! Your Sponsor knows you as an individual. Your Sponsor may have tools not included in this booklet.

Steps One, Two and Three

DR. BOB'S REVIEW

- Get a notebook and writing gear.

- Set a committed schedule (time, day, hours per week, etc.) and then stick to it. Discuss your time commitment with your Sponsor.

- Write your personal information on Page 1.

Step Four

SESSION WORK

- Commit to your Sponsors how much time you will spend working your inventory. Daily, Weekly or however much time you will actually devote to writing your Inventory. Minimum.

- Pray before you begin each session - get quiet and do whatever your personal spiritual practice suggests.

- Pages two and three are the first two-page spread. Draw a line down the right page approximately in the middle.

- Begin on the left side of the left page margin line to serve as Column One and begin to write names - people, places, institutions, principles, etc. If it comes to mind, write it down. Even if you covered something on a previous Inventory - if it comes up write it down!

- Write a name, skip a line, write a name, skip a line - no matter how dramatic or complex you feel that entry to be.

- Always work down, not across.

- When you cannot think of a name to add to Column One for 20 minutes, begin Column Two.

- Column Two will have why this name is on your list. Do not use more than 19 words. If you think of a new name for inclusion on your list in Column One while doing Column Two, write it at the end of your current list of names.

- When you have completed the list of names with entries in Column Two, go to Column Three.

- Go down the list and read Column One, the item in Column Two related to Column One, and write down in Column Three what this affected. Describe what it affected in your own words - the Seven Deadly Sins or other list. These must mean something to you, personally.

- Hold Column Four until you sit down with your Sponsor for Step Five.

- On a new page, list your assets the same way you listed the names in the previous section of the Inventory.

- When you can look at the list for ten minutes and not come up with another asset, start the second column of how you have used, or abused, that gift. Keep the entries in this column to a maximum of 19 words.

Step Five

- Let your Sponsor (or the other person with whom you are doing a Fifth Step) set the time, location and conditions of your Fifth Step. You may want to have soda, water or coffee available, and you may want to plan on sharing a meal if the Fifth will take a long time. Your Fifth Step may require more than one session, but usually the full Fifth can be done in a single face-to-face session.

- Pray before you begin your Fifth, or whatever your spiritual practice requires.

- As you and your Sponsor discuss the first three columns, write into Column Four exactly what your part was in the item under discussion.

- You may want a 2nd page to write a list of recurring defects that come up during your Fifth Step. You may need to keep yet another page available to list items that will be required for your Eighth Step - the things for which you must make amends.

- Listen to your Sponsor - a Sponsor's experience will be your strongest guide as to how you can deal with your own history.

- When your have completed Column Four, discuss what the results will mean for your Recovery - what you have learned.

- End your Fifth Step with a Prayer or Meditation before you leave to do the first hour of your Sixth Step.

Step Six

- Review your Fifth Step, particularly Column Four, and spend a quiet hour meditating on what you have learned about yourself.

- Consider the benefits you get from the defects, shortcomings and the abuse of assets you have identified in your Inventory. Are you willing to surrender those manipulated benefits and have your Higher Power be in charge of your life and rewards? Are you willing to simply do what you are supposed to do without satisfaction of your desires, damage to others or as part of your selfish behaviors?

Step Seven

- Pray the full 3rd and 7th Step Prayers, with the personal words necessary for you to truly believe your Prayer. If your belief has other practices or rituals to serve this purpose, do those.

- Remember this is not a one time action, so continue to look for your own selfishness, defects, shortcomings or abuse of your gifts and remain willing to surrender those actions.

Continue Your Inventory as Needed.

Recovery Reader – Second Edition

sober.org

Steps Eight and Nine

Step Eight - Made a list of all persons we had harmed and became willing to make amends to them all.

Step Nine –Made direct amends to such people, wherever possible, except when to do so would injure them or others.

It is time now to clear away the wreckage of our past. We do this by making amends and restitution. Restitution is defined as "the giving back of something that was taken away."

Step Eight: Made a list of all persons we had harmed, and became willing to make amends to them all.

For Step Eight, we'll give you a guide in order for you to have one last opportunity to be certain that all has been uncovered. Please complete the guide on your own as soon as possible.

Now, please take out your Inventory forms, as they are the heart of our Eighth Step amends list. But we also need to ask God to reveal to us any others we have harmed but who are not yet on our list. We'll add their names now as we move on to Step Nine.

As part of our effort to be thorough, we must define the word "amend," and according to dictionary.com, we find:

a·mend [uh-mend]

—*verb (used with object)*

1. *to alter, modify, rephrase, or add to or subtract from (a motion, bill, constitution, etc.) by formal procedure: Congress may amend the proposed tax bill.*

2. *to change for the better; improve: to amend one's ways.*

3. *to remove or correct faults in; rectify.*

—*verb (used without object)*

4. *to grow or become better by reforming oneself: He amends day by day.*

Focus on Others

We can see that our purpose is not just to relieve ourselves of the guilt and shame from the effects of our past actions, but we are to "alter," "repair," "to change for the better; improve," "to correct faults in; rectify" and "become better."

Moving into our Ninth Step amends we step from the self-absorption of the first eight steps to the real world. To this point I admitted, I came to believe, I did an Inventory, I shared it, I became willing, I asked to have my defects removed, and I made the list of my harms while active in my alcoholism.

But in Step Nine our goal is to heal the damage we have done.

We hurt real people; I did not just hurt "my mother." Before she ever had me she was a woman with a life and goals and hopes, and I hurt that woman. That real woman.

Now I review my list and come to see these people as independent from me. What do I do to make it better, to improve, to repair, to set right, the real damage I did to these real people. How do I do this without making it more about "me?"

Some people coming into AA are told they do not have to do amends if it will be difficult, embarrassing, or expensive. Many people follow that direction and, since they have not done the work required by the Step, soon find themselves drunk again – and very surprised.

"Reminding ourselves that we have decided to go to any lengths to find a spiritual experience, we ask that we be given strength and direction to do the right thing, no matter what the personal consequences might be." Page 79

To do The Work means to Do The Work! Not to come up with reasons why the one attempting to achieve lasting sobriety is different and can explain their way out of doing that work.

In the Ninth Step, we focus on the one we have hurt. Sometimes this means that we have to pay money, lose the reputation we had built by hiding the truth, or even serve time in prison to make amends for a real crime.

But we become free, without the guilt, shame, and doom that comes from continuing our life hiding the truth. We can walk down the street without fear of being exposed, face the people we meet, and know that we have done what was in our power to right our wrongs.

More Action

The amends process is explained as the Big Book tells us what to do next:

"...Now we go out to our fellows and repair the damage done in the past. We attempt to sweep away the debris which has accumulated out of our effort to live on self-will and run the show ourselves. If we haven't the will to do this, we ask until it comes. Remember, it was agreed at the beginning that we would go to any lengths for victory over alcohol." Page 88, 89

The Big Book divides the amends that we need to make into five types. We'll list each of the amends that you need to make according to the type. Then, before approaching anyone, reread the advice offered by the Big Book regarding each type. Also, seek counsel from your Sponsor, spiritual advisor, or another member of the group that's gone through the amends process. Finally, pray each morning regarding all the items listed. Now, label each with a plus (+) or a minus (-), depending on your willingness to make the amends — a plus indicating immediate readiness and the minus noting the ones you feel more hesitant about.

Review

- Whom did I hurt?
- What did I do?
- Where was I at fault?

- Where had I been selfish, dishonest, or inconsiderate?

- Did I arouse: Jealousy? Suspicion? Bitterness?

- What Should I have done differently?

Step Eight: Types of Amends

Amend type (a) — People We Hate / Resent

- It may be some have done us more harm than we have done them.

- With a person we dislike, we take the bit in our teeth.

- It is harder to go to an enemy than a friend, but the benefit is greater.

- Go in a helpful, forgiving spirit.

- Do not criticize or argue.

- We are there to sweep off OUR side of the street.

- Nothing can be accomplished until we do so.

- Discuss your faults, not his or hers.

- Be calm, frank, open.

- It doesn't matter if they accept the apology or throw us out of the office. We've done our part.

Now transfer the names from your resentment and other lists, except for family members. Add any other names that have come to you that you have harmed or owe amends.

Write your list.

Amend type (b) — The People / Institutions / Owed Money Most alcoholics owe money.

- We don't dodge anyone.

- In some cases, some of us had to disclose our alcoholism by way of explaining what drove us and what we are now trying to do.

- We do not try to beat anyone out of anything, but we arrange a deal that we can live up to. Arranging time payments has worked for many of us.

- Let them know you're sorry.

- Drinking made us slow to pay.

- If we fear facing our creditors, we often drink.

Write your list.

Amend type (c) — Incidents of criminal offense

- Some of us padded expense accounts, fell behind on child support, wrote bad checks, and committed other offenses of the law.

- We remind ourselves that we must be willing to go to any lengths to correct these mistakes if we are to stay sober.

- We don't have the power to do this.

- We ask God for strength and direction.

- We don't worry about the consequences. We know God will protect us if we try to do the right thing for a change.

- We may lose position or reputation, though most of us have experienced that already.

- We are willing anyway.

- We must not shrink at anything.

Write your list.

Amend Type (d) — Incidents of Domestic Trouble

- We may have committed adultery.

- After years with a drunk, spouses get worn out, resentful, and uncommunicative.

- We begin to feel self-pity .

- So we look around for another, feeling justified, when WE were really the source of the problem in the first place.

- Sometimes that leads to feelings of guilt.

- We have to do something about this.

- If the spouse does not know, we do not always say it is best to tell.

- If she knows something, we admit our fault.

- We have no right to name the others involved.

Write your list.

Keep in mind we are dealing with the most horrible human emotion: jealousy.

- Don't risk more combat over this.

- Some think just being sober in the home now is enough. It isn't.

- We have treated spouses and family in a shocking way.

- We have been like a tornado.

- We broke hearts and uprooted affection, and our selfishness kept the home in turmoil.

- Just saying we are sorry will not do.

- We sit with the family and analyze the past, not criticizing any of them.

- Yes, they may have defects, but many of them were inspired by our behaviors.

- We pray each morning for God to show us the way of patience, tolerance, kindliness, and love.

Amend Type (e) — Wrongs We Can Never Fully Right

Be very careful about listing anyone or anything here. We only list someone here if we can HONESTLY say that the wrong cannot be righted, usually when to do so would further injure them or another person. We are willing (or pray for the willingness to become willing) to make the amend if we can.

- If the case is that they cannot be seen, we write them an honest letter.

- We don't delay if it can be avoided.

- We do not have to be scraping, but we do have to be sensible, tactful, considerate, and Humble.

Discuss the circumstances surrounding the amends with your Sponsor or the meeting facilitator before you list anyone here.

Caution Where Others Are Concerned

Sometimes others are involved (spouses, children, other family members). We don't sacrifice them to save ourselves. Before taking drastic action that might affect another we get their consent, we consult others, and we ask God to help. If the drastic step is still indicated, we move ahead.

This guide may be copied and distributed freely so long as the content is not altered and the price, except for photocopying fees if desired, is not charged.

Step Nine - Doing It!

Reading for Step Nine

Our experience with Step Nine prompts us to emphasize four ideas about this step.

Token amends will not do! Just what is an amend? Here is what our trusty dictionary said:

a-mend :(uh mend') v. v.t.

> *1. to change for the better; improve.*
>
> *2. to remove or correct faults in; rectify.*
>
> *3. to grow or become better by reforming oneself.*

Later in this document you will see an extraction of words and phrases that the authors of the Big Book used to describe what they meant by the word amend. Their true meaning, while including the definition above, is more like the synonyms for the word, "rectify:"

rectify : v.

> *1. right, set right, put right, make right, correct, adjust, regulate, straighten, square; focus, attune; mend, amend, emend, fix, repair, revise; remedy, redress, cure, reform.*

One might even use the definition of the word, "repair," to express their meaning:

re-pair :[1] (ri pâr') -paired, -pair-ing . v.t.

> *1. to restore to a good or sound condition after decay or damage; mend.*
>
> *2. to restore or renew.*
>
> *3. to remedy; make up for; compensate for.*

Extracted words and phrases as examples of "amends:"

BB = the Big Book of AA, Alcoholics Anonymous

12&12 = Twelve Steps and Twelve Traditions

Self-Correction

...*sweep away the debris which has accumulated out of our effort to live on self-will.*   [BB, page 76, line 22]

...*demonstration of good will*   [BB, page 77]

...*sweep off our side of the street*   [BB, page 77]

...*sit down with the family and frankly analyze the past as we now see it.*   [BB, page 83,]

...*We clean house with the family.*   [BB, page 83]

...*asking each morning in Meditation that our Creator show us the way of patience, tolerance, kindliness and love.*   [BB, page 83]

...*The spiritual life is not a theory. We have to live it...*   [BB, page 83]

...*Our behavior will convince them more than our words.*   [BB, page 83]

...*There may be some wrongs we can never fully right.*   [BB, page 83]

...*Some people cannot be seen—we send them an honest letter.*   [BB, page 83]

...*We should be sensible, tactful, considerate and Humble without being servile or scraping.*   [BB, page 83]

Restitution

...*repair the damage [we have] done in the past*   [BB, page 76]

...*set right the wrong*   [BB, page 77, line]

...*straighten out the past*   [BB, page 77]

...*arranging the best deal... [of repayment] ... we can*   [BB, page 78]

...*reparations*   [BB, page 79]

...*sent...money*   [BB, page 79]

...willing to go to jail   *[BB, page 79]*

...make a public statement   *[BB, page 80]*

... [make]...good to the wife or parents   *[BB, page 82]*

...reconstruction   *[BB, page 83]*

Apology

...confessing our former ill feeling [BB, page 77]

...expressing our regret   *[BB, page 77]*

...we let these people know we are sorry   *[BB, page 78]*

...admitting faults   *[BB, page 79]*

...admit our faults   *[BB, page 81]*

...asking forgiveness   *[BB, page 79]*

...A remorseful mumbling that we are sorry won't fill the bill at all.

[BB, page 83]

Don't rush into amends without guidance. You can mess up yourself and others unless the best judgment is used. When we are new to sobriety, our judgment is often not so swift. Please read again the words we offered for Step Eight, which is the planning of your amendment step.

Your amends must never harm others. Both of the books make clear that we cannot seek atonement at the expense of others. Be especially careful not to implicate or injure other people in your wrong-doing.

Don't forget to take the hidden step – forgiveness. You will recall that in Step Four you listed the people who had harmed you as part of your resentment matrix. None of the steps emphasizes sufficiently that the ultimate process of resentment eradication (and they must be wiped out) is forgiveness of those we resent. If you have not yet cleaned up your resentments, finish them off in Step Nine. It then becomes the double-edged sword that cuts you free from all harms done by you and to you.

However, there is a difference between being forgiven and forgiving. Our amends to those we have harmed are made at our own initiative and directly to the person harmed, whenever possible. On the other hand, when we are forgiving others, it is rarely appropriate to approach them to let them know they are forgiven. Why?

They might have no idea that we have resented them. After all, the resentment is ours. Letting them in on our problem cannot do them any good, and may cause them considerable hurt feelings or aggravation – even anger.

We have been learning not to play God and to avoid Ego-serving activities. Approaching others to let them know they are forgiven would usually be thought of as self-serving. This we avoid.

If, on the other hand, the injuring party has let us know that they feel guilt about what they have done, it can often be a true act of kindness to let them know they are off the hook as far as we are concerned. We do this with true Humility and compassion. We never give the impression that they owe us something for our act of forgiveness. We then try to treat them the way we want others to forgive us for our own wrongs.

Some of our members believe that the other side of the forgiveness coin, that we are forgiven for our transgressions, is a necessary goal of Step Nine. There is no need at all that we be forgiven by the person we have harmed after we make an amend. If they choose to tell us we are forgiven, that is a fine gesture – one we might cherish. However, the real goal here is that you cease to know guilt stemming from your prior acts or omissions. The removal of guilt is the exclusive domain of your spiritual power.

On your way. Your Step Nine can last from several weeks to many years. Start it when you have finished Step Eight and are told to do so. Continue until you are done.

Promises of Step Nine

Here are the 20 promises starting at the bottom of page 83 in the Big Book. Some people think these are the only promises the Big Book makes. Little do they realize that each step has a set of promises, and that there are many more besides. There are even a few guarantees. Drop us a line if you have found the 173 promises and guarantees in the Big Book that we have found.

If we are painstaking about this phase of our development,

- We will be amazed before we are half way through.
- We are going to know a new freedom

- And a new happiness.

- We will not regret the past

- Nor wish to shut the door on it.

- We will comprehend the word serenity and we will know peace.

- No matter how far down the scale we have gone, we will see how our experience can benefit others.

- That feeling of uselessness (will disappear).

- And self-pity will disappear.

- We will lose interest in selfish things and (we will) gain interest in our fellows.

- Self-seeking will slip away.

- Our whole attitude and outlook upon life will change.

- Fear of people (will leave us) and

- (Fear) of economic insecurity will leave us.

- We will intuitively know how to handle situations which used to baffle us.

- We will suddenly realize that God is doing for us what we could not do for ourselves.

- Are these extravagant promises? We think not. They are being fulfilled among us—sometimes quickly, sometimes slowly.

- They will always materialize if we work for them.

Writing: It would be a good idea to update your amendment plan (Step Eight) when each amendment is done. Check it off. Make a note as to their reaction. If an agreement was reached concerning further action on your part, write it down. We even know one Sponsor who keeps Step Eight lists of his Step partners on a computer (on an encrypted file for total privacy). Every month or so, the list is made current.

Forgiveness – The Missing Step

This is a discussion of forgiveness. First, we point out, as if you didn't already know, that alcoholics tend to feel victimized by people, places, things, and the cosmos in general. As if this were not enough, we alcoholics also carry a grudge about what has been done to us or not done for us.

In the paragraphs that follow, we explore the implications of carrying resentments around with us. If we cannot get rid of our resentments any other way, we are sometimes faced with the ultimate resentment eradication tool forgiveness– we forgive those whom we resent. The nature of forgiveness is investigated, and finally, techniques to achieve forgiveness are presented. Our discussion of forgiveness is elaborated upon through links to four additional pages below. It is best, we think, that they be viewed in the order listed.

Alcoholics are Resentment–Prone

Most alcoholics have a deep (almost pathological) sense of justice. If we are wronged (meaning often that we did not get what we wanted) or if we even conjure up the notion that we might have been wronged, we find full justification to express anger or harbor resentment. It then seems almost a duty to carry a justified resentment. Otherwise, those who have wronged us would get off scot-free. And that wouldn't be right, would it? So, we waste our God-given lives judging and punishing our fellows. Relinquishing a justified resentment is one of the most difficult experiences known to the alcoholic.

If you explore the origins of the word resentment in our dictionary your will find:

Resent has also been used in other senses that seem strange to us, such as "to feel pain" or "to perceive by smell." The thread that ties the senses together is the notion of feeling or perceiving. Again.

For the alcoholic, resentment is a reliving of the offense that injured us in the first place. Think about it. We perceive that we are punishing that person for their wrong, when in fact, we are simply willing ourselves to feel the hurt again, and again, and again. Get the point? Resenting makes no more sense than our drinking did. Something is twisted in brainsville, we think.

Methods of Resentment Removal

How are resentments removed? Here are the customary methods and they are presented in increasing order of difficulty (to the alcoholic, that is):

NEGLECT

Yes, benign neglect removes most of our thoughts of the day. We simply forget about things that are not important to us. As we grow in our sobriety we are less interested in harboring resentments and they follow a natural order of elimination, unless they are captured by our perverse habits.

REFLECTION

If we are aware of our resentment and, if we wish to get rid of it, we are wise to think about it. Did we really hear what the other person said? Did they really say what they meant? Was what we heard just a rumor? Does the offending action fit a pattern, or might it have been a fluke? Was the offender in distress? Are we giving this person the benefit of the doubt? If not, why are we better off carrying resentment?

INVESTIGATION

Maybe we need more substantiation or facts? Is there independent verification of what happened? Have we mentioned to the perceived offending person that we are taken aback by their action and we would like to see if we understood correctly? Do the facts substantiate that we were really harmed on purpose? If not, why not just drop the whole thing?

BENEFIT/COST ANALYSIS

If there was a real offense, especially an intentional one, what is the benefit to us of carrying a resentment? Should it be a big resentment? What should be its ranking among the other justified resentments we already have? Will its insertion into our resentment Inventory mean we should discard a resentment of lesser injury? How long should we carry this resentment? Does it justify vengeance? Are we willing to suffer loss of friendship, destruction of property, expense, arrest, or social disfavor as a consequence of being judge, jury, and executioner? Would it simply be nicer to be rid of the resentment?

FORGIVENESS

Yes, it is possible to be rid of residual resentments through forgiveness. The reference links below will describe how this can be done. Here are a few pointers though:

ANONYMITY

The person you resent need not know of your resentment. In fact, it is much better and simpler if they do not know. A grudge nurtured in secret is much sweeter anyway.

PRIVACY

Unless the person whom you resent has asked for your forgiveness or, if you are absolutely certain that they will cherish your forgiveness, you should keep your forgiving private. It can be a gross form of arrogance to approach another person in order to tell them that they are forgiven. Usually, they will have no idea of having committed an offense and they will wonder who the dickens you think you are forgiving them – God, perhaps?

FINALITY

Once you have forgiven another person the act is final. It need never be repeated nor should you permit the resentment to recur.

Of course, there is the old standby – Prayer. After the discussion of each step in the Big Book, a number of methods to alleviate or remove problems are set forth. The persistent and fundamental tool "suggested" to us is Prayer. Prayer should have been in the list above, but we didn't know how to rank it in order of difficulty. For some of us, Prayer is the easy and natural tool for straightening out our lives. For others, it is an alien, even hostile, prospect. Whatever one's feeling about Prayer might be, there should be steady effort to make it a primary ingredient in our consciousness.

What is Forgiveness

for-give (fuhr giv′) v. <-gave, -giv-en, -giv-ing>
1. to grant pardon for or remission of (an offense, sin, etc.);
absolve.

2. *to cancel or remit (a debt, obligation, etc.): to forgive the interest owed on a loan.*

3. *to grant pardon to (a person).*

4. *to cease to feel resentment against: to forgive one's enemies.*

5. *to pardon an offense or an offender.*

Who is the Keeper of Our Wrongs

There may be a bit of our personal theology here. If yours is different, please don't be offended. You might just be right.

When we commit an offense (or fail to fulfill an obligation), the wrong is recorded. The party(s) we have offended, if any, might keep score – most people do. We also add to the bag of guilt, shame, remorse, and self-loathing that we haul around with us.

But the real recorder has been built into the system of the universe by its Creator. It is automatic and inevitable that all wrongs are recorded and the one and only thing that can remove them is amendment (correction or repair) of the wrong. Period.

In the East, they call this system Karma. In metaphysics, they might call it the Akasha. Whatever it is called and wherever it is located (most likely within us), it works, and it always works without fail.

Objectives of Forgiveness

Just who is being forgiven, and by whom?

Forgiving others

If an act of courtesy on our part will help others feel better about themselves, then perhaps we should let them know we have no negative feelings about their actions. But we should never believe that we can, in fact, interfere in their being forgiven in accordance with God's plan for them. Our beliefs and actions are not part of that plan.

Being forgiven by others

The same logic applies as with forgiving others. Cosmetic forgiveness between humans can be a compassionate act. However, genuine forgiveness is a very personal matter.

Being forgiven by God

God does not keep records nor does He carry grudges. The universal system of justice He has created takes care of correction and forgiveness automatically. He does not intervene. He simply loves us all the time.

Forgiving ourselves

Just as humans cannot truly forgive each other, self-forgiveness is not possible, either. However, there is more to be said here. We assuredly agree that many, if not most, alcoholics know guilt, shame, remorse, and self-loathing to excess. We MUST be rid of these before we can truly see the perfection of the Creator within ourselves as we are intended to do. We must also be enabled to look into the mirror and smile at the creature emerging from the slime of self-centered assertion into the service of the Father through his fellows. Knowing that we are forgiven is a requirement for the sober life.

The first thing to do is to clear away the false crimes of which we have convicted ourselves. A solid Step Five will produce a list of our defects of character and a preliminary list of persons we have harmed. If we feel bad about ourselves for anything not on these lists, the lists are either incomplete or we are caught up in the defect of senseless self-condemnation. Feeling bad about oneself, which might have been justified when we were doing our damage, is often an emotional hangover that needs to be discarded. You can create a self-respect (not pride) list. It might be next to the mirror and it might say, "I have cause to respect myself today because I have ... (list of good deeds, steps taken, persons helped, Prayers, etc.)." But, be sure never to put yourself on your Step Eight list.

The second thing to do is to take Step Nine (after completing Step One through Step Eight with your Sponsor, of course). Why? Because an amend is the only means of gaining forgiveness.

Our "Right" to Forgive

We feel that when a wrong is committed there is an immediate creation of a record of the act. This record cannot be prevented NOR can it be eradicated through forgiveness. The injured party cannot remove the record, and God will not do so either, because He created the system of records in the first place. It works just fine for Him.

So, how are you and others absolved from your wrongs? You guessed it. Step Nine. Amendment (repair/correction) of the offense removes the record automatically. Forgiveness plays no part whatsoever in absolution.

Why all this talk about forgiveness then? The fact is that we are not forgiving offenses against ourselves by removing the need for amendment on the part of the offender. That we cannot do. Only amendment can do that. Our act of forgiving is to clean out ourselves. That's right. We remove from ourselves the curse we have imposed upon ourselves to punish the offender. Our forgiveness absolves not their act but removes our own personal reaction to it.

Wow, what a concept! It is not their karma we correct, but our own!

Here are some additional sources we have found genuinely helpful. You might notice that some of them don't agree completely with what we have said. That doesn't make them, or us, wrong. It does make it necessary for you to dwell deeply upon your own convictions.

The Big Book on Forgiveness

Our Big Book (Alcoholics Anonymous) has a great deal to say about resentments and forgiveness. Enjoy.

Harboring Resentments is Fatal

We are reluctant to repeat the book.

However, some of the points it makes cannot be left without comment: If we were to read page 66 again, we would note the power of resentment far exceeds any conception we had of negative thinking. Were you aware that:

...a life which includes deep resentment leads only to futility and unhappiness.

The hours in which we allow futility and unhappiness in our lives are not worthwhile. Resentments waste our lives.

Resentments shut us off from the sunlight of the Spirit, thereby preventing the maintenance and growth of a spiritual experience.

When shadowed from the sunlight of the Spirit, the insanity of alcohol returns, we drink again, and we die.

Harboring of resentments is fatal.

Yet, freeing ourselves of resentment must be done! There is striking evidence that resentment creates a physical poison in our bodies in addition to the mental and spiritual maladies it feeds.

Eradicating Resentments

How do we rid ourselves of resentments? Hopefully, this process began in Step Four. Our list holds the key.

Note the message of the column headings in our Inventory:

Column #1) Who do you hold a grudge against?

Column #2) What did they do that you found offensive?

Column #3) How did you contribute to their action? and

Column #4) Why did you react with a resentment?

The first lesson is that resentments cannot be cleared up until we know we have them and why. The second lesson is that we have made ourselves vulnerable to the outside world to an extraordinary extent. Our entire self-concept has been molded by the opinions and actions of others, and our old thinking as to what we ought to be and were.

Next, it is necessary to be willing to let go of the resentment. You will learn more about this in Step Six. Moreover (and the Big Book doesn't give as much help here as it might), we must forgive the person we resent. There will be more discussion of forgiving others in Step Eight. Just accept right now that you are going to have to do it! There is no other course.

The ultimate key given you in the Big Book is the oft repeated notion that your life is now on a different basis. A basis is a foundation – that upon which all the rest stands. Your new basis is trusting and relying upon God.

The Art of Forgiveness
Reprinted from the Big Book (Alcoholics Anonymous) and the 12&12

> *We cannot be helpful to all people, but at least God will show us how to take a kindly and tolerant view of each and every one. Referring to our list again. Putting out of our minds the wrongs others had done, we resolutely looked for our own mistakes. Where had we been selfish, dishonest, self-seeking, and frightened? Though a situation had not been entirely our fault, we tried to disregard the other person involved entirely. Where were we to blame? The Inventory was ours, not the other man's.*   *Page 67, line 11*

> *If we are sorry for what we have done, and have the honest desire to let God take us to better things, we believe we will be forgiven and will have learned our lesson. If we are not sorry, and our conduct continues to harm others, we are quite sure to drink. We are not theorizing. These are facts out of our experience.*   *Page 70, line 8*

> *The question of how to approach the man we hated will arise. It may be he had done us more harm than we have done him and, though we may have acquired a better attitude toward him, we are still not too keen about admitting our faults. Nevertheless, with a person we dislike, we take the bit*

*in our teeth. It is harder to go to an enemy than to a friend, but we find it
much more beneficial to us. We go to him in a helpful and forgiving spirit,
confessing our former ill feeling and expressing our regret. Under no condition
do we criticize such a person or argue.*

Page 77, line 18

*When we retire at night, we constructively review our day. Were we resentful,
selfish, dishonest, or afraid? Do we owe an apology? Have we kept something
to ourselves which should be discussed with another person at once? Were we
kind and loving toward all? What could we have done better? Were we
thinking of ourselves most of the time? Or were we thinking of what we could
do for others, of what we could pack into the stream of life? But we must be
careful not to drift into worry, remorse or morbid reflections, for that would
diminish our usefulness to others. After making our review we ask God's
forgiveness and inquire what corrective measures should be taken.*

Page 86, line 5

Step Five

*"This vital Step was also the means by which we began to get the feeling that we
could be forgiven, no matter what we had thought or done. Often it was
while working on this Step with our Sponsors or spiritual advisers that we
first felt truly able to forgive others, no matter how deeply we felt they had
wronged us. Our moral Inventory had persuaded us that all-round
forgiveness was desirable, but it was only when we resolutely tackled Step
Five that we inwardly knew we'd be able to receive forgiveness and give it,
too."*

12 & 12, page 57

*"These obstacles, however, are very real. The first, and one of the most difficult,
has to do with forgiveness. The moment we ponder a twisted or broken
relationship with another person, our emotions go on the defensive. To escape
looking at the wrongs we have done another, we resentfully focus on the
wrong he has done us. This is especially true if he has, in fact, behaved badly
at all. Triumphantly we seize upon his misbehavior as the perfect excuse for
minimizing or forgetting our own.*

*"Right here we need to fetch ourselves up sharply. It doesn't make much sense
when a real tosspot calls a kettle black. Let's remember that alcoholics are not
the only ones bedeviled by sick emotions. Moreover, it is usually a fact that our*

behavior when drinking has aggravated the defects of others. We've repeatedly strained the patience of our best friends to a snapping point, and have brought out the very worst in those who didn't think much of us to begin with. In many instances we are really dealing with fellow sufferers, people whose woes we have increased. If we are now about to ask forgiveness for ourselves, why shouldn't we start out by forgiving them, one and all?"   12 & 12, page 78

Step Eight

We shall want to hold ourselves to the course of admitting the things we have done, meanwhile forgiving the wrongs done us, real or fancied. We should avoid extreme judgments, both of ourselves and of others involved. We must not exaggerate our defects or theirs. A quiet, objective view will be our steadfast aim.   12 & 12, page 81]

In all these situations we need self-restraint, honest analysis of what is involved, a willingness to admit when the fault is ours, and an equal willingness to forgive when the fault is elsewhere.
12 & 12, page 91

...that where there is wrong, I may bring the spirit of forgiveness 12 & 12, page 99

... It is by forgiving that one is forgiven.
12 & 12, page 99

Then he asked for the grace to bring love, forgiveness, harmony, truth, faith, hope, light, and joy to every human being he could.
12 & 12, page 101

He thought it better to give comfort than to receive it; better to understand than to be understood; better to forgive than to be forgiven.   12 & 12, page 101

At last, acceptance proved to be the key to my drinking problem. After I had been around AA for seven months, tapering off alcohol and pills, not finding the program working very well, I was finally able to say, "Okay, God. It is true that I–of all people, strange as it may seem, and even though I didn't give my permission–really, really am an alcoholic of sorts. And it's all right with me. Now, what am I going to do about it?" When I stopped living in the problem and began living in the answer, the problem went away. From that moment on, I have not had a single compulsion to drink.

And acceptance is the answer to all my problems today. When I am disturbed, it is because I find some person, place, thing, or situation--some fact of my life -- unacceptable to me, and I can find no serenity until I accept that person, place, thing, or situation as being exactly the way it is supposed to be at this moment. Nothing, absolutely nothing happens in God's world by mistake. Until I could accept my alcoholism, 1 could not stay sober; unless I accept life completely on life's terms, I cannot be happy. I need to concentrate not so much on what needs to be changed in the world as on what needs to be changed in me and in my attitudes. .   *Page 448*

One morning, however, I realized I had to get rid of (my resentment), for my reprieve was running out, and if I didn't get rid of it I was going to get drunk--and I didn't want to get drunk any more. In my Prayers that morning I asked God to point out to me some way to be free of this resentment. During the day a friend of mine brought me some magazines to take to a hospital group I was interested in, and I looked through them and a "banner" across the front of one featured an article by a prominent clergyman in which I caught the word resentment

He said, in effect: "If you have a resentment you want to be free of, if you will pray for the person or the thing that you resent, you will be free. If you will ask in Prayer for everything you want for yourself to be given to them, you will be free. Ask for their health, their prosperity, their happiness, and you will be free. Even when you don't really want it for them, and your Prayers are only words and you don't mean it, go ahead and do it anyway. Do it every day for two weeks and you will find you have come to mean it and to want it for them and you will realize that where you used to feel bitterness and resentment and hatred, you now feel compassionate understanding and love."

It worked for me then, and it has worked for me many times since, and it will work for me every time I am willing to work it. Sometimes I have to ask first for the willingness, but it too always comes. Because it works for me, it will work for all of us. As another great man says, "The only real freedom a human being can ever know is doing what you ought to do because you want to do it."

This great experience that released me from the bondage of hatred and replaced it with love is really just another affirmation of the truth I know: I get everything I need in Alcoholics Anonymous everything I need I get--and when I get what I need I invariably find that it was just what I wanted all the time. Page 552

Forgiveness

REPRINTED FROM THE SERMON ON THE MOUNT, BY EMMET FOX

*"Forgive Us Our Trespasses, as We Forgive Them
that Trespass Against Us"*

This clause is the turning point of the Prayer. It is the strategic key to the whole Recovery. Let us notice here that Jesus has so arranged this marvelous Prayer that it covers the entire ground of the enfoldment of our souls completely, and in the most concise and telling way. It omits nothing that is essential for our salvation, and yet, so compact is it that there is not a thought or a word too much. Every idea fits into its place with perfect harmony and in perfect sequence. Anything more would be redundant; anything less would be incompleteness, and at this point, it takes up the critical factor of forgiveness.

Having told us what God is, what man is, how the universe works, how we are to do our own work (the salvation of humanity and of our own souls), he then explains what our true nourishment or supply is, and the way in which we can obtain it. Now, he comes to the forgiveness of sins.

The forgiveness of sins is the central problem of life. Sin is a sense of separation from God and is the major tragedy of human experience. It is, of course, rooted in selfishness. It is essentially an attempt to gain some supposed good to which we are not entitled in justice. It is a sense of isolated, self-regarding, personal existence, whereas the Truth of Being is that all are One. Our true selves are at one with God, undivided from Him, expressing His ideas, witnessing to His nature – the dynamic Thinking of that Mind. Because we are all one with the great Whole of which we are spiritually a part, it follows that we are one with all men. Just because in Him we live and move and have our being, we are, in the absolute sense, all essentially one.

Evil, sin, the fall of man, in fact, are essentially the attempt to negate this Truth in our thoughts. We try to live apart from God. We try to do without

Him. We act as though we had a life of our own, as separate minds, as though we could have plans, purposes, and interests separate from His. All this, if it were true, would mean that existence is not one and harmonious, but a chaos of competition and strife. It would mean that we are quite separate from our fellow man and could injure him, rob him, or hurt him, or even destroy him, without any damage to ourselves. In fact, the more we took from other people the more we should have for ourselves. It would mean that the more we considered our own interests, and the more indifferent we were to the welfare of others, the better off we should be.

Of course it would then follow naturally that it would pay others to treat us in the same way, and that accordingly we might expect many of them to do so. Now if this were true, it would mean that the whole universe is only a jungle; that sooner or later it must destroy itself by its own inherent weakness and anarchy. But, of course, it is not true and therein lays the joy of life.

Undoubtedly, many people do act as though they believed it to be true, and a great many more who would be dreadfully shocked if brought face to face with that proposition in cold blood, have nevertheless, a vague feeling that such must be very much the way things are even though they, themselves, are personally above consciously acting in accordance with such a notion. Now, this is the real basis of sin, of resentment, of condemnation, of jealousy, of remorse, and all the evil brood that walk that path.

This belief in independent and separate existence is the arch sin, and now, before we can progress any further, we have to take the knife to this evil thing and cut it out once and for all. Jesus knew this, and with this definite end in view, he inserted at this critical point a carefully prepared statement that would encompass our end and his, without the shadow of a possibility of miscarrying. He inserted what is nothing less than a trip clause. He drafted a declaration that would force us, without any conceivable possibility of escape, evasion, mental reservation, or subterfuge of any kind, to execute the great sacrament of forgiveness in all its fullness and far-reaching power.

As we repeat the Great Prayer intelligently, considering and meaning what we say, we are suddenly, so to speak, caught up off our feet and grasped as though in a vise, so that we must face this problem – and there is no escape. We must positively and definitely extend forgiveness to everyone to whom it is possible that we can owe forgiveness, namely, to anyone that we think can have injured us in any way. Jesus leaves no room for any possible glossing of this fundamental thing. He has constructed his Prayer with more skill than ever yet lawyer displayed in the casting of a deed. He has so contrived it that once our attention has been drawn to this matter, we are inevitably obliged either to forgive our enemies in sincerity and truth, or never again to repeat that Prayer. It is safe to say that no one who reads this booklet with understanding will ever again be able to use the Lord's Prayer unless and until he has forgiven. Should you now attempt to repeat it without forgiving, it can safely be predicted that you will not be able to finish it. This great central clause will stick in your throat.

Notice that Jesus does not say, "forgive me my trespasses and I will try to forgive others," or "I will see if it can be done," or "I will forgive generally, with certain exceptions." He obliges us to declare that we have actually forgiven, and forgiven all; and he makes our claim to our own forgiveness to depend upon that. Who is there that has grace enough to say his Prayers at all, who does not long for the forgiveness or cancellation of his own mistakes and faults? Who would be so insane as to endeavor to seek the Kingdom of God without desiring to be relieved of his own sense of guilt? No one, we may believe. So, we see that we are trapped in the inescapable position that we cannot demand our own release before we have released our brother.

The forgiveness of others is the vestibule of Heaven, and Jesus knew it, and has led us to the door. You must forgive everyone who has ever hurt you if you want to be forgiven yourself; that is the long and the short of it. You have to get rid of all resentment and condemnation of others, and not least, of self-condemnation and remorse. You have to forgive others and, having discontinued your own mistakes, you have to accept the forgiveness of God for them too, or you cannot make any progress. You have to forgive yourself, but you cannot forgive yourself sincerely until you have forgiven others first. Having forgiven others, you must be prepared to forgive yourself too. To refuse to forgive oneself is only spiritual pride. "And by that sin fell the angels."

We cannot make this point too clear to ourselves; we have got to forgive. There are few people in the world who have not at some time or another been hurt, really hurt, by someone else, or been disappointed, or injured, or deceived, or misled. Such things sink into the memory where they usually cause inflamed and festering wounds, and there is only one remedy – they have to be plucked out and thrown away. The one and only way to do that is by forgiveness.

Of course, nothing in the entire world is easier than to forgive than people who have not hurt us very much. Nothing is easier than to rise above than the thought of a trifling loss. Anybody will be willing to do this but what the Law of Being requires of us is that we forgive not only these trifles, but also the very things that are so hard to forgive that at first it seems impossible to do it at all. The despairing heart cries, "It is too much to ask. That thing meant too much to me. It is impossible. I cannot forgive it." But the Lord's Prayer makes our own forgiveness from God, which means our escape from guilt and limitation, dependent upon just this very thing. There is no escape from this, and so forgiveness there must be, no matter how deeply we may have been injured, or how terribly we have suffered. It must be done.

If your Prayers are not being answered, search your consciousness and see if there is not someone whom you have yet to forgive. Find out if there is not some old thing about which you are very resentful. Search and see if you are not really holding a grudge (it may be camouflaged in some self-righteous way) against some individual, or some body of people, a nation, a race, a social class, some religious movement of which you disapprove perhaps, a political party, or what-not. If you are doing so, then you have an act of forgiveness to perform, and when this is done, you will probably take your action. If you cannot forgive at present, you will have to wait for your demonstration until you can. You will have to postpone finishing your recital of the Lord's Prayer, as well, or involve yourself in the position that you do not desire the forgiveness of God.

Setting others free means setting yourself free because resentment is really a form of attachment. It is a Cosmic Truth that it takes two to make a prisoner; the prisoner – and a jailer. There is no such thing as being a prisoner on one's own account. Every prisoner must have a jailer, and the jailer is as much a prisoner as his charge. When you hold resentment against anyone, you are bound to that person by a cosmic link, a real, though mental chain. You are tied by a cosmic tie to the thing that you hate.

The one person perhaps in the whole world whom you most dislike is the very one to whom you are attaching yourself by a hook that is stronger than steel. Is this what you wish? Is this the condition in which you desire to go on living? Remember, you belong to the thing with which you are linked in thought. At some time or other, if that tie endures, the object of your resentment will be drawn again into your life, perhaps to wreak further havoc. Do you think that you can afford this? Of course, no one can afford such a thing and so the way is clear.

You must cut all such ties by a clear and spiritual act of forgiveness. You must loose him and let him go. By forgiveness you set yourself free; you save your soul. Because the law of love works alike for one and all, you also help to save his soul, making it so much easier for him to become what he ought to be.

But how, in the name of all that is wise and good, is the magic act of forgiveness to be accomplished, when we have been so deeply injured that, though we have long wished with all our hearts that we could forgive, we have nevertheless found it impossible; when we have tried and tried to forgive, but have found the task beyond us.

The technique of forgiveness is simple enough, and not very difficult to manage when you understand how. The only thing that is essential is willingness to forgive. Provided you desire to forgive the offender, the greater part of the work is already done. People have always made such a misunderstanding of forgiveness because they have been under the erroneous impression that to forgive a person means that you have to compel yourself to like him.

Happily this is by no means the case – we are not called upon to like anyone whom we do not find ourselves liking spontaneously, and indeed, it is quite impossible to like people to order. You can no more like people to order than you can hold the winds in your fist. If you endeavor to coerce yourself into doing so, you will finish by disliking or hating the offender more than ever. People used to think that when someone had hurt them very much, it was their duty, as good Christians, to pump up, as it were, a feeling of liking for him. Since such a thing is utterly impossible, they suffered a great deal of distress, and ended, necessarily, with failure and a resulting sense of sinfulness. We are not obliged to like anyone, but we are under a binding obligation to love everyone. Love, or charity as the Bible calls it, meaning a vivid sense of impersonal good will. This has nothing directly to do with the feelings. It is always followed, sooner or later, by a wonderful feeling of peace and happiness.

The method of forgiving is this: Get by yourself and become quiet. Repeat any Prayer or treatment that appeals to you, or read a chapter of the Bible. Then quietly say, "I fully and freely forgive X (mentioning the name of the offender); I loose him and let him go. I completely forgive the whole business in question.

"As far as I am concerned, it is finished forever. I cast the burden of resentment upon the Christ within me. He is free now, and I am free too. I wish him well in every phase of his life. That incident is finished. The Christ Truth has set us both free. I thank God."

Then get up and go about your business. On no account repeat this act of forgiveness, because you have done it once and for all, and to do it a second time would be tacitly to repudiate your own work. Afterward, whenever the memory of the offender or the offense happens to come into your mind, bless the delinquent briefly and dismiss the thought.

Do this however many times the thought may come back. After a few days it will return less and less often, until you forget it altogether. Then, perhaps after an interval, shorter or longer, the old trouble may come back to memory once more. You will find that now all bitterness and resentment have disappeared and you are both free with the perfect freedom of the children of God. Your forgiveness is complete. You will experience a wonderful joy in the realization of the demonstration.

Everybody should practice general forgiveness every day as a matter of course. When you say your daily Prayers, issue a general amnesty, forgiving everyone who may have injured you in any way, and on no account particularize. Simply say: "I freely forgive everyone." Then, in the course of the day, should the thought of grievance or resentment come up, bless the offender briefly, and dismiss the thought.

The result of this policy will be that very soon you will find yourself cleared of all resentment and condemnation and the effect upon your happiness, your bodily health, and your general life will be nothing less than revolutionary.

Step Ten

"Continued to take personal Inventory, and when we were wrong, promptly admitted it."

The last three steps are frequently called the "Maintenance" Steps. They are also summarized as "Body, Mind and Spirit."

Step Ten deals with the "Mind" part of the Body–Mind–Spirit of our daily life. The Mind is supposed to monitor our daily life. This is where we ask ourselvse about our interactions with other people, monitor our own attitudes and behaviors.

On a daily basis we exercise the Steps to show the new thinking and actions we have received in Recovery. This means we remain vigilant to keep our Recovery fresh and avoid falling back into old thinking and actions, to the benefit of ourselves and others.

Admitting to being an alcholic is a foundation of truth where we must be aware of our tendency to be selfish and self-serving, that our life is unmanageable when under our own brains. (Step One)

There is a power, greater than ourselves that can return, or deliver, us to sanity. (Step Two)

Every day we have the choice to surrender our own Ego and desire to the care and direction of God as we understand God. (Step Three)

We must track our actions, attitudes, resentments and effects to make ourselves more beneficial to God and the people around us. This can be written down or simply observed – most people in Recovery do both. This is also called "Keeping Your Side of the Street Clean." (Step Four)

Running under the isolation and Ego of our own brain can be deadly, so we use our Sponsor and the small group of people in the fellowship to sound out our reactions, thinking and planned actions. The reflection we receive from the people with whom we share will guide us into correcting our own thought and actions. (Step Five)

We look at our willingness to surrender our defects, to give up the benefits we receive through those defects, and make ourselves willing to have those shortcomings removed, without reservation. (Step Six)

Actively include in our daily Prayer and Meditations the desire to have our defects removed, knowing that we do not get to limit what parts of our personality or behaviors will be removed. We make the effort to make oursevles Humble, not demanding. (Step Seven)

We review our list of people we have harmed and see where names should be removed or added. We must be honest, neither avoiding responsibility for the results of our actions, nor inflating our value to make us seem more important in the lives of others. (Step Eight)

We review what actions we can take to correct the damage we may have caused, note our experience in previous corrections we have made, and then discuss such actions with our Sponsor and others before taking what we think would be actions to repair or make better what has appeared on our list. We do direct amends where possible, and indirect amends where we are unable to correct damage from our past behaviors. (Step Nine)

Step Ten leads us through the first Nine Steps like a well stocked toolbox to prevent new damage when possible and live a new life as a benefit to ourselves and the people around us.

sponsormagazine.info

Step Eleven

"Sought, through Prayer and Meditation, to improve our conscious contact with God, as we understand Him, praying only for knowledge of His will for us and the power to carry that out."

Prayer and Meditation are personal actions that reflect your understanding of your Higher Power.

If you are a member of a recognized faith, you will probalby find guidelines on when and how to pray and meditate.

If you are not a member of a system of belief or thought that gives a specific regimen for Prayer and Meditation, you have options to adopt systems that fit within your understanding of a 'spritual life.'

Prayer

Many members of our fellowship refer to Prayer as talking to God, Meditation is listening.

Some people believe in a diety which they call God. If their Higher Power, God, is in charge, is everywhere, knows everything and makes all decisions, what is their purpose in Prayer? They cannot tell God something God does not know. They cannot negotiate a 'better deal' than what God has decided. They cannot go somewhere God will not see what they do.

If you are one of these people, Prayer is the time you make yourself honest. You can tell God that you are scared. You can be honest about your desires and try to make yourself willing to accept what you do or do not receive.

Almost all members of AA say that the best Prayer is "Thank you."

Meditation

Meditation can confuse many people. It can include a formal system of words, music or actions, or it can be a simple way of calming the inner turmoil to find a calmness from which healthy decisions can be made. If you have a tradition that gives you guidelines and methods, you may benefit from applying those guidelines to your own practice of Meditation. If you have not had a method of Meditation before getting into Recovery, there are many books, recordings and classes you can consider to learn a method that works for you.

The most important thing about Meditation is that you make the effort. Meditation is a tool to provide calm in turmoil, quiet in chaos, and a foundation on which to build healthy decisions and actions.

In the early days of AA, while it was emerging from the Oxford Group, the members observed "quiet time," at home to start the day, and at the gatherings to begin the meeting. This was a group Meditation, after which the member of the group would discuss any guidance that had been received on his or her problems. Many groups maintain the orginal Oxford Group observance of quiet time at the beginning of their meetings.

Steps Ten and Eleven
Together

The Steps are structured to provide recognition of our problem (alcoholism and the spiritual poverty that accompanies that disease), and the corrective measures to heal our past as far as humanly possible.

Beyond the humanly possible we turn to our spiritual life as an everyday reality. Whether clothed in the official structure of an established religion, or the method of moral living dictated by another sense of authority, we change our approach to daily life to live on a spiritual basis.

A basic definition of "spiritual" is given elsewhere, but it does no good to do the work of Steps 1 through 9 if we do not proceed to live in "a design for living that really works."

The articles in this section are intended to help you with your ongoing spiritual growth and not as an indoctrination into an "authorized" spirituality.

When AA began, its members were all Christian. With the publication of the Big Book and the change of wording to allow for "God as you understand God," or "A Higher Power," Recovery has expanded into every known religion and school of moral thought.

Standing with Christians in our meetings we have sober Jews, Muslims, Buddhists, Hindus, native beliefs, and organized schools on non-belief.

Those who have not settled the question of religion within their alcoholic haze find that they can first focus on the simplicity of not picking up one drink one day at a time and of following the direction of the people who arrived before them.

They may jump through the "religion" hoop later, or they may not. They can still remain sober.

Even Atheists and Antitheists stay sober provided they recognize their sobriety as a consequence of a power greater than themselves. For some, this has been the fellowship of AA – the dozens of men and women they encounter who can do what the new person cannot do – stay sober!

It is the purpose of the following section to help expand your Recovery by exercising the steps in your daily practice of spiritual growth and interaction with the people of this world.

Spot Check Inventory

Am I...	or Am I?
Into self-pity	*Grateful for Blessings*
Resentful	*Forgiving*
Critical	*Accepting*
Suspicious	*Trusting*
Tactless and Disrespectful	*Loving and Understanding*
Narrow-Minded	*Open-Minded*
Avoiding People	*Comfortable with Others*
Envious	*Aware of My Own Worth*
Pessimistic	*Optimistic*
Procrastinating	*Prompt*
Prone to Gossip	*Respectful of Other's Privacy*
Self-Centered	*Helpful to Others*
Impulsive and Self-Indulgent	*Self-Disciplined*
Selfish	*Generous*
Self-Righteous and Intolerant	*Tolerant*
Domineering	*Considerate*
Arrogant	*Humble*
Impractical	*Realistic*
Self-Deceiving	*Honest with Myself*
Impatient	*Patient*
Stubborn	*Willing to Compromise*
Aimless and Indifferent	*Purposeful*
Dishonest	*Truthful*

Step Twelve

Having had a spiritual awakening as the result of these steps, we tried to carry this message to alcoholics, and to practice these principles in all our affairs.

There are three parts to the Twelfth Step:

Body, Mind and Spirit

Your Mind is supposed to be focused in the Tenth Step. How are you behaving? Review your behavior as you go through your day. Do you owe an amends? Do you need to correct something before it winds up on a new Inventory? Did you do something right? (You need to keep doing that.)

Your Spirit is supposed to be focused in the Eleventh Step. This is not just time spent when rising and retiring, but all through the day working to keep your Spiritual Life expressed in your daily behavior. Take moments for guidance and gratitude throughout your day.

Your Body should be on the front lines - carrying the message to the alcoholic who still suffers. Carrying your beliefs in the form of your actions to be of service to God (as you undestand God) and others, not just alcoholics.

This means you have more action in the practice of your Recovery.

- Do Service, to your Home Group and where possible.

- Sponsor others - share what you have been given.

- Continue to build your Spiritual Life.

- Having had a spiritual awakening as the result of the first eleven Steps. (An explanation can be found in Appendix II of the Big Book) Step Twelve helps us stay focused on what the Step calls THE result. THE ONLY result. A spiritual awakening.

There is a teaching story that applies here:

A young student visited a monk to ask the questions that had come up during the process of learning. The monk immediately offered a cup of tea. The student held the cup and monk began to pour. The cup began to fill and then went over the brim, spilling out.

"Stop!" the disciple yelled. "It's going all over the floor!"

The monk stopped pouring and smiled. "How can I give you more tea if you do not give me an empty cup?"

Carrying this message to other alcoholics, and to practice the principles of the first Eleven Steps in all our affairs, are the Legacy of the process of the Steps to allow us to live a life of Recovery. It is offering an empty cup to receive what comes next.

As you live the result of the active cleaning of the past, reordering the present under the new direction provided by the High Power of your own understanding, you build up a reservoir of hope, happiness and satisfaction at becoming a responsible, adult member of your community.

Like the story of the monk giving his visitor a cup of tea, we cannot receive what comes next until we give away what we have been given so far. The St. Francis Prayer says "Make me a channel;" and a channel must have both an intake and an outflow. If there is no input, the reservoir dries up. If there is no outflow, the reservoir becomes stagnant.

But it is important that you understand that you do not do Service because you are being nice – you do it to get what comes next!

If you've had a Spiritual Awakening as the result of taking the actions in Steps One through Eleven, then you're ready to carry our life-saving and life-changing message to others.

Let's concentrate on carrying this message to other alcoholics as the basis of our discussion of Step Twelve.

Chapter Seven of the Big Book tells us exactly how to make a "Twelve Step Call." Here are some of the main points it describes. (I suggest you read the chapter in its entirety and discuss its contents with your Sponsor or other members of the group.)

"Practical experience shows that nothing will so much insure immunity from drinking as intensive work with other alcoholics. It works when other

activities fail. This is our twelfth suggestion: Carry this message to other alcoholics! You can help when no one else can. You can secure their confidence when others fail.”

Page 89

More promises are given in the next paragraph:

"Life will take on new meaning. To watch people recover, to see them help others, to watch loneliness vanish, to see a fellowship grow up about you, to have a host of friends—this is an experience you must not miss. We know you will not want to miss it. Frequent contact with newcomers and with each other is the bright spot of our lives.

Page 89

There is more to read about doing a classic Twelve Step Call. Read it so you know what to do when you have the chance to make one.

Step Twelve - the part about carrying the message - is not only the focus of this Chapter, it is the focus of the rest of the book!

The last chapter of the front of the book, "A Vision for You," talks about what we hope every newcomer will experience, but it is also the message of what all of us hope will be true in our own lives.

There is more. There is sharing of the message FROM the authors of the stories TO YOU! All those stories in the back of all four editions of the Big Book are past members carrying their message TO YOU. When you cannot get out to a meeting and feel you need one – let them share their message with you and read one of their stories.

From this point, you will do exactly the same kind of mix of what we earlier said was the mix of staying alive. Breathing. Pumping blood. Eating food. Getting rid of wastes. Speaking with others. Listening to others. Doing what is in front of you for your job, your family, your spirit.

By working these Steps, on a daily basis:

You will abstain from the substance that triggers your physical allergy.

You will be free of your mental obsession and another downward spiral.

You will see where you have a chance to identify damage from your past life, share your discovery with your Sponsor and, possibly, other trusted members of the Fellowship.

You will take the actions you and your Sponsor agree will repair or make better the situation you are dealing with. Sometimes the correct action will be to keep your hands off the situation, sometimes it will be a change in you to avoid repeating the error, sometimes it will be making a direct amends, sometimes it will require an indirect amends.

You will find new things that fill your life and your time, whether it is a return to family, or living with the full consequences of past actions. You will find people with whom to share new interests. You will make time to reflect on your actions, pray and meditate to maintain your emotional sobriety. You will find that you have something to share with someone newer than yourself – possibly as a Sponsor, possibly as being a good friend.

You will become a man among men, a worker among workers, a member of your immediate society and your larger world who can be a man of his word. You may get to the point where someone who doesn't know your story, never has to calculate "but he's an alcoholic, he's an addict" in their dealings with you.

You will find yourself, possibly for the first time.

You will see where the dozens of promises in the Big Book are coming true for you.

You will understand the word serenity, and you will know peace.

The Tenth Step is the practice of Steps 1 through 9, as needed. You will review your behavior, hopefully correct it before you have a new amends to make.

The Eleventh Step is maintenance of your source, your guidance, your Higher Power as you understand that Higher Power. We encourage you to schedule your week to allow for a minimal, formal contact with that Higher Power daily - or more frequently: every morning before you get out of bed, or while brushing your teeth, or sitting with your breakfast; every evening before retiring, reviewing the day and setting goals for the day to come.

The Twelfth Step tells you what actions you will need to take to carry the message - to share your own story and Recovery, and to help those around you.

Living in the Twelfth Step

There is only one result of working the Twevle Steps – the Spiritual Awakening. We are charged to "carry this message" and to "practice these principles in all our affairs."

It becomes necessary to understand exactly what these terms mean to you.

The "Spiritual Awakening" is not about adhering to definitions or limits outside your own life, but it is about creating a new foundation of the new life where you actually belong. Unlike the old life of isolaton and grief, we have the chance to be "happy, joyous and free."

Sometimes we become all three – happy, joyous and free – at the same time. Sometimes we have tragedies that happen in our life that can damage a sense of joy or happiness. Such trials are not restricted to people in Recovery. Everyone has crises and challenges in their life, but if we surrender to despair and indulgent wallowing in those difficult emotions we risk losing the foundation of our new life.

During these times we must accept what is true and use our fellowship, Prayer and Meditation to get through the bad times. Being honest about how we feel during difficulties, and applying the tools we have been given to live a new life carries our message to others. Our life becomes an example of the application of the princples.

Our actions carry our message better than our words – how we carry ourselves, how we keep our word, how we do what is expected of a non-alcoholic in the same position.

Service is the most common form of 'carrying the message'. Carrying the message is the purpose of service and can mean speaking at a meeting, talking with one other person, or quietly doing the service work that makes meetings possible. Setting out chairs, making coffee, greeting people at the door when they arrive, sharing in meetings, Sponsoring and being Sponsored are all forms of service.

Taking a service position within one's local fellowship is a more formal kind of service. This can be as a Secretary, Treasurer, or Literature person within the meeting, or as a representative to our local service committee, Intergroup, district or area serviceboards. It is suggested we not hold any one position for more than two years – leave room to allow new people a chance to do the same service.

Service can be personal – sharing our experience, strength and hope, one on one. This can mean actually being a Sponsor, but it can also mean talking with a newcomer or a member of the Program who simply needs to take the risk of sharing honestly and being heard. The person who needs to talk with us may not be a newcomer, but someone with considerable time in the program who has entered a situation that is bothering them.

Above all , when we talk with someone, we must make an effort to actually listen. We do not simply wait for them to stop talking so we get to say something - consider what they have said and share only from our own experience. If we do not have an answer they need, we must be honest and say 'I don't know', then offer to help them find someone who has the experience they need. This simple form of Service may be the strongest in reaching and being a real benefit to the person we are trying to help.

Service does not just mean within the structure of the meeting and fellowship. We can also do service in the larger society of our community, with our neighbors, and other public groups in need of our time and talents.

AA Traditions

The Traditions module is, as are all subjects in this syllabus, a presentation of a single position on the meaning and application of the Traditions. As such subjective material requires, the reader may accept or reject such portions as he or she feels is appropriate for their intended use.

There are few things that prove true of alcoholics, but it can be said that they do not like being told what to do.

The Traditions were not an attempt to tell AAs what to do, or even set the standard for AA groups. The Traditions were a result of errors made in groups and by individuals that resulted in the loss of early groups, and the loss of an unknown number of alcoholics who were driven away by those mistakes.

When the meetings were limited to the original two, Akron, OH and New York, the problems addressed by the two primary founders and their fellowships were frequently discussed between the groups before any alcoholics were made to create a formal standard.

The original meetings changed. At first they required a medical detox and working the equivalent of the first six steps before attending meetings. When that standard was dropped, the fellowship continued to grow.

The need for a personal connection to someone in the Oxford Group was never a formal requirement, but it was the only entry for the first two groups. Clarence Snyder's group, which was unaffiliated with the Oxford Group, eliminated that requirement.

The membership limitation to upper class, white males was never formal, but the reality was that these people first gathered to use this process to get and remain sober.

The Traditions began as a series of articles published in The Grapevine, the AA 'meeting-in-print,' during the first decade or so of AA meetings, first within the Oxford Group and later as an independent entity. Bill Wilson, the author of those articles, drew heavily from the volume of correspondence maintained with groups around the world and individuals involved in the sudden growth of the AA Program.

After the Saturday Evening Post article in 1941, the membership exploded from a few hundred to several thousand, guided by the book, Alcoholics Anonymous. In that explosion, groups began to raise the number of qualifications for membership, which kept people away. Alcoholics who otherwise might have stayed to hear the message, and might have worked the Steps to stay sober left the meetings.

These new requirements were not to assure "the right kind of alcoholic" would join, but they were written as the result of fears – personal fears and cultural fears of the time.

The lack of understanding of a healthy fellowship led to a number of impressive blunders in meeting-building. One meeting in the 1940s served beer at their meetings. The meeting quickly vanished and a new AA group did not form for several years. Even in recent news, an AA group was accused of the systematic sexual abuse that they touted as being part of the program.

Clearly, such acts are not part of the AA program, but the newcomer has no way of knowing this.

To this day, there are groups who do not subscribe to the Traditions and the Traditions are not required to form an AA meeting.

The purpose of this discussion is to explore the intent and application of the principles contained in the Traditions.

The Twelve Traditions are copyrighted by the central office for Alcoholics Anonymous. This article is based on the "Long Form" of each Tradition, which may not be as familiar as the Traditions read in most meetings.

"Our AA experience has taught us that: "

First Tradition

Each member of Alcoholics Anonymous is but a small part of a great whole. AA must continue to live or most of us will surely die. Hence our common welfare comes first. But individual welfare follows close afterward.

Without the fellowship, the history of alcoholism tells us long and tragic stories of individuals who have tried to remove alcohol and its effects from their lives, and failed. Here and there people succeeded and their stories were notable by the rarity.

Founded by the strictly Christian Oxford Group members, Alcoholics Anonymous made the concept of "willing submision" the foundation of the Twelve Step Program.

This means that despite an individual's religious or political beliefs, personal opinions of individuals or movements within the Program, our united stance of Recovery as our common binding agent.

Whatever stands we take on public issues, we accept the common focus that requires AA be there when we need it and if we do not stand together we will eventually die drunk or high, often cold and alone.

We "carry this message" to insure our own Recovery and to make Recovery possible to others.

"We" succed where "I" have failed.

The fellowship continues to be a resource for us as we face new situations in the new life, and where we meet the newcomers to whom we "give it away." It is the "giving it away" that makes room for our next lesson and next revelation.

This almost never means sacrificing what we know to be true , but exercising the "restraint of tongue and pen" that tends to divide our fellowship into factions, hurt feelings, or drives wedges between those who would otherwise be part of our sobriety.

We may never learn to like everyone in the meeting. There will be people you encounter in meetings that will test your ability to accept to its limit. But we are required to love them as expressions of our new trust in a Higher Power and our level of acceptance.

Second Tradition

For our group purpose there is but one ultimate authority-a loving God as He may express Himself in our group conscience.

Related to the First Tradition, the Second has us put our authority into the combined personal Higher Power expressed through the members of the Group and the Fellowship, and not in the loudest voice, the strongest passion, or the entrenched authority of a deluded Bleeding Deacon.

There is a desire to make that trust in our Higher Power about other people's refusal to submit to group conscience, or drive to get others to see the right way. But that direction is for us to keep our hands off the results of the Group Conscience – it is about our restraint of tongue and pen.

Groups can become ill, as can individuals. The Group that does not correct its behavior may cease to exist. The group that changes according to whim, fashion, or some passing concept of political correctness may also risk ceasing to exist.

Group Inventory is suggested by World Service to keep each Group active as a reflection of its membership and the need that group serves.

Third Tradition

> Our membership ought to include all who suffer from alcoholism. Hence we may refuse none who wish to recover. Nor ought AA membership ever depend upon money or conformity. Any two or three alcoholics gathered together for sobriety may call themselves an AA Group, provided that, as a group, they have no other affiliation.

The Third Tradition was the most protective of all AA's service legacies. The single requirement of having the desire to stop drinking does not exclude desire for Recovery from other problems, but identifies the qualification of that individual for the very reason the AA group is gathered.

This means you may be an alcoholic, AND an addict, AND a compulsive gambler, AND an over-eater, AND a sexual compulsive, AND have any number of other problems. Many of these problems are addressed with other 12-Step programs where the membership shares those specific problems, but a "singleness of purpose" is inclusive.

But the requirement to be in an AA meeting is the desire to stop drinking. Beyond that, it is about their willingness to perform the work outlined in the Twelve Steps to find and maintain sobriety.

The Big Book is often misunderstood as saying that ONLY an alcoholic can be in the meetings. A member is not even required to identify as anything, other than by local custom. The only question of identity is whether or not he or she identifies with the reason for this AA meeting's existence; to carry the message to the alcoholic who still suffers, and that he or she satisfies the only requirement for membership - to have the desire to stop drinking.

Any additional qualification is an outside issue for the group, but may be vital to one's own Recovery process.

Here are two examples of attempts to control membership prior to adopting the Third Tradition

Early Membership Agreement

—◆— *Application for Membership* —◆—

ALCOHOLICS ANONYMOUS

Having read the twelve steps and having taken Step No. 1, I apply for membership in the Montreal Group of Alcoholics Anonymous.

When admitted to membership it will be my desire to co-operate with the group as fully as possible and not to harm it, interfere with its work or impede its progress in any way.

Therefore:

1. I agree not to attend any meeting on a day on which I have taken anything whatsoever to drink of an alcoholic nature.

2. In the interests of complete honesty, if I do any drinking whatsoever at any time, I will make the fact known to my sponsor, or in his absence, to some other senior member of the group, and will not attempt to deliberately hide such drinking from the group.

3. Further, in the event that I continue drinking intermittently while ostensibly a member of this group, I agree to relinquish my membership if asked to do so by the group through my sponsor or the group secretary.

4. Understanding that although the aims and objects of A.A. are well known, names and affairs of the group are definitely secret, I agree not to divulge names of members to outsiders or to discuss private affairs of the group with non-members.

5. I undertake to introduce new members to the group only after they have fulfilled whatever qualifications for membership the group may from time to time require.

6. I undertake to familiarize myself with the duties and obligations of a sponsor and when called upon to sponsor an applicant will make every effort to see that he becomes a good member.

_____
Applicant

Date _____   _____
Sponsor

Proposed Application from early AA Group

Banned from AA

In an effort to enforce their own vision of AA, some early groups wrote official letters of expulsion from the fellowship, as shown in this example:

```
December 5, 1941

From The Executive Committee
of the Los Angeles Group of
Alcoholics Anonymous

Dear Mrs. Irma Lavone,

At a meeting of the Executive Committee of
the Los Angeles Group of Alcoholics
Anonymous held December 4, 1941, it was
decided that your attendance at group
meetings was no longer desired until certain
explanations and plans for the future were
made to the satisfaction of this Committee.
This action has been taken for reasons which
should be most apparent to yourself.

It was decided that, should you so desire,
you may appear before members Committee and
state your attitude. This opportunity may be
afforded you between of this now and
December 15, 1941.

You may communicate with us at the above
address by that date. In case you do not
wish to appear, we shall consider the matter
closed and that your membership is
terminated.
```

Source: Wally P.

Fourth Tradition

> *With respect to its own affairs, each AA group should be responsible to no other authority than its own conscience. But when its plans concern the welfare of neighboring groups also, those groups ought to be consulted. And no group, regional committee, or individual should ever take any action that might greatly affect AA as a whole without conferring with the Trustees of the General Service Board. On such issues our common welfare is paramount.*

Independence of the individual groups has been hailed as a march of immature anarchy, but the truth has been new meeting formats have evolved to suit the needs of particular fellowships. A group that creates conditions or a format that others find unacceptable will either

> *a) prove their value as they find support, or*

> *b) fade away as the new meeting succeeds or fails, according to its value to its local community.*

Throughout the country, people open meetings with different readings, or with no readings. They announce their name and that they are alcoholic, or make no identification at all. They have book readings, speaker meetings, writing meetings, discussion-only meetings (men only, women only, gay only, lawyer only, teacher only), and special meetings put on as classes or workshops for the local fellowship.

Every group has someone move into their area from another region where things are done differently, who tries to make people "do it right!"

Every meeting is free to form and format as it sees fit, provided it does not affect another group or the overall structure of AA. This means it is a courtesy for a meeting starting on a night where another meeting already exists to let that group know of its intent so the first meeting is acknowledged. But neither group can claim any authority to approve or disapprove the other meeting.

Meetings are free to change the readings from AA, but cannot claim that their revised materials represent AA as a whole – it is simply not true. But such changes may serve their Group's needs in Recovery.

In many respects, relationships between Groups are entirely optional and usually considered an "Outside Issue" as explained in the Tenth Tradition. That Group A passes the Seventh Tradition at the beginning of the meeting, and

Group B passes the Seventh Tradition basket at the end of the meeting, is not the concern of the other meeting.

Fifth Tradition

Each Alcoholics Anonymous group ought to be a spiritual entity having but one primary purpose-that of carrying its message to the alcoholic who still suffers.

Groups become entrenched in their own glory, particularly when members have remained sober for many years. There is a real danger that members of a group may set themselves up as the judges of all things good for local and international AA.

It is never the purpose of an AA group to prove their superiority or ranking over other groups. The Fifth Tradition keeps the focus on the ability of the group, by whatever composition or format, to serve the alcoholic who still suffers.

"The alcoholic who still suffers" does not mean only newcomers, although newcomers are usually in the most identifiable distress. Members with long term sobriety face new problems in life and may need the combined experience, strength, and hope of their group to face the new problem. Someone with a few months of sobriety may blossom with new fears that had been kept asleep by drunkenness and now need their group to get them into the next Step or the next exercise of Principles.

The newcomer is always the first thought with this Tradition. Does the Group carry the message of Recovery to that newcomer? Is the meeting set up and open at the time promised? Is there a personal 'hello' for the new man or woman walking or rolling through the door for the first time?

Are they confident that the newcomer will find that meeting there the next time?

Some Groups further carry the message to treatment centers, hospitals, or the homes or hospital rooms of alcoholics who cannot attend. Such outreach is up to a Group Conscience, as expressed in Tradition Four.

Sixth Tradition

Problems of money, property, and authority may easily divert us from our primary spiritual aim. We think, therefore, that any considerable property of genuine use to AA should be separately incorporated and managed, thus dividing the material from the spiritual. An AA group, as such, should never go into business. Secondary aids to AA, such as clubs or hospitals which require much property or administration, ought to be incorporated and so set apart that, if necessary, they can be freely discarded by the groups. Hence such facilities ought not to use the AA name. Their management should be the sole responsibility of those people who financially support them. For clubs, AA managers are usually preferred. But hospitals, as well as other places of recuperation, ought to be well outside AA-and medically supervised. While an AA group may cooperate with anyone, such cooperation ought never go so far as affiliation or endorsement, actual or implied. An AA group can bind itself to no one.

Alcoholics are notorious for being power-grabbing Egotists. The purpose of the Sixth Tradition is to avoid the perils of position, notoriety, or other benefits from association with an outside group.

Linked directly to the non-affiliation of Tradition Eight, the Sixth Tradition prevents the threats of money, property, or prestige that have caused other public benefit concerns to vanish over the years.

We are not an organization in the traditional sense. We have a policy of cooperation with outside organizations that must never take the form of an "endorsement" by name, material, funds, or public statements to or from such outside groups. The name AA should not be linked in any public or business sense with any outside organization, no matter how attractive or beneficial it may seem at the moment.

AA has learned to function on a principle known to Native Americans for many years – "It must be good for seven generations." This means what seems beneficial or attractive at the moment may become a liability that will cause unity of the fellowship to suffer, and may cause groups or areas to lose their ability to serve the alcoholics who still suffer.

Seventh Tradition

The AA groups themselves ought to be fully supported by the voluntary contributions of their own members. We think that each group should soon achieve this ideal; that any public solicitation of funds using the name of Alcoholics Anonymous is highly dangerous, whether by groups, clubs, hospitals, or other outside agencies; that acceptance of large gifts from any source, or of contributions carrying any obligation whatever, is unwise. Then too, we view with much concern those AA treasuries which continue, beyond prudent reserves, to accumulate funds for no stated AA purpose. Experience has often warned us that nothing can so surely destroy our spiritual heritage as futile disputes over property, money, and authority.

Accepting money from outside organizations opens the door to have to conform to the donor's requirements to get the next donation. While many sources may claim non-involvement and a lack of requirements for the money, it creates an open door for a donor who has made such a contribution to dictate that only certain people, a certain class of person, a certain race, a certain religious group, political affiliation, or class, be reached with the contributor's money.

Independence from outside support, to be self-supporting, is required for the adult responsibility of any individual attempting to achieve a mature, healthy sobriety. The collection of alcoholics in their search for this same kind of healthy responsibility can only benefit from the same responsibility for their group's financial health.

Eighth Tradition

Alcoholics Anonymous should remain forever non-professional. We define professionalism as the occupation of counseling alcoholics for fees or hire. But we may employ alcoholics where they are going to perform those services for which we may otherwise have to engage non-alcoholics. Such special services may be well recompensed. But our usual AA "Twelfth Step" work is never to be paid for.

When AA grew from a few hundred people to several thousand in the weeks after the appearance of the Saturday Evening Post article by Jack Alexander, it became clear that someone had to answer the mail, answer the phones, and perform the unglamorous work of responding.

As with other changes in AA, it was a huge controversy as to whether someone being paid for secretarial work was performing a Twelfth Step job, which should never be subject to a paycheck.

Bill Wilson explains the principle of responsible services in his chapter on the Eighth Tradition in Twelve Steps and Twelve Traditions, but confirmed that no one should ever be paid for Twelfth Step Work. But it was also a violation of the Seventh Tradition to expect someone to do non-Twelfth Step work for free.

"Our own contributions" slowly began to mean paying for the phone bill for an AA phone, the box rent for an AA mailing address, or (when local meetings need a physical location for local services) rent for a reasonable local office.

Speakers for AA are not to be paid for their talk, but it is reasonable to provide for transportation costs and, when needed, a local sleeping spot. If the speaker travelled to that city, the gas, rail, or airfare would still apply. If the local community cannot host the speaker in a member's home, it may be appropriate for the local group to provide a motel room.

Despite the spiritual nature of the Program, it is not appropriate to suddenly expect loggers to cut down trees to make paper for AA literature as a free service to the Fellowship, nor can we expect buildings to be built with contributed electricity for local meetings.

The Eighth Tradition protects from the same big-shotism that is the focus of Tradition Six, while acknowledging the real financial costs of providing our services.

Ninth Tradition

> *Each AA group needs the least possible organization. Rotating leadership is the best. The small group may elect its Secretary, the large group its Rotating Committee, and the groups of a large Metropolitan area their Central or Intergroup Committee, which often employs a full-time Secretary. The trustees of the General Service Board are, in effect, our AA General Service Committee. They are the custodians of our AA Tradition and the receivers of voluntary AA contributions by which we maintain our AA General Service Office in New York. They are authorized by the groups to handle our over-all public relations and they guarantee the integrity of our principle newspaper, "The AA Grapevine." All such representatives are to be guided in the spirit of service, for true leaders in AA are but trusted and experienced servants of the whole. They derive no real authority from their titles; they do not govern. Universal respect is the key to their usefulness.*

Many AA groups have a regular Home Group meeting where group issues are decided, but some have chosen to create a committee to conduct the group's business. The decision to handle operational issues this way is up to the Group.

But such a committee is not vested with permanent authority. The Group needs to be able to create, or dissolve, such service bodies, as needed.

A few groups in an area may want to host a Round-Up, a Conference, or an Assembly, and create a committee to carry out their issues and do the work. They may even vote to continue the committee from year to year, as needed. Such committees need to reflect the groups they serve in an open, accessible, and democratic manner.

Groups in an area may choose to create an Intergroup with representatives from member groups to carry out services for the local fellowships. As I write, a local Intergroup provides a depository where groups can go to buy books, literature, current meeting guides (which the Intergroup edits and publishes), and outside items like bumper stickers, anniversary chips, posters, and other items the local Intergroup has approved for sale. Like individual meetings, service boards are not the authority of groups outside their service area and need not be approved by anyone other than the groups they serve.

It should also be said that opinions on the right and wrong way to carry out services abound, and anyone on the losing side of a vote is free to express their opinion and displeasure.

But the Second Tradition remains our authority, as expressed in the group conscience. Dissenting opinions are invited and may win a later vote.

Tenth Tradition

No AA group or member should ever, in such a way as to implicate AA, express any opinion on outside controversial issues–particularly those of politics, alcohol reform, or sectarian religion. The Alcoholics Anonymous groups oppose no one. Concerning such matters they can express no views whatever.

An earlier fellowship, the Washingtonian Temperance Society failed to find the common focus we have for groups and, as a result, competed with each other for members, took public positions on public issues, took both sides of public arguments in very public disagreements, and managed to be lost to history because of massive disunity.

Alcoholics Anonymous does not have opinions on public issues. Members of Alcoholics Anonymous have lots of opinions and will frequently express them at the top of their lungs, sometimes even in meetings.

As a Fellowship, in the name of Unity (First Tradition), Service (Twelfth Step, Fifth Tradition), and Recovery (the sum goal of all of the Steps and Traditions), we remove outside issues from our interior discussions.

Alcoholics Anonymous has no position on political issues. Members have lots of opinions on political issues.

Alcoholics Anonymous has no position on religious issues. Members have lots of opinions on religious issues.

Alcoholics Anonymous has no position on social issues or private therapies. Members have lots of opinions on social issues and private therapies.

We want the newcomer to find a meeting that is united on Recovery, not divided by politics, religion, controversy, or a self-righteousness that prevents the members from carrying the message.

AA must protect its primary purpose (Fifth Tradition) by keeping the meetings open and inviting to the newcomer. None of us want to be responsible for the newcomer leaving his or her first meeting feeling unwelcome because there was an argument over an outside issue, particularly if it makes them believe they are on the wrong side of the issue for AA. Outside issues can include politics, religion, substances other than alcohol, behaviors, or psychological theories.

Having no opinion prevents AA from being on the right side or the wrong side of outside issues. Members always have the freedom to discuss such issues among themselves and outside the framework of the Meeting.

Eleventh Tradition

> Our relations with the general public should be characterized by personal anonymity. We think AA ought to avoid sensational advertising. Our names and pictures as AA members ought not be broadcast, filmed, or publicly printed. Our public relations should be guided by the principle of attraction rather than promotion. There is never need to praise ourselves. We feel it better to let our friends recommend us.

Anonymity of the membership does not mean no one ever knows about AA. The neighbors knew you were drunk; they probably noticed you aren't drunk now. They may suspect why. Your family probably knows what you are doing. You may have an abundance of gratitude for the Program and AA.

But this does not give permission to make public pronouncements on behalf of AA, hoping to get others into AA, or to build up the membership of any group.

Avoiding promotion and campaigning for membership means the responsibility for the attraction of AA remains with the result of the group's actions (the Steps and Recovery) and not clever campaigns or slogans. This does not mean you will not see public service announcements on television, or hear them on the radio. Those services let people know that AA exists and is available if they want to seek out help.

Non-promotion does not eliminate a policy of "cooperation with the professional community." This means that the local service boards can provide information to requests from groups of educational, religious, medical, legal, or public service groups. It also means a phone number is available in most AA communities for more information about local AA meetings.

Twelfth Tradition

> *And finally, we of Alcoholics Anonymous believe that the principle of Anonymity has an immense spiritual significance. It reminds us that we are to place principles before personalities; that we are actually to practice a genuine Humility. This to the end that our great blessings may never spoil us; that we shall forever live in thankful contemplation of Him who presides over us all.*

Anonymity was originally intended to protect members from the public stigma of alcoholism, but proved to be a powerful tool that allowed newcomers to enter the program, even if they did not give their right name when they entered the doors. Anonymity was seen as a way to take away the markers of social position, legal standing, or background. They became "an alcoholic in Recovery," rather that Name / Occupation / Address / Bank Balance / Connections who is an alcoholic.

In the early years, local and national celebrities achieved sobriety and revealed their membership in AA, only to get drunk again to give the message "AA didn't work for XX, so it probably won't work for you..." The most notable case was Rolle H., a national baseball star who achieved highly publicized sobriety, and drank again.

Anonymity became a defense for the alcoholic to clear away distractions to achieve sobriety and to protect the fellowship from the actions of a single person to taint the public perception of that person representing AA.

Misconceptions about AA 'Tradition'

Many people repeat "Who you see here, what you hear here, let it stay here" as their understanding of anonymity. It is better used as a statement of confidentiality. But the words are not from AA. They came from signs placed outside war plants in World War II to keep workers from speaking of the sensitive jobs they were doing.

Sponsorship

People who are starting to help others through the steps must first look at how their Sponsor sponsored them.

But a basic truism of Recovery is that we can always do better.

This is a collection of information for the Sponsor for improving his or her value to the Sponsee.

Sponsorship

BY CLARENCE SNYDER, 1944

This is slightly edited from the first pamphlet ever written concerning Sponsorship. It was written by Clarence H. Snyder in early 1944. Its original title was to be "AA ... Its Obligations and Its Responsibilities." It was printed by the Cleveland Central Committee under the title:"AA ... Its Opportunities and Its Responsibilities."

The masculine form is used throughout for simplicity, although it is intended to include women as well.

The guide was written for the original concept of the 12-Step Call, where the recovering members would accept the invitation of the family or prospective member or seek out those with drinking problems from local doctors (before HIPPA prevented revealing anything about a patient's medical condition). Many of the points still apply to talking with the likely candidate through whatever source they may be contacted.

Preface

Each member of Alcoholics Anonymous is a potential Sponsor of a new member and should clearly recognize the obligations and duties of such responsibility.

The acceptance of an opportunity to take the AA plan to a sufferer of alcoholism entails very real and critically important responsibilities. Each member, undertaking the Sponsorship of a fellow alcoholic, must remember that he is offering what is frequently the last chance for rehabilitation, sanity, or maybe life itself.

Happiness, Health, Security, Sanity, and Life are the things we hold in the balance when we Sponsor an alcoholic.

No member among us is wise enough to develop a program that can be successfully applied in every case. However, in the following pages, we have outlined a suggested procedure, which supplemented by the member's own experience, has proven successful.

Personal Gains of Being a Sponsor

No one reaps the full benefits from any fellowship he is connected with unless he wholeheartedly engages in its important activities. The expansion of Alcoholics Anonymous to wider fields of greater benefit to more people results directly from the addition of new, worthwhile members or associates.

Any AA who has not experienced the joys and satisfaction of helping another alcoholic regain his place in life has not yet fully realized the complete benefits of this fellowship.

On the other hand, it must be clearly kept in mind that the only possible reason for bringing an alcoholic into AA is for that person's gain. Sponsorship should never be undertaken:

1. *To increase the size of the group*

2. *For personal satisfaction and glory*

3. *Because the Sponsor feels it his duty to remake the world*

Until an individual has assumed the responsibility of setting a shaking, helpless human being back on the path toward becoming a healthy, useful member of society, he has not enjoyed the complete thrill of being an AA.

Source of Names

Most people have among their own friends and acquaintances someone who would benefit from our teachings. Others have names given to them by their church, by their doctor, by their employer, or by some other member, who cannot make a direct contact.

Because of the wide range of the AA activities, the names often come from unusual and unexpected places.

These cases should be contacted as soon as all facts such as: marital status, domestic relations, financial status, drink habits, employment status, and others readily obtainable, are at hand.

Is the Prospect a Candidate?

Much time and effort can be saved by learning as soon as possible if:

1. *The man really has a drinking problem;*

2. The man knows he has a problem;

3. The man wants to do something about his drinking;

4. The man wants help.

Sometimes the answers to these questions cannot be made until the prospect has had some AA instruction and an opportunity to think. Often we are given names, which upon investigation, show the prospect is in no sense an alcoholic or is satisfied with his present plan of living. We should not hesitate to drop these names from our lists. However, be sure to let the man know where he can reach us at a later date.

Who Should Become Members?

AA is a fellowship of men and women bound together by their inability to use alcohol in any form sensibly, or with profit or pleasure. Obviously, any new members introduced should be the same kind of people, suffering from the same disease.

Most people can drink reasonably, but we are only interested in those who cannot. Party drinkers, social drinkers, celebrators, and others who continue to have more pleasure than pain from their drinking, are of no interest to us.

In some instances, an individual might believe himself to be a social drinker when he definitely is an alcoholic. In many such cases, more time must pass before that person is ready to accept our program. Rushing such a man before he is ready might ruin his chances of ever becoming a successful AA. Do not ever deny future help by pushing too hard in the beginning.

Some people, although definitely alcoholic, have no desire or ambition to better their way of living, and until they do, AA has nothing to offer them.

Experience has shown that age, intelligence, education, background, or the amount of liquor drunk, has little, if any, bearing on whether or not the person is an alcoholic.

Presenting the Plan

In many cases, a man's physical condition is such that he should be placed in a hospital, if at all possible. Many AA members believe hospitalization, with ample time for the prospect to think and plan his future, free from domestic and business worries, offers a distinct advantage. In many cases, the hospitalization period marks the beginning of a new life. Other members are equally confident that any man who desires to learn the AA plan for living can do it in his own home or while engaged in normal occupation. Thousands of cases are treated in such a manner and have proved satisfactory.

Suggested Steps

The following paragraphs outline a suggested procedure for presenting the AA plan to the prospect, at home or in the hospital.

Qualify as an Alcoholic

In calling upon a new prospect, it has been found best to qualify oneself as an ordinary person who has found happiness, contentment, and peace of mind through AA.

Immediately make it clear to the prospect that you are a person engaged in the routine business of earning a living. Tell him your only reason for believing yourself able to help him is because you, yourself, are an alcoholic and have had experiences and problems that might be similar to his.

Tell Your Story

Many members have found it desirable to launch immediately into their personal drinking story as a means of getting the confidence and wholehearted cooperation of the prospect.

It is important in telling the story of your drinking life to tell it in a manner that will describe an alcoholic, rather than a series of humorous drunken parties. This will enable the man to get a clear picture of an alcoholic, which should help him to more definitively decide whether or not he is an alcoholic.

Inspire Confidence in AA

In many instances, the prospect will have tried various means of controlling his drinking, including hobbies, church, changes of residence, change of associations, and various control plans. These will, of course, have been unsuccessful. Point out your series of unsuccessful efforts to control drinking, their absolute fruitless results; and yet, you were able to stop drinking through the application of AA principles. This will encourage the prospect to look forward, with confidence, to sobriety in AA in spite of the many past failures he might have had with other plans.

Talk About "Plus" Values

Tell the prospect frankly that he cannot quickly understand all the benefits that are coming to him through AA. Tell him of the happiness, peace of mind, health, and in many cases, material benefits that are possible through understanding and application of the AA way of life.

Show Importance of Reading Our Book

Explain the necessity of reading and rereading the AA book. Point out that this book gives a detailed description of the AA tools, and the suggested methods of using these tools to build a foundation of rehabilitation for living. This is a good time to emphasize the importance of the twelve steps and the four absolutes.

Qualities Required for Success in AA

Convey to the prospect that the objectives of AA are to provide the ways and means for an alcoholic to regain his normal place in life. Desire, patience, faith, study, and application are most important in determining each individual's plan of action in gaining the full benefits of AA.

Introduce Faith

Since the belief of a Power greater than oneself is the heart of the AA plan, and since this idea is often very difficult for a new man, the Sponsor should attempt to introduce the beginnings of an understanding of this all-important feature.

Frequently, this can be done by the Sponsor relating his own difficulty in grasping a spiritual understanding and the methods he used to overcome his difficulties.

Listen to His Story

While talking to the newcomer, take time to listen and study his reactions in order that you can present your information in a more effective manner. Let him talk too. Remember – Easy Does It.

Take to Several Meetings

To give the new member a broad and complete picture of AA, the Sponsor should take him to various meetings within a convenient distance of his home. Attending several meetings gives the new man a chance to select a group in which he will be most happy and comfortable. It is extremely important to let the prospect make his own decision as to which group he will join. Impress upon him that he is always welcome at any meeting and can change his home group if he so wishes.

Explain AA to Prospect's Family
A successful Sponsor takes pains and makes any required effort to make certain that those people closest and with the greatest interest in their prospect (mother, father, wife, etc.) are fully informed of AA, its principles and its objectives. The Sponsor sees that these people are invited to meetings and keeps them in touch with the current situation regarding the prospect at all times.

Anticipate Hospital Experience[7]
A prospect will gain more benefit from a hospitalization period if the Sponsor describes the experience and helps him anticipate it, paving the way for those members who will call on him.

Consult Older Members in AA
These suggestions for Sponsoring a new man in AA teachings are by no means complete. They are intended only for a framework and general guide. Each individual case is different and should be treated as such. Additional information for Sponsoring a new man can be obtained from the experience of older men in the work. A co-Sponsor, with an experienced and newer member working on a prospect, has proven very satisfactory.

Before undertaking the responsibility of Sponsoring, a member should make certain that he is able and prepared to give the time, effort, and thought such an obligation entails. It might be that he will want to select a co-Sponsor to share the responsibility, or he might feel it necessary to ask another to assume the responsibility for the man he has located.

- Clarence H. Snyder

IF YOU ARE GOING TO BE A SPONSOR – BE A GOOD ONE![8]

---

[7] In early AA you were not allowed to start 'The Program' unless you had gong gone through a recognized hospital detoxification The first time someone simply showed up to get and stay sober, it resulting resulted in a major controversy within the fellowship.

[8] There has been one change in this article from its original appearance; it was originally presented within a "Christian-only" context. This has been modified to conform with the "God as you understand himHim" now used in A.A.

Zen and the Art of Sponsorship

"God, Make me a Channel of Thy Peace..." -- *St. Francis Prayer*

To be a channel is to allow what is being channeled to flow through. If it is water, it must include input and outflow. In Sponsorship, it must provide the principles as received into your life through your Sponsor, your experience within the Program, and carrying that message to those you would Sponsor.

How to Not Know

The most difficult answer for any alcoholic is "I don't know," but it is "not knowing" that opens the possibility of learning. Even the answer that was perfect yesterday may not be the right answer for today.

Your Sponsee will learn more about truth if you say "I don't know, let's find someone with experience with that," and together you seek the answer with your Sponsee. If you search together through the tools available to you - through Prayer, literature, the fellowship, and professional sources - your Sponsee will learn how to find an answer by experience and improvisation.

To "not know" is to agree to be a student and makes it possible for you and your Sponsee to learn from your Higher Power.

"Not knowing" how to live without a drink brought you to your Recovery. Recognition of your own limits and the willingness to find the new answer will improve your own Recovery and that of your Sponsee.

Some groups and Sponsors use "Rev. Mychal's Prayer"

"God, take away everything

I think I know about you

and about me, and teach me."

Essential

Sponsorship is a concept of one member of the Program helping another member of the Program through the process of the Steps and applying those Steps and principles into their daily life.

Sponsorship requires the ability to see the Now and use the Program to help the Sponsee (sometimes called "pigeon," "baby," "cookie," or "protégé") to move through the Recovery process using the Twelve Steps.

Essential Improvisation

Improvisation is a specific way of approaching theater, based on the book "Improvisation for the Theatre" by Viola Spolin. Today, improvisation is best known through improv comedy, such as The Second City.

The essence of improvisation is always to support – never deny -- what came before. There is no "one size fits all" philosophy and there are countless ways to successfully carry the message to your Sponsee.

An attitude of improvisation will allow you to take whatever progress the Sponsee makes with the Steps and application of those Steps to his/her life as a way to learn the lesson, and then move on and move forward.

Essential Zen

Zen is defined by the Free Online Dictionary as "Buddhist doctrine that enlightenment can be attained through direct intuitive insight." Zen is not a religion. Zen is an approach based on recognition of the moment, the immediate moment, the "Now."

Sponsorship is the challenge of matching the experience of the Sponsor with the situation of the Sponsee. Zen requires that you be focused on the Now, the Sponsee's actions, and the tools of the Program, to eliminate the actions that created the current situation, clean up the baggage of the past which interferes with life in the Now, and taking the action required for the personal change Recovery demands.

Improvisation requires the Sponsor be armed with information and a wide variety of specific examples and answers that address the need of the Now. In the Big Book, it says "obviously you can't carry something you haven't got," so it is necessary that the Sponsor become saturated in a variety of material in addition to the Sponsor's own experience.

The combination of Sponsorship, Zen, and improvisation allows the Sponsor to listen to the Sponsee, to respond in a way that includes the "yes, and..." of improv, and direct the Sponsee toward taking new action to correct his negative actions by using the available tools of meetings, fellowship, Prayer, literature, and phone - whatever suits the moment.

Over-prepare

Get into your Program as never before. You will be amazed at how the themes you find in reading, listening to speakers, attending discussion meetings, and conversations you have with other people in the Program will tie into the obstacles and questions in the "Now" of your Sponsee and yourself.

Dallas B., Pacific Group, Mar Vista, CA

Clancy's Seven Questions

Several years ago, Clancy I., was explaining to me that guilt, resentment, fear, feelings of personal inadequacy and loneliness were the five areas that seem to cause the most serious problems for people in recovery.

He shared with me seven questions that he uses to help a person start writing and he emphasized that the questions and the writing are not intended to replace AA's Fourth Step, they just help the person get started.

Most of the people who approach Clancy or who are referred to him, are very hardcore cases who have tried numerous times and approaches to solve their problems.

Here are the Seven Questions:

1. *In looking back over your life – what memories are still painful, guilty, dirty?*

2. *In what ways do you consider yourself an inadequate person?*

3. *Who do you resent – and why? Be specific.*

4. *What do you conceive to be your defects of character – as you see them today?*

5. *What is the nature of the ongoing problems you have with people close to you – in human relations – what seems to always happen when you have these things that blow up?*

6. *In what way do you believe that AA can help you with any of these problems?*

7. *In what way do you believe that AA can begin to change things?*

I have been using these "Seven Questions" with the people that I sponsor ever since Clancy shared them with me.

I've discovered that they are very effective when dealing with rock-bottom newcomers and with the high-bottom intellectual types. I have also used them numerous times in helping old-timers who were struggling through a difficult period.

I never give the newcomer the questions without also setting a time for them to complete their writing. Normally, I'll give them the questions and expect them to be finished with their writing by the next day, and I'll have them call me so that we can get together and discuss their answers and apply the solution to their problems.

If the newcomer procrastinates and doesn't meet the deadline for the questions, I usually consider that they are not yet serious enough to approach their problem and I move on to help someone else.

I pass them on to you with the hope that they will help you in helping others as much as they have helped me. Dallas B.

P.S. Thank you Clancy for all of your help, and for the structure, responsible behavior and discipline that you've taught me, and for all that you do for Alcoholics Anonymous! My life would not be so good without you!

To New Sponsors

So, someone has asked you to be their Sponsor. What do you do?

First, remember you cannot carry something you haven't got. Do you have a Sponsor? Your ability to share with a new prospect is limited to your own experience, so you cannot show a newcomer how to work with a Sponsor if you do not work with a Sponsor.

Call your Sponsor as soon as someone asks you and whimper, "What do I do?" Your Sponsor is your best guide to being a Sponsor.

Do you have a network of people in the Program with whom you can discuss your life and options in Recovery? Do you continue to do step work with your Sponsor, even after years of sobriety? Do you have a spiritual life? Will you be able to share what you have with newcomers, even if they are not of the same faith as you?

The experience of a Sponsor and Sponsee working together is unique and should be between equals, one of whom has more experience in Recovery than the other. It is a close teacher / student relationship that may evolve into a friendship, but it is not necessary to become friends for successful Sponsorship.

Being a Sponsor does not mean you are superior to the newcomer – you are just someone who is a little further along the path than the Sponsee and who is willing to share with the newcomer what you've done.

A Sponsor helps the Sponsee understand the basics of the Program and works the Sponsee through the Steps (particularly the 4th and 5th Steps).

A Sponsor shares basic information in the Big Book, most often by sitting with the Sponsee and going through the first 181 pages out loud, defining the words and concepts to make the Sponsee aware of the tools being laid at his feet.

A Sponsor is not a bank. Loaning or borrowing money between a Sponsor and a Sponsee can taint the relationship. The two of you will talk about financial issues, but money can ruin what could be a working relationship that could help you both.

A Sponsor is not a taxi service. A Sponsor may take a Sponsee to meetings, particularly to the Sponsor's Home Group, but the Sponsee should be encouraged to develop a new network of people in the Program for rides and discussion.

A Sponsor is not a counselor. That means marriage- or employment-counselor. You will discuss the Sponsee's issues and problems, but you do not have any authority to share anything other than your own experience and background in the Steps. Even if you are a licensed counselor, this is not a professional relationship.

A Sponsor is not a therapist. Again, even if the Sponsor is a licensed therapist, this is not a professional relationship. The Sponsor's job is to help the newcomer through Recovery using the Steps, and the principles in daily living. This will cover areas of money, relationships, employment, sex, desire, defects, and spiritual life.

A Sponsor Is Not Perfect

No one in our Program has attained perfection, but progress is our ongoing goal. You may make mistakes, but learn from them and share with your Sponsee how mistakes can be used as part of the lessons required for Recovery.

What your Sponsee sees you do is every bit as important as anything you say.

If you do not know something, be honest. Your willingness to seek an answer for something you do not know can be a powerful lesson for your prospect.

Successful Sponsorship

Having a Sponsor or being a Sponsor does not guarantee that the prospect will stay sober.

If your Sponsee goes out and starts drinking again, find someone else to work with who may want what you have to offer.

If you stay sober, the Sponsorship has been effective.

If your Sponsee stays sober, it is not because of your wonderful Sponsorship. It is because you have helped the Sponsee find and develop his spiritual awakening and personal relationship to a Higher Power.

Recovery Reader – Second Edition

To New Speakers

So, you have been asked to speak as a sober member of Alcoholics Anonymous. Congratulations! You've seen it done a hundred times, but how do you get up there to deliver a message of your experience, strength, and hope.

This is simply one member's attempt to share Experience, Strength, and Hope with someone else, regardless of how many listeners he or she may have. A member speaking for the first time, or who wants to re-examine how they present their story when they speak to a group, might benefit from a few words from those with previous experience.

What Do You Say?

First, introduce yourself. You may choose to say your first name or your full name. Give your sobriety date and the information for your Home Group.

In the Big Book, we are told that we are to carry the message and a speaker needs to be clear on what his/her message is. In its simplest form, that message will be "This works."

Your talk should be broken into the three basic phases; "What it was like...," "What happened...," and "What it is like now." It is not the purpose of your talk to explain everything – you won't be able to do that. But you will take some key moments from your story to share. You may want to mention if you have had previous bouts of sobriety.

Preparation

You really do not need to write a script for everything you are going to say. A simple list of words in some approximate order that makes sense to you will remind you what you want to say. You will then be able to tell that part of your story as if you were telling the story to some friends.

Because, you are.

Many speakers do a short Prayer before they talk, sometimes alone in the bathroom or a quiet place, sometimes at the beginning of their talk. The best public Prayer I have heard is a variation on Fr. Mychal's Prayer.

"God, take away everything I think I know about you, and take away everything I think I know about me, and teach me."

Language

The book says "We will tell, in our own words..." and no one can tell you what you cannot say. Well, some may try, but their authority is to tell you what they have done, not their theories on forbidden language.

But in the Raleigh area there is a sign some meetings use, "A lack of profanity offends no one."

My language was rough when I arrived in the south. And my story included a lot of the language I used in the streets. After a talk where my Sponsor's wife had brought a friend to hear what I had to say, she could only remember that I had used the Queen-Mother of swear words in my talk. My Sponsor's wife came up to me to suggest I watch my language.

So I became righteous and brought up the direction from the book, "We will tell, in our own words..." She agreed. "It also says you are to carry the message, and people won't hear the message if you are offending them."

At first I wanted to justify my language but realized that speaking was not about me and how wonderful I was. I was told to carry the message and voluntarily began restricting my language. The result was a better talk about the Program and what it has given me.

You have to make up your own mind.

Who Are You Talking To?

First, remember who you are talking to. A room full of alcoholics is going to be far too self-involved to bother noticing much of what you are saying. In fact, there may be only a small number of people who are really listening – and you will never know who they are. You may be fooled that the folks who are sitting in the front, bright-eyed and apparently paying attention, are not the people who will really get your message.

But don't be too sure of that. Sometimes you may plant a seed that won't take root for months or years, but something from your story may sink in with someone who is new, or who has been around for a while, secretly suffering and ready to try something desperate – like using someone else's story to apply our Program to their own life.

Get sober quickly

Many speakers take the opportunity to tell war stories, and some of the things we have done are exactly what give us the authority of experience. But some never leave the "and I got so drunk that I..." phase - you risk the newcomer leaving the meeting wondering if you ever got sober.

Whatever the length of time you have to talk, we offer this guideline:

Try to keep your personal drunk-a-logue down to 1/3 of the available time. "We will tell you what we were like..." does not mean talk about your career as a budding alcoholic all night. So, if you are speaking for 45 minutes, use no more than 15 minutes for your drunk stories. With 30 minutes, you need no more than 10 minutes of drunk stories.

The Beginning of Your Own Sobriety

The "What happened..." phase of your talk should run no more than 1/3 of the total time, but may be less if you had hit a solid bottom and only had to have one sobriety date. With more than one sobriety date you may want to share on why you had to change your date.

Benefits

Sometimes a speaker will only talk about the struggles he/she must face in sobriety. Many of us have to share that we are not examples of success with jobs or relationships or behavior.

But never forget that you are talking to a room full of people who already know how to suffer.

Talk about your story in Recovery. Share how you worked your Steps, talk about your Home Group, your Sponsor, your Inventory, and Step Work. Share the personal pain that finally gave you the desire to stop drinking. Really!

Your honesty will reach your audience. To stand there and visibly be better than the drunk you are describing will carry a message.

Do not share on Steps or problems you have not had. No one needs more theory. You are there to carry the message of how the actions you have taken – how using the Big Book, the Steps, your Sponsor, and the other tools – have taken you to this new place in your life.

Do not be afraid to share your real past, but do not involve the names or positions of other people in your story by name. You are telling your story, not theirs.

If you have a secret you learned to give up, you are not required to tell that secret from the podium. No one can make that decision but you. If you can share a past secret, it may carry a stronger message to someone in your audience who may need to hear how you found freedom from the poison of secrets.

Tell them how the Program has given you what nothing else has. Talk about feeling at peace inside your own skin. Share the healing you have experienced, the changes in your relationships (family, friends, or work) or health.

Avoid presenting your story so that getting a new car, a new job, or more money is the reward of working your Program. People can become confused with the benefits of the Program and material things. Your job is to share your message, your Recovery, offer a solution, and "the" result of our Program.

"Having had a spiritual awakening as the result of these Steps..."   T e n t h Step

Above all, talk of your hope and belief that the Program succeeded where nothing else could. Share your sense that you felt it would not work for you but that it brought you to where you are now and your hope for the future.

Tools, Steps, and Service

Try to include how you have used the Steps and Tools of the Program (meetings, fellowship, literature, Sponsor, etc.):

- Meetings
- Fellowship
- Sponsorship
- Phone
- Literature
- Writing
- Steps and Steps and Steps

Talk about Service and how it has affected your Recovery. Keep it within your own experience and tell how you have done Service. This can include carrying meetings into institutions, setting up for meetings, giving rides, talking with newcomers, making and receiving phone calls,

Afterwards

If people come up to thank you, say "Thank you." It is not your job to explain to them why they are wrong, just say "Thank you."

If they say they got something from your talk, they know better than you what is in their own head.

The Three Talks

Almost all speakers say they had three talks:

- *The talk they wanted to give;*

- *The talk they actually gave;*
- *The talk based on things they remembered after the meeting – what they think they should have said.*

That is common. Like life, you do as well as you can and do it a little bit better the next time. Do your best and learn. You can do it better the next time.

Emptying your Cup

There is an old teaching story of a petitioner coming to see a monk for wisdom. The monk offered him a cup of tea and the petitioner held out a cup. The monk poured until the cup was full, then kept pouring until the cup overflowed and the tea spilled all over the floor.

When the teapot was empty, the monk shook his head and looked at the petitioner. He said:

"How can I give you any tea if you do not give me an empty cup?"

Speaking is your opportunity to empty your cup to get the next blessing or lesson.

Write A List

You may want to write down a simple list of things you want to say and put them on an index card or a sheet of note paper to help you, should your mind go blank looking at the faces staring at you.

Just show up on time and tell the truth. You'll do fine.One Speaker's Personal List

This is an example of the 'list' it is suggested for you to use when you need to keep your talk moving forward. Your items on your list will be personalized, of course.

Give sobriety date, home group
Mama's suicide
Growing up with an active alcoholic
Molested age 4
Never feeling "real" inside my own skin
Family moved every year, no long term friends
Drugs in high school, relief
Drinking college, THE relief. It worked for me
Hating AA (Dad)
Going to AA for Inspiration, but not an alcoholic

The 20 Questions – was "I" an alcoholic?
Four years plus not able to stay sober in Program
Two poor choices of Sponsors I could "out think"
Sponsor #3
Day one of my Sobriety
My real Inventory
Service, non-negotiable
Sponsoring to stay Sober
Moving from state to state, new Sponsors, more service
Traveling – finding new meetings
Diagnosed diabetic – Stayed Sober
Moving here, local home group and Sponsor
Commitment to Service and
Threatened with amputation and stayed sober; heart attack and stayed sober; how my heart attack meant I didn't have the amputation; COPD and stayed sober; Three cancer scares, stayed sober
Message to the newcomer.
Wrap at... [Stop time for speaker at this meeting]

DO YOUR OWN LIST - It could even be shorter

Active Listening

OBJECTIONS AND QUESTIONS

Ultimately, you cannot get anyone sober. If they do not do the work, they will not get the result. You can't coddle anyone, either.

Every Sponsor encounters repeating questions or situations. Over time, your experience dealing with certain issues will be the most valuable thing you can offer a new Sponsee. There are different responses to different types of off topic questions.

Specific guidance can make a difference. These are samples of specifics we have encountered, more than once. They are not the only questions, but they can serve as models to build your own aresenal of answers for people who will come to you in the future.

You can also try to remember the more odd questions you are asked or the comments that may play into your own experience in Recovery.

A few samples of such questions or comments might be.

"I'll never be able to do Step Four..."

When the time comes, when you have really done Steps One, Two, and Three you will be able to do the next step. You might even look forward to it.

There is nothing in Step Four you have not already thought about. The purpose of Step Four is to get those thoughts out of your head and onto paper, where they stop moving. When we only tell and retell our story without writing it down, our version changes just a little every time we tell it.

By writing it all in one place, you see what a big steaming pile your life has become. When you see that pile, you'll be ready to sit down with your Sponsor or the person with whom you do Step Five, to have them help you make sense of what is there.

"I'll never be able to do Step Five…"

In Step Five, you get to see your personal, steaming pile in 3D. You need two eyes to see things in 3D, so you need a second viewpoint to see your Fourth Step in three dimensions. The person you're doing Step Five with will have some experience and be able to help you separate the things that come up:

a) *What is yours and what is not? We tend to become the center of the universe (we think) and everything is about "me." We take on responsibility for other people's thoughts or actions, or try to escape our own responsibility by claiming it was really so-and-so, not "me." You may be surprised to see what gets taken out of your Fourth Step, and what remains.*

b) *Not everything in your Fourth Step are bad things. The Big Book and the Twelve and Twelve both tell us we must Inventory our assets, too. The purpose of identifying assets is to see where we were given gifts or developed good abilities, and usually how we have not used these assets properly, or turned them into a weapon against other people.*

c) *We hear the person we have chosen for our Fifth Step share his own experience with the issues we are facing and are surprised to find how we have reacted as simple humans, not monsters or saints. We find that we are imperfect, as are the other people in AA, but need to take responsibility for what is ours, discard excess baggage that is not ours to repair, and identify all the aspects of our lives, good and bad.*

Sometimes a participant will challenge you with a rumor he has heard about AA. Answer that rumor truthfully; either with the facts and cite your source for your answers, or admit you do not have the answer now and agree to look for the real story behind the rumor.

"I heard Bill Wilson used LSD."

Yep. In the 1960s, before Timothy Leary and black light posters, researchers believed LSD would be useful in treating alcoholism and depression, and might be a tool to use in finding the "Spiritual Experience" most AAs were seeking. Bill took LSD under supervision, often with Aldous Huxley (author of "The Doors of Perception") in California. Lois participated in some of those lab sessions.

The story is in Chapter 23 of Pass It On, which is Bill Wilson's history of AA. When it became controversial, Bill stopped participating in the experiment. It is also covered in Ernie Kurtz' unofficial history of AA, "Not God."

In other sessions, you may have someone who wants to explore some non-Recovery related question, or wants to show how smart they are by asking a question to which they already know the answer, but want to have the chance to be the one to tell the class.

"Isn't it true Bill Wilson was a Mason?"

I really don't know. It's never been part of my understanding of how to do the Steps or to deal with my own Recovery. But I'm sure it has been documented if it is true.

Does that change whether you will do your Steps, or the information being presented here? Can we focus on Steps and Recovery?

"Shouldn't alcoholism simply be classified as a Mental Illness?"

I'm not a medical person and am not qualified to diagnose either medically or psychiatrically. The AMA (American Medical Association) does define alcoholism as a separate diagnosis with mental and physical factors. The mental obsession might be on the level of a mental illness. An alcoholic can have additional problems, such as schizophrenia, neurosis, etc., but that does not change the diagnosis of "alcoholic."

Would you use the fact the disease is not classified the way you want it to be classified as a reason not do the Steps? If you think psychiatry would help you more than the Steps, you are free to try that.

I, personally, have done three rounds of psychotherapy and several class/ workshop sessions in sobriety. I found having my AA program in place, and telling the doctor the truth (which was a whole new concept) to be very useful in getting the benefit of a good therapist.

Sometimes the question will be heartfelt and, if you have made the class a safe place to ask real questions, may be instrumental in helping the participant overcome his or her block on doing the work of Recovery.

"I don't understand all that "thee" and "thine" stuff. What does that mean?"

It would never have occurred to me to ask that question. I was raised in a good, church-going family and "thee" and "thine" were part of the language from the very early days.

Let's take the suggested Third Step Prayer on Page 63:

> *"God, I offer myself to Thee – to build with me and to do with me as Thou wilt. Relieve me of the bondage of self, that I may better do Thy will. Take away my difficulties, that victory over them may bear witness to those I would help of Thy Power, Thy Love, and Thy Way of life. May I do Thy will always!"*

Now, let's do that in current English to get the meaning without the 16th Century English.

> *"God, I offer myself to You – to build with me and to do with me as You will. Relieve me of the bondage of self, that I may better do Your will. Take away my difficulties, that victory over them may bear witness to those I would help of Your Power, Your Love, and Your Way of life. May I do Your will always!"*

If you have a more personal way to phrase this Prayer, so that it is clear to you and you mean the words, you have an obligation to make this Prayer as strong as you can.

If you don't know an answer, don't claim that you do. You can always help someone find an answer you do not already have. You can help them find someone who can answer their questions. You aren't expected to know everything.

Remember that a lot of the newcomer's early objections to AA are based on information from people who may not be fans of AA, or may be a result of fear of admitting there might be answers of which the newcomer do not already have.

Sometimes, it can also be useful to ask if the answer to the question has anything to do with getting and staying clean and sober. If they do not get the answer they like, will it justify staying drunk and high with all that means in their own life and the lives of the people they affect?

Or a newcomer's arguments may even a delaying tactic – a distraction to avoid the serious self appraisal required to deflate the Ego. They may require some time to believe they are going to be able to take the actions to repair past damage and become a new and useful member of the society in which they find themselves.

Build Your Arch

For the first fifteen years of my Recovery, the internet was not much of a thing. I used email, but websites were strange and alien things that other people made. And archives were just starting to appear, brimming with files of art and poetry and writings and research and more.

In time, web pages began to appear on every possible topic. Including Recovery.

And in one of these I found this image.

I understood the intent. I understood that the artist wanted to repesent the arch through which we will walk into the new life, given to us by Recovery.

But I am a problem child and my only thought was "How can you build an arch like that?"

It looked to me like this arch would fall down around the First Step. Before the First Step. It would fall apart about the point of the empty stone above 'Notes' on the left side.

So I wondered how I could build an arch that did not fall down. A lasting arch that represented the work I was doing through the Steps, using the Tools, and keeping the structure, the combination of spirituality and action, topped by the three "maintenance" Steps: Ten, Eleven and Twelve.

I found a way to make my arch[9].

Maybe you will be able to use it.

Maybe you will build your own arch. An arch that makes sense to you and gives you lasting peace and shelter.

---

9 This arch was used for the first time as an illustration in the relapse prevention class, The Work. This is the second version, with a slight adjustment on the positioning of the Steps. It is available as a free download from the home website for this book, http://sponsormagazine.info

Do The Work, You Get The Result

"Most Good ideas are simple, and this concept was the keystone of the new and triumphant arch through which we passed to freedom." - Page 62

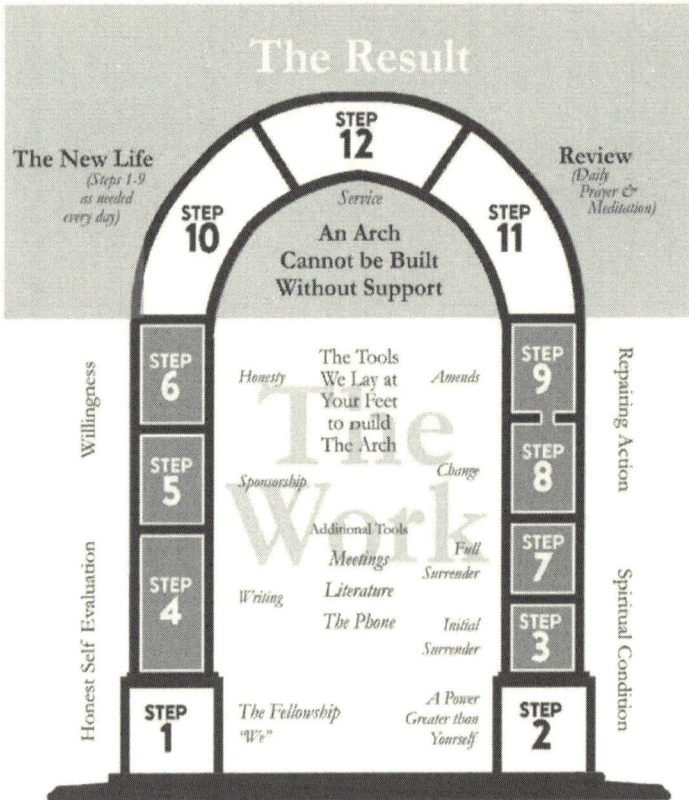

The Result

STEP 12

The New Life
(Steps 1-9
as needed
every day)

STEP 10

Service

Review
(Daily
Prayer &
Meditation)

STEP 11

An Arch Cannot be Built Without Support

Willingness

STEP 6

Honesty

The Tools We Lay at Your Feet to build The Arch

Amends

STEP 9

Repairing Action

STEP 5

Sponsorship

Change

STEP 8

The Work

Additional Tools

Honest Self Evaluation

STEP 4

Writing

Meetings
Literature
The Phone

Full Surrender

Initial Surrender

STEP 7

STEP 3

Spiritual Condition

STEP 1

The Fellowship "We"

A Power Greater than Yourself

STEP 2

YOUR FOUNDATION
"The Moment of Clarity"
"Hitting Bottom"
"Step Zero"

Why Carry This Message?

The best way to learn a subject, no matter what that subject may be, is to teach that subject to others. As you teach, as you share, as you Sponsor, you reap the benefits. Maybe the one to whom you carry the message does not succeed, but you do!

You "carry this message" to ensure your own Recovery.

Repeatedly the story returns to where someone finds Sobriety and begins a life in Recovery, but maintains a basic attitude of selfishness - "I got mine – you're on your own." And those people show up in the familiar story of a Relapse.

Even if you are not working closely with one person as a "Sponsor" you can share your Recovery with them as a friend. They may listen to you as they would not listen to anyone else. As with Step One - the Step Twelve success is based on "We."

Working with others, actively supporting the meetings and service structure, donating, and doing Service are the ways we improve our own understanding of Recovery. We get more by giving it away.

This chart from the National Training Laboratories may help you understand.

THE LEARNING PYRAMID
AVERAGE RETENTION RATES

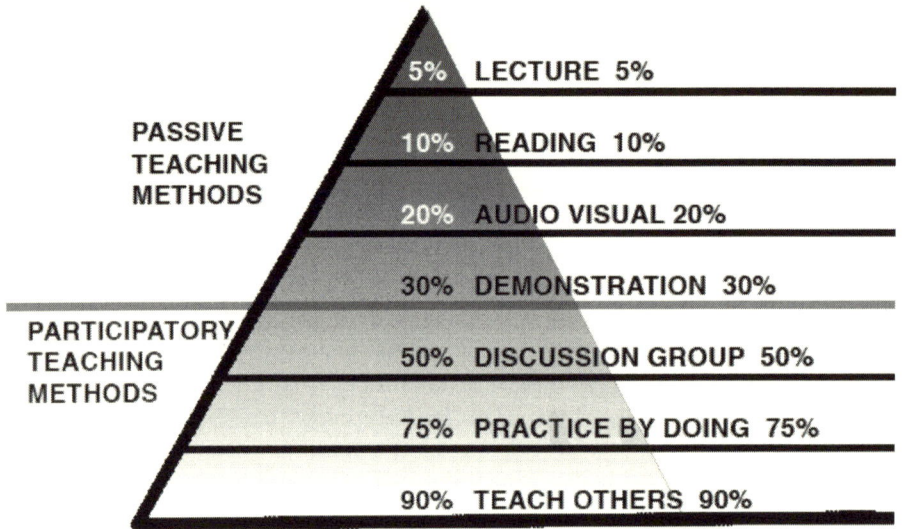

PASSIVE TEACHING METHODS

5% LECTURE 5%

10% READING 10%

20% AUDIO VISUAL 20%

30% DEMONSTRATION 30%

PARTICIPATORY TEACHING METHODS

50% DISCUSSION GROUP 50%

75% PRACTICE BY DOING 75%

90% TEACH OTHERS 90%

ADAPTED FROM **NATIONAL TRAINING LABORATORIES,** BETHEL, MAIN

That Ain't in the Book!

We hear a lot of stuff said in meetings that can't be reconciled with the Program as described in the Big Book of Alcoholics Anonymous. What follows are some of the things we often hear, along with what the 1st Edition of our basic text has to say on the subject.

This list includes the corresponding page and paragraph from the Big Book that deals with the subject.

"Remember your last drunk."

> *"We are unable, at times, to bring into our consciousness with sufficient force the memory of the suffering and humiliation of even a week or a month ago. We are without defense against the first drink."* *Page 24*

"I choose not to drink today."

> *"The fact is that most alcoholics, for reasons yet obscure, have lost the power of choice in drink."* *Page 24*

"Play the tape all the way through."

> *"The almost certain consequences that follow taking even a glass of beer do not crowd into the mind to deter us. If these thoughts do occur, they are hazy and readily supplanted with the old threadbare idea that this time we shall handle ourselves like other people. There is a complete failure of the kind of defense that keeps one from putting his hand on a hot stove."* *Page 24*

"Think through the drink."

> *"Once more: The alcoholic at certain times has no effective mental defense against the first drink. Except in a few rare cases, neither he nor any other human being can provide such a defense. His defense must come from a Higher Power."* *Page 43*

"I will always be recovering, never recovered."

"The Story of How Many Thousands of Men and Women Have Recovered from
   Alcoholism"   Title Page

"Doubtless you are curious to discover how and why, in face of expert opinion to
   the contrary, we have recovered from a hopeless condition of mind and body."
                                                                 Page 20

"We, of Alcoholics Anonymous, are more than one hundred men and women who
   have recovered from a seemingly hopeless state of mind and body."
                                                 Forward, First Edition

"Further on, clear-cut directions are given showing how we recovered." Page 132

"We have recovered, and have been given the power to help others."   Page 132

"We are all just an arm's length away from a drink."

"And we have ceased fighting anything or anyone - even alcohol. For by this time
   sanity will have returned. We will seldom be interested in liquor. If tempted,
   we recoil from it as from a hot flame. We react sanely and normally, and we
   will find that this has happened automatically. We will see that our new
   attitude toward liquor has been given us without any thought or effort on our
   part. It just comes! That is the miracle of it. We are not fighting it, neither are
   we avoiding temptation. We feel as though we had been placed in a position
   of neutrality - safe and protected. We have not even sworn off. Instead, the
   problem has been removed. It does not exist for us."   Page 84

"I don't have an alcohol problem, I have a living problem."

"In our belief, any picture of the alcoholic which leaves out this physical factor is
   incomplete."   Page xxiv

"Don't drink and go to meetings."

"Many of us felt we had plenty of character. There was a tremendous urge to cease
   forever. Yet we found it impossible. This is the baffling feature of alcoholism as
   we know it—this utter inability to leave it alone, no matter how great the
   necessity or the wish."   Page 34

"Whether such a person can quit upon a non-spiritual basis depends upon the extent to which he has already lost the power to choose whether he will drink or not."
Page 34

"Unlike the feelings of the ship's passengers, however, our joy in escape from disaster does not subside as we go our individual ways. The feeling of having shared in a common peril is one element in the powerful cement which binds us. But that in itself would never have held us together as we are now joined."
Page 17

"This is a selfish program."

"Our very lives, as ex-problem drinkers depend upon our constant thought of others and how we may help meet their needs."
Page 20

"Helping others is the foundation stone of your Recovery. A kindly act once in a while isn't enough. You have to act the Good Samaritan every day, if need be. It may mean the loss of many nights' sleep, great interference with your pleasures, interruptions to your business. It may mean sharing your money and your home, counseling frantic wives and relatives, innumerable trips to police courts, sanitariums, hospitals, jails and asylums. Your telephone may jangle at any time of the day or night. "
Page 97

"For if an alcoholic failed to perfect and enlarge his spiritual life through work and self-sacrifice for others, he could not survive the certain trials and low spots ahead."
Page 14-15

"Selfishness, self-centeredness! That, we think, is the root of our troubles." Page 62

"So our troubles, we think, are basically of our own making. They arise out of ourselves, and the alcoholic is an extreme example of self-will run riot, though he usually doesn't think so. Above everything, we alcoholics must be rid of this selfishness. We must, or it kills us!"
Page 62

"Meeting makers make it."

"Here are the steps we took, which are suggested as a program of Recovery."
Page 59

"I'm powerless over people, places, and things."

"We have recovered, and have been given the power to help others." Page 132

"Years of living with an alcoholic is almost sure to make any wife or child neurotic." Page 122

"The alcoholic is like a tornado roaring his way through the lives of others. Hearts are broken. Sweet relationships are dead. Affections have been uprooted. Selfish and inconsiderate habits have kept the home in turmoil. We feel a man is unthinking when he says that sobriety is enough." Page 89

"You can help when no one else can. You can secure their confidence when others fail." Page 103

"You're in the right place."

"Then we have a certain type of hard drinker. He may have the habit badly enough to gradually impair him physically and mentally. It may cause him to die a few years before his time. If a sufficiently strong reason - ill health, falling in love, change of environment, or the warning of a doctor - becomes operative, this man can also stop or moderate, although he may find it difficult and troublesome and may even need medical attention."

"If anyone who is showing inability to control his drinking can do the right-about-face and drink like a gentleman, our hats are off to him." Page 20-21

"We do not like to pronounce any individual as alcoholic, but you can quickly diagnose yourself. Step over to the nearest barroom and try some controlled drinking. Try to drink and stop abruptly. Try it more than once. It will not take long for you to decide, if you are honest with yourself about it. It may be worth a bad case of jitters if you get a full knowledge of your condition." Page 31

"Your husband may be only a heavy drinker. His drinking may be constant or it may be heavy only on certain occasions. Perhaps he spends too much money for liquor. It may be slowing him up mentally and physically, but he does not see it. Sometimes he is a source of embarrassment to you and his friends. He is positive he can handle his liquor, that it does him no harm, that drinking is necessary in his business. He would probably be insulted if he were called an alcoholic. This world is full of people like him. Some will moderate or stop altogether, and some will not. Of those who keep on, a good number will become true alcoholics after a while." Page 92

"If you are satisfied that he is a real alcoholic."

"If he thinks he can do the job in some other way, or prefers some other spiritual approach, encourage him to follow his own conscience."   Page 95

"If an alcoholic wants to get sober, nothing you say can make him drink."

"A spirit of intolerance might repel alcoholics whose lives could have been saved, had it not been for such stupidity. We would not even do the cause of temperate drinking any good, for not one drinker in a thousand likes to be told anything about alcohol by one who hates it."   Page 103

"We must change playmates, playgrounds, and playthings."

"Assuming we are spiritually fit, we can do all sorts of things alcoholics are not supposed to do. People have said we must not go where liquor is served; we must not have it in our homes; we must shun friends who drink; we must avoid moving pictures which show drinking scenes; we must not go into bars; our friends must hide their bottles if we go to their houses; we mustn't think or be reminded about alcohol at all. Our experience shows that this is not necessarily so. We meet these conditions every day. An alcoholic who cannot meet them, still has an alcoholic mind; there is something the matter with his spiritual status. His only chance for sobriety would be some place like the Greenland Ice Cap, and even there an Eskimo might turn up with a bottle of scotch and ruin everything!"   Page 100-101

"I'm a people pleaser. I need to learn to take care of myself."

"Is he not really a self-seeker even when trying to be kind?"   Page 61

"Don't drink, even if your ass falls off." or "Don't drink, no matter what."

"Many of us felt we had plenty of character. There was a tremendous urge to cease forever. Yet we found it impossible. This is the baffling feature of alcoholism as we know it—this utter inability to leave it alone, no matter how great the necessity or the wish."   Page 34

"I haven't had a drink today, so I'm a complete success today."

"The elimination of drinking is but a beginning. A much more important demonstration of our principles lies before us in our respective homes, occupations and affairs."   Page 19

"It's my opinion that..." or "I don't know anything about the Big Book, but this is the way I do it..."

"We have concluded to publish an anonymous volume setting forth the problem as we see it. We shall bring to the task our combined experience and knowledge. This should suggest a useful program for anyone concerned with a drinking problem." Page 19

"We need to give up planning; it doesn't work."

"On awakening let us think about the twenty-four hours ahead. We consider our plans for the day. Before we begin, we ask God to direct our thinking, especially asking that it be divorced from self-pity, dishonest or self-seeking motives. Under these conditions we can employ our mental faculties with assurance, for after all God gave us brains to use. Our thought-life will be placed on a much higher plane when our thinking is cleared of wrong motives. In thinking about our day we may face indecision. We may not be able to determine which course to take. Here we ask God for inspiration, an intuitive thought or a decision. We relax and take it easy. We don't struggle. We are often surprised how the right answers come after we have tried this for a while." Page 86

"I have a choice to not drink today."

"We alcoholics are men and women who have lost the ability to control our drinking. We know that no real alcoholic ever recovers control. All of us felt at times that we were regaining control, but such intervals - usually brief - were inevitably followed by still less control, which led in time to pitiful and incomprehensible demoralization. We are convinced to a man that alcoholics of our type are in the grip of a progressive illness. Over any considerable period we get worse, never better." Page 30

"If all I do is stay sober today, then it's been a good day."

"Sometimes we hear an alcoholic say that the only thing he needs to do is to keep sober. Certainly he must keep sober, for there will be no home if he doesn't. But he is yet a long way from making good to the wife or parents whom for years he has so shockingly treated." Page 82

"We feel a man is unthinking when he says sobriety is enough." Page 82

"You don't need a shrink. You have an alcoholic personality. All you will ever need is in the first 164 pages of the Big Book."

"But this does not mean that we disregard human health measures. God has abundantly supplied this world with fine doctors, psychologists, and practitioners of various kinds. Do not hesitate to take your health problems to such persons. Most of them give freely of themselves, that their fellows may enjoy sound minds and bodies. Try to remember that though God has wrought miracles among us, we should never belittle a good doctor or psychiatrist. Their services are often indispensable in treating a newcomer and in following his case afterward."   Page 133

"AA is the only way to stay sober."

"If he thinks he can do the job in some other way, or prefers some other spiritual approach, encourage him to follow his own conscience. We have no monopoly on God; we merely have an approach that worked with us."   Page 95

"Our book is meant to be suggestive only. We realize we know only a little."
                                                                    Page 164

"My Sponsor told me that, if in making amends I would be harmed, I could consider myself as one of the 'others' in Step Nine."

"Reminding ourselves that we have decided to go to any lengths to find a spiritual experience, we ask that we be given strength and direction to do the right thing, no matter what the personal consequences might be."   Page 79

"I need to forgive myself first." or "You need to be good to yourself."

"The rule is we must be hard on ourself, but always considerate of others."Page 74

"Take what you want and leave the rest."

"The tremendous fact for every one of us is that we have discovered a common solution. We have a way out upon which we can absolutely agree, and upon which we can join in brotherly and harmonious action. This is the great news this book carries to those who suffer from alcoholism."   Page 17

"Just do the next right thing."

"We may not be able to determine which course to take. Here we ask God for inspiration, an intuitive thought or a decision."   Page 86

"Being still inexperienced and having just made conscious contact with God, it is not probable that we are going to be inspired at all times. We might pay for this presumption in all sorts of absurd actions and ideas."   Page 87

"Don't make any major decisions for the first year."

(a) – That we were alcoholic and could not manage our own lives.

(b) – That probably no human power could have relieved our alcoholism.

(c) – That God could and would if He were sought. Being convinced, we were at Step Three, which is that we decided to turn our will and our life over to God as we understood Him."   Page 60

"When ready, we say something like this: 'My Creator, I am now willing that you should have all of me, good and bad. I pray that you now remove from me every single defect of character which stands in the way of my usefulness to you and my fellows. Grant me strength, as I go out from here, to do your bidding. Amen.' We have then completed Step Seven."   Page 76

"Stay out of relationships for the first year!"

"We do not want to be the arbiter of anyone's sex conduct."   Page . 69

"In Meditation, we ask God what we should do about each specific matter. The right answer will come if we want it."   Page 69

"God alone can judge our sex situation.   Page 69

"Counsel with other persons is often desirable, but we let God be the final judge."   Page 69-70

"We earnestly pray for the right ideal, for guidance in each questionable situation, for sanity, and for the strength to do the right thing."   Page 70

"Alcohol was my drug of choice."

"The fact is that most alcoholics, for reasons yet obscure, have lost the power of choice in drink."   Page 24

"Keep coming back, eventually it will rub off on you."

"Though our decision was a vital and crucial step, it could have little permanent effect unless at once followed by a strenuous effort to face, and to be rid of, the things in ourselves which had been blocking us"   Page 64

"Ninety Meetings in Ninety Days."

"We meet frequently so that newcomers may find the fellowship they seek."
Page 15

"None of us makes a sole vocation of this work, nor do we think its effectiveness would be increased if we did."
Page 19

"Here are the steps we took, which are suggested as a program of Recovery."
Page 59

"You only work one step a year." or "Take your time to work the steps."

"What often takes place in a few months can hardly be brought about by himself alone."
Page 569

"Next we launched on a course of vigorous action."
Page 63

"If that is so, this step may be postponed, only, however, if we hold ourselves in complete readiness to go through with it at the first opportunity"
Page 74

"Returning home we find a place where we can be quiet for AN HOUR, carefully reviewing what we have done." "Make sure to put something good about yourself in your 4th Step Inventory."
Page 75

"First, we searched out the flaws in our make-up which caused our failure."
Page 64

"The Inventory was ours, not the other man's. When we saw our faults we listed them."
Page 71

"If you have already made a decision, and an Inventory of your grosser handicaps, you have made a good beginning."
Page 67

"You need to stay in those feelings and really feel them."
Page 84

"When these crop up, we ask God at once to remove them."
Page. 125

Notes and Essays

These short snippets are introductions to the rich lore of AA/ Twelve Step history and personal observations on the process of Twelve Step Recovery.

Dozens of excellent books and websites are available to give you a more substantive education in the viewpoints, documentations and even the disagreements over the details of our history.

It has not been the purpose of this book to present the 'One Truth' of the Program and the process of Recovery, but to share with you the varieties of experience and different, sometimes opposing, positions taken by various reporters and historians.

How the Big Book Was Put Together

A TALK BY BILL WILSON

AA Co-Founder Bill Wilson

I think I'm on the bill for tonight's show with a talk on the 12 Traditions of AA. But you know drunks, like women, have the prerogative, or at least seize the prerogative of changing their minds - I'm not going to make any such damn talk! For something very festive I think the Traditions 1-12 would be a little too grim, might bore you a little. As a matter of fact, speaking of Traditions, when they were first written back there in 1945 or 1946 as tentative guides to help us hang together and function, nobody paid any attention except a few "againers" who wrote me and asked what the hell are they about?

Nobody paid the slightest attention. But, little by little as these Traditions got around we had our clubhouse squabbles, our little rifts, this difficulty and that, it was found that the Traditions indeed did reflect experience and were guiding principles. So, they took hold a little more and a little more and a little more so that today the average AA coming in the door learns at once what they're about; about what kind of an outfit he really has landed in and by what principles his group and AA as a whole are governed.

But, as I say, the dickens with all that. I would like to just spin some yarn and they will be a series of yarns which cluster around the preparation of the good old AA bible and when I hear that it always makes me shudder because the guys who put it together weren't a damn bit biblical. I think sometimes some of the drunks have an idea that these old timers went around with almost visible halos and long gowns and they were full of sweetness and light. Oh boy, how inspired they were, oh yes. But wait till I tell you. I suppose the book yarn really started in the living room of Doc and Annie Smith.

As you know, I landed there in the summer of '35, a little group caught hold. I helped Smithy briefly with it and he went on to found the first AA group in the world. And, as with all new groups, it was nearly all failure, but now and then, somebody saw the light and there was progress. Pampered, I got back to New York, a little more experienced group started there, and by the time we got around to 1937, this thing had leaped over into Cleveland, and began to move south from New York.

But, it was still, we thought in those years, flying blind, a flickering candle indeed, that might at any moment be snuffed out. So, on this late fall afternoon in 1937, Smithy and I were talking together in his living room, Anne sitting there, when we began to count noses. How many people had stayed dry; in Akron, in New York, maybe a few in Cleveland? How many had stayed dry and for how long? And when we added up the total, it sure was a handful of, I don't know, 35 to 40 maybe. But enough time had elapsed on enough really fatal cases of alcoholism, so that we grasped the importance of these small statistics. Bob and I saw for the first time that this thing was going to succeed. That God in his providence and mercy had thrown a new light into the dark caves where we and our kind had been and were still by the millions dwelling.

I can never forget the elation and ecstasy that seized us both. And when we sat happily talking and reflecting, we reflected, that well, a couple of score of drunks were sober but this had taken three long years. There had been an immense amount of failure and a long time had been taken just to sober up the handful. How could this handful carry its message to all those who still didn't know? Not all the drunks in the world could come to Akron or New York. But how could we transmit our message to them, and by what means? Maybe we could go to the old timers in each group, but that meant nearly everybody, to find the sum of money - somebody else's money, of course and say to them "Well now, take a sabbatical year off your job if you have one, and you go to Kentucky, Omaha, Chicago, San Francisco and Los Angeles and where ever it may be and you give this thing a year and get a group started."

It had already become evident by then that we were just about to be moved out of the City Hospital in Akron to make room for people with broken legs and ailing livers; that the hospitals were not too happy with us. We tried to run their business perhaps too much, and besides, drunks were apt to be noisy in the night and there were other inconveniences, which were all tremendous. So, it was obvious that because of drunks being such unlovely creatures, we would have to have a great chain of hospitals.

And as that dream burst upon me, it sounded good, because you see, I'd been down in Wall Street in the promotion business and I remember the great sums of money that were made as soon as people got this chain idea. You know, chain drug stores, chain grocery stores, chain dry good stores. That evening Bob and I told them that we were within sight of success and that we thought this thing might go on and on and on, that a new light indeed was shining in our dark world. But how could this light be a reflection and transmitted without being distorted and garbled? At this point, they turned the meeting over to me, and being a salesman, I set right to work on the drunk tanks and subsidies for the missionaries, I was pretty poor then.

We touched on the book. The group conscience consisted of 18 men good and true. And the good and true men, you could see right away, were dammed skeptical about it all. Almost with one voice, they chorused "let's keep it simple, this is going to bring money into this thing, this is going to create a professional class. We'll all be ruined."

"Well," I countered, "that's a pretty good argument. Lots to what you say... but even within gunshot of this very house, alcoholics are dying like flies. And if this thing doesn't move any faster than it has in the last three years, it may be another 10 before it gets to the outskirts of Akron. How in God's name are we going to carry this message to others? We've got to take some kind of chance.

We can't keep it so simple it becomes anarchy and gets complicated. We can't keep it so simple that it won't propagate itself, and we've got to have a lot of money to do these things."

So, exerting myself to the utmost, which was considerable in those days, we finally got a vote in that little meeting and it was a mighty close vote by just a majority of maybe 2 or 3. The meeting said with some reluctance, "Well Bill, if we need a lot of dough, you better go back to New York where there's plenty of it and you raise it."

Well, boy, that was the word that I'd been waiting for. So I scrammed back to the great city and I began to approach some people of means describing this tremendous thing that had happened. And it didn't seem so tremendous to the people of means at all. What? 35 or 40 drunks sober up? They have sobered them up before now, you know. And besides, Mr. Wilson, don't you think it's kind of sweeping up the shavings? I mean, wouldn't something for the Red Cross be better?

In other words, with all of my ardent solicitations, I got one hell of a freeze from the gentlemen of wealth. Well, I began to get blue and when I begin to get blue my stomach kicks up as well as other things.

I was lying in the bed one night with an imaginary ulcer attack (this used to happen all the time - I had one the time the 12 steps were written) and I said, "My God, we're starving to death here on Clinton Street." By this time the house was full of drunks. They were eating us out of house and home. In those days we never believed in charging anybody anything - so Lois was earning the money, I was being the missionary and the drunks were eating the meals. "This can't go on. We've got to have those drunk tanks, we've got to have those missionaries, and we've got to have a book. That's for sure."

The next morning I crawled into my clothes and I called on my brother-in-law. He's a doctor and he is about the last person who followed my trip way down. The only one, save of course, the Lord. "Well," I said, "I'll go up and see Leonard." So I went up to see my brother-in-law Leonard and he pried out a little time between patients coming in there. I started my awful bellyache about these rich guys who wouldn't give us any dough for this great and glorious enterprise.

It seemed to me he knew a girl and I think she had an uncle that somehow was tied up with the Rockefeller offices. I asked him to call and see if there was such a man and if there was, would he see us. On what slender threads our destiny sometimes hangs. So, the call was made. Instantly there came onto the other end of the wire the voice of dear Willard Richardson - one of the loveliest Christian gentlemen I have ever known.

And the moment he recognized my brother-in-law he said, "Why Leonard, where have you been all these years?"

Well, my brother-in-law, unlike me, is a man of very few words, so he quickly said to dear old Uncle Willard, he had a brother-in-law who had apparently some success sobering up drunks and could the two of us come over there and see him.

"Why certainly," said dear Willard.

"Come right over."

So we go over to Rockefeller Plaza. We go up that elevator - 54 flights or 56 I guess it was, and we walk promptly into Mr. Rockefeller's personal offices, and ask to see Mr. Richardson. Here sits this lovely, benign old gentleman, who nevertheless had a kind of shrewd twinkle in his eye. So I sat down and told him about our exciting discovery, this terrific cure for alcoholics that had just hit the world, how it worked and what we have done for them. And, boy, this was the first receptive man with money or access to money - remember we were in Mr. Rockefeller's personal offices at this point - and by now, we had learned that this was Mr. Rockefeller's closest personal friend. So he said, "I'm very interested. Would you like to have lunch with me, Mr. Wilson?"

Well, now you know, for a rising promoter, that sounded pretty good - going to have lunch with the best friends of John D. Things were looking up. My ulcer attack disappeared. So I had lunch with the old gentleman and we went over this thing again and again and, boy, he's so warm and kindly and friendly.

Right at the close of the lunch he said, "Well now Mr. Wilson or Bill, if I can call you that, wouldn't you like to have a luncheon meeting with some of my friends? There's Frank Amos, he's in the advertising business but he was on a committee that recommended that Mr. Rockefeller drop the prohibition business. And there's Leroy Chipman, he looks after Mr. Rockefeller's real estate. And there's Mr. Scotty, Chairman of the Board of the Riverside Church and a number of other people like that. I believe they'd like to hear this story."

So a meeting was arranged and it fell upon a winter's night in 1937. And the meeting was held at 30 Rockefeller Plaza. We called in, posthaste, a couple of drunks from Akron - Smithy included, of course - heading the procession. I came in with the New York contingent of four or five. And to our astonishment we were ushered into Mr., Rockefeller's personal boardroom right next to his office. I thought to myself "Well, now this is really getting hot." And indeed I felt very much warmed when I was told by Mr. Richardson that I was sitting in a chair just vacated by Mr. Rockefeller.

I said "Well, now, we really are getting close to the bankroll." Old Doc Silkworth was there that night too, and he testified what he had seen happen to these new friends of ours, and each drunk, thinking of nothing better to say, told their stories of drinking and recovering and these folk listened. They seemed very definitely impressed. I could see that the moment for the big touch was coming. So, I gingerly brought up the subject of the drunk tanks, the subsidized missionaries, and the big question of a book or literature.

Well, God moves in mysterious ways, his wonders to perform. It didn't look like a wonder to me when Mr. Scott, head of a large engineering firm and Chairman of the Riverside Church, looked at us and said "Gentlemen, up to this point, this has been the work of goodwill only. No plan, no property, no paid people, just one carrying the good news to the next. Isn't that true? And may it not be that that is where the great power of this society lies? Now, if we subsidize it, might it not alter its whole character? We want to do all we can, we're gathered for that, but would it be wise?"

Well then, the salesmen all gave Mr. Scott the rush and we said, "Why, Mr. Scott, there're only 40 of us. It's taken 3 years. Why millions, Mr. Scott, will rot before this thing ever gets to them unless we have money and lots of it."

And we made our case at last with these gentlemen for the missionaries, the drunk tanks and the book. So one of them volunteered to investigate us very carefully, and since poor old Dr. Bob was harder up than I was, and since the first group and the reciprocal community was in Akron, we directed their attention out there. Frank Amos, still a trustee in the Foundation, at his own expense, got on a train, went out to Akron and made all sorts of preliminary inquiries around town about Dr. Bob. All the reports were good except that he was a drunk that recently got sober. He visited the little meeting out there. He went to the Smith house and he came back with what he thought was a very modest proposal.

He recommended to these friends of ours that we should have at least a token amount of money at first, say $50,000, something like that. That would clear up the mortgage on Smith's place. It would get us a little rehabilitation place. We could put Dr. Smith in charge. We could subsidize a few of these people briefly, until we got some more money. We could start the chain of hospitals. We'd have a few missionaries. We could get busy on the book, all for a mere 50,000 bucks. Well, considering the kind of money we were backed up against, that did sound a little small, but, you know, one thing leads to another and it sounded real good. We were real glad.

Mr. Willard Richardson, our original contact, then took that report into John D. Jr. as everybody recalls. And I've since heard what went on in there. Mr. Rockefeller read the report, called Willard Richardson and thanked him and said: "Somehow I am strangely stirred by all this. This interests me immensely." And then looking at his friend Willard, he said, "But isn't money going to spoil this thing? I'm terribly afraid that it would. And yet I am so strangely stirred by it."

Then came another turning point in our destiny. When that man whose business is giving away money said to Willard Richardson, "No," he said, "I won't be the one to spoil this thing with money. You say these two men who are heading it are a little 'stressed', I'll put $5,000 in the Riverside Church treasury. Those folks can form themselves into a committee and draw on it, as they like. I want to hear what goes on. But, please don't ask me for any more money."

Well, with fifty thousand that then was shrunk to five, we raised the mortgage on Smithy's house for about three grand. That left two and Smith and I commenced chewing on that too. Well, that was a long way from a string of drunk tanks and books. What in thunder would we do? Well, we had more meetings with our newfound friends, Amos, Richardson, Scott, Chipman and those fellows who stuck with us to this day, some of them now gone. And, in spite of Mr. Rockefeller's advice, we again convinced these folks that this thing needed a lot of money. What could we do without it?

So, one of them proposed, "Well, why don't we form a foundation, something like the Rockefeller Foundation?"

I said, "I hope it will be like that with respect to money."

And then one of them got a free lawyer from a firm who was interested in the thing. And we all asked him to draw up an agreement of trust, a charter for something to be called the Alcoholic Foundation. Why we picked that one, I don't know. I don't know whether the Foundation was alcoholic, it was the Alcoholic Foundation, not the Alcoholics Foundation. And the lawyer was very much confused because in the meeting, which formed the Foundation, we made it very plain that we did not wish to be in the majority. We felt that there should be non-alcoholics on the board and they ought to be in a majority of one.

"Well, indeed," said the lawyer, "What is the difference between an alcoholic and a non-alcoholic?"

And one of our smart drunks said, "That's a cinch, a non-alcoholic is a guy who can drink and an alcoholic is a guy who can't drink."

"Well," said the lawyer, "how do we state that legally?"

We didn't know. So at length, we have a foundation and a board which I think then was about seven, consisting of four of these new friends, including my brother-in-law, Mr. Richardson, Chipman, Amos and some of us drunks. I think Smithy went on the board but I kind of coyly stayed off it thinking it would be more convenient later on.

So we had this wonderful new foundation. These friends, unlike Mr. Rockefeller, were sold on the idea that we needed a lot of dough, and so our salesmen around New York started to solicit some money, again, from the very rich. We had a list of them and we had credentials from friends of Mr. John D. Rockefeller. "How could you miss, I ask you, salesmen?"

The Foundation had been formed in the spring of 1938 and all summer we solicited the rich. Well, they were either in Florida or they preferred the Red Cross, or some of them thought that drunks were disgusting and we didn't get one damn cent in the whole summer of 1938, praise God! Well, meantime, we began to hold trustee meetings and they were commiseration sessions on getting no dough. What with the mortgage and with me and Smithy eating away at it, the five grand had gone up the flu, and we were all stone-broke again. Smithy couldn't get his practice back either because he was a surgeon and nobody likes to be carved up by an alcoholic surgeon - even if he was three years sober. So things were tough all around, no fooling. Well, what would we do?

One day, probably in August 1938, I produced at a Foundation meeting, a couple of chapters of a proposed book along with some recommendations of a couple of doctors down at Johns Hopkins to try to put the bite on the rich. And we still had these two book chapters kicking around. Frank Amos said, "Well now, I know the religious editor down there at Harpers, an old friend of mine, Gene Exman." He said, "Why don't you take these two book chapters, your story and the introduction to the book, down there and show them to Gene and see what he thinks about them."

So I took the chapters down. To my great surprise, Gene who was to become a great friend of ours, looked at the chapters and said, "Why Mr. Wilson, could you write a whole book like this?"

"Well," I said, "Sure, sure."

There was more talk about it. I guess he went in and showed it to Mr. Canfield, the big boss, and another meeting was had. The upshot was that Harpers intimated that they would pay me as the budding author, fifteen hundred in advance royalties, bringing enough money in to enable me to finish the book. I felt awful good about that. It made me feel like I was an author or something. I felt real good about it but after a while, not so good. Because I began to reason, and so did the other boys, if this guy Wilson eats up the fifteen hundred bucks while he's doing this book, after the book gets out, it will take a long time to catch up. And if this thing gets him publicity, what are we going to do with the inquiries? And, after all, what's a lousy 10% royalty anyway? The fifteen hundred still looked pretty big to me. Then we thought too, now here's a fine publisher like Harpers, but if this book if and when done, should prove to be the main textbook for AA, why would we want our main means of propagation in the hands of somebody else? Shouldn't we control this thing? At this point, the book project really began.

I had a guy helping me on this thing who had red hair and ten times my energy and he was some promoter. He said, "Bill, this is something, come on with me."

We walk into a stationery store, we buy a pad of blank stock certificates and we write across the top of them 'Works Publishing Company'- Par Value Twenty-five Dollars. So we take the pad of these stock certificates, (of course we didn't bother to incorporate it, that didn't happen for several more years) we took this pad of stock certificates to the first AA meeting where you shouldn't mix money with spirituality. We said to the drunks "Look, this thing is gonna be a cinch. Parker will take a third of this thing for services rendered. I, the author will take a third for services rendered, and you can have a third of these stock certificates par 25 if you'll just start paying up on your stock. If you only want one share, it's only five dollars a month, 5 months, see?"

And the drunks all gave us this stony look that said, "What the hell? You mean to say you're only asking us to buy stock in a book that you ain't written yet?"

"Why sure," we said. "If Harpers will put money in this thing why shouldn't you? Harpers said it's gonna be a good book."

But the drunks still gave us this stony stare. We had to think up some more arguments.

"We've been looking at pricing costs of the books, boys. We get a book here, ya know, 400 or 450 pages, it ought to sell for about $3.50."

Now back in those days we found on inquiry from the printers that that $3.50 book could be printed for 35 cents making a 1,000% profit. Of course, we didn't mention the other expenses, just the printing costs. "So boys, just think on it, when these books move out by the carload we will be printing them for 35 cents and we'll be selling them direct mail for $3.50. How can you lose?"

The drunks still gave us this stony stare. No salt. Well, we figured we had to have a better argument than that. Harpers said it was a good book, you can print them for 35 cents and sell them for $3.50, but how are we going to convince the drunks that we could move carload lots of them? Millions of dollars.

So we get the idea we'll go up to the Reader's Digest, and we got an appointment with Mr. Kenneth Paine, the managing editor there. Gee, I never forget the day we got off the train up at Pleasantville and were ushered into his office. We excitedly told him the story of this wonderful budding society. We dwelled upon the friendship of Mr. Rockefeller and Harry Emerson Fosdick. You know we were traveling in good company with Paine. The society, by the way, was about to publish a textbook, then in the process of being written and we were wondering, Mr. Paine, if this wouldn't be a matter of tremendous interest to the Reader's Digest? Having in mind of course that the Reader's Digest has a circulation of 12 million readers and if we could only get a free ad of this coming book in the Digest we really would move something, ya see?

"Well," Mr. Paine said, "this sounds extremely interesting, I like this idea, why I think it'll be an absolutely ideal piece for the Digest. How soon do you think this new book will be out Mr. Wilson?"

I said, "We've got a couple of chapters written, ahem, if we can get right at it, Mr. Paine, uh, you know, uh, probably uh, this being October, we ought to get this thing out by April or next May. Why?"

Mr. Paine said, "I'm sure the Digest would like a thing like this. Mr. Wilson, I'll take it up with the editorial board, and when the time is right and you get already to shoot, come up and we'll put a special feature writer on this thing and we'll tell all about your society."

And then my promoter friend said, "But Mr. Paine, will you mention the new book in the piece?"

"Yes," said Mr. Paine, "we will mention the book."

Well, that was all we needed, we went back to the drunks and said, "now look, boys, there are positively millions in this - how can you miss? Harpers says it's going to be a good book. We buy them for 35 cents from the printer, we sell them for $3.50 and the Reader's Digest is going to give us a free ad in its piece and boys, those books will move out by the carload. How can you miss? And after all, we only need four or five thousand bucks."

So we began to sell the shares of Works Publishing, not yet incorporated, par value $25 and at $5 per month to the poor people. Some people bought as few as one and one guy bought ten shares. We sold a few shares to non-alcoholics and my promoter friend who was to get one-third interest was a very important man in this transaction because he went out and kept collecting the money from the drunks so that little Ruthie Hock and I could keep working on the book and Lois could have some groceries (even though she was still working in that department store).

So, the preparation started and some more chapters were done and we went to AA meetings in New York with these chapters in the rough. It wasn't like chicken-in-the-rough; the boys didn't eat those chapters up at all. I suddenly discovered that I was in this terrific whirlpool of arguments. I was just the umpire - I finally had to stipulate. "Well boys, over here you got the Holy Rollers who say we need all the good old-fashioned stuff in the book, and over here you tell me we've got to have a psychological book, and that never cured anybody, and they didn't do very much with us in the missions, so I guess you will have to leave me just to be the umpire. I'll scribble out some roughs here and show them to you and let's get the comments in."

So we fought, bled and died our way through one chapter after another. We sent them out to Akron and they were peddled around and there were terrific hassles about what should go in this book and what should not. Meanwhile, we set drunks up to write their stories or we had newspaper people to write the stories for them to go in the back of the book. We had an idea that we'd have a text and all and then we'd have stories all about the drunks who were staying sober.

Then came that night when we were up around Chapter 5. As you know I'd gone on about myself, which was natural after all. And then the little introductory chapter and we dealt with the agnostic and we described alcoholism, but, boy, we finally got to the point where we really had to say what the book was all about and how this deal works. As I told you this was a six-step program then.

On this particular evening, I was lying in bed on Clinton Street wondering what the deuce this next chapter would be about. The idea came to me: Well, we need a definite statement of concrete principles that these drunks can't wiggle out of. Can't be any wiggling out of this deal at all. And this six-step program had two big gaps in-between they'll wiggle out of. Moreover if this book goes out to distant readers, they have to have, got to have an absolutely explicit program by which to go.

This was while I was thinking these thoughts, while my imaginary ulcer was paining me and while I was mad as hell at these drunks because the money was coming in too slow. Some had the stock and weren't paying up. A couple of guys came in and they gave me a big argument and we yelled and shouted and I finally went down and laid on the bed with my ulcer and I said, "Poor me."

There was a pad of paper by the bed and I reached for that and said, "You've got to break this program up into small pieces so they can't wiggle out. So I started writing, trying to bust it up into little pieces. And when I got the pieces set down on that piece of yellow paper, I put numbers on them and was rather agreeably surprised when it came out to twelve. I said, "That's a good significant figure in Christianity and mystic lore." Then I noticed that instead of leaving the God idea to the last, I'd got it up front but I didn't pay much attention to that, it looked pretty good.

Well, the next meeting comes along; I'd gone on beyond the steps trying to amplify them in the rest of that chapter to the meeting and boy, pandemonium broke loose.

"What do you mean by changing the program, what about this, what about that, this thing is overloaded with God. We don't like this, you've got these guys on their knees - stand them up! A lot of these drunks are scared to death of being Godly, let's take God out of it entirely."

Such were the arguments that we had. Out of that terrific hassle came the Twelve Steps. That argument caused the introduction of the phrase that has been a lifesaver to thousands; it was certainly none of my doing. I was on the pious side then, you see, still suffering from this big hot flash of mine. The idea of "God as you understand Him" came out of that perfectly ferocious argument and we put that in.

Well, little by little things ground on, little by little the drunks put in money and we kept an office open in Newark, which was the office of a defunct business where I tried to establish my friend. The money ran low at times and Ruthie Hock worked for no pay. We gave her plenty of stock in the Works Publishing of course. All you had to do is tear it off the pad, par 25 have a week's salary, dear. So, we got around to about January 1939. Somebody said, "Hadn't we better test this thing out; hadn't we better make a pre-publication copy, a Multilith or mimeographed copy of this text and a few of the personal stories that had come in - try it out on the preacher, on the doctor, the Catholic Committee on Publications, psychiatrists, policemen, fishwives, housewives, drunks, everybody. Just to see if we've got anything that goes against the grain anyplace and also to find out if we can't get some better ideas here?"

So at considerable expense, we got this pre-publication copy made; we peddled it around and comments came back, some of them very helpful. It went, among other places, to the Catholic Committee on Publications in New York and at that time we had only one Catholic member to take it there and he had just gotten out of the asylum and hadn't had anything to do with preparing the book.

The book passed inspection and the stories came in. Somehow we got them edited; somehow we got the galleys together. We got up to the printing time. Meanwhile, the drunks had been kind of slow on those subscription payments and a little further on I was able to go up to Charlie Towns where old Doc Silkworth held forth. Charlie believed in us so we put the slug on to Charlie for 2,500 bucks. Charlie didn't want any stocks; he wanted a promissory note on the book not yet written.

So, we got the $2,500 from Charlie routed around through the Alcoholic Foundation so that it could be tax exempt. Also, we had blown $6,000 in these nine months in supporting the three of us in an office and the till was getting low. We still had to get this book printed. So, we go up to Cornwall Press, which is the largest printer in the world, where we'd made previous inquiries and we asked about printing and they said they'd be glad to do it and how many books would we like? We said that was hard to estimate. Of course our membership is very small at the present time and we wouldn't sell many to the membership but after all, the Reader's Digest is going to print a plug about it to its two million readers. This book should go out in carloads when it's printed.

The printer was none other than dear old Mr. Blackwell, one of our Christian friends and Mr. Blackwell said, "How much of a down payment are you going to make? How many books would you like printed?"

"Well," we said, "we'll be conservative, let's print 5,000 just to start with."

Mr. Blackwell asked us what we were going to use for money. We said that we wouldn't need much; just a few hundred dollars on account would be all right. I told you; after all, we're traveling in very good company, friends of Mr. Rockefeller and all that.

So, Blackwell started printing the 5,000 books; the plates were made and the galleys were read. Gee, all of a sudden we thought of the Reader's Digest, so we go up to there, walk in on Mr. Kenneth Paine and say, "We're all ready to shoot."

And Mr. Paine replies "Shoot what - Oh yes, I remember you two, Mr. Marcus and Mr. Wilson. You gentlemen were here last fall. I told you the Reader's Digest would be interested in this new work and in your book. Well, right after you were here, I consulted our editorial board and to my great surprise they didn't like the idea at all and I forgot to tell you!"

Oh boy, we had the drunks with 5,000 bucks in it, Charlie Towns hooked for 2,500 bucks and $2,500 on the cuff with the printer. There was $500 left in the bank, what in the deuce would we do?

Morgan Ryan, the good-looking Irishman who had taken the book over to the Catholic Committee on Publication, had been in an earlier time a good ad man. He said that he knew Gabriel Heatter. "Gabriel is putting on these three minute heart to heart programs on the radio. I'll get an interview with him and maybe he'll interview me on the radio about all this," said Ryan.

So, our spirits rose once again. Then all of a sudden we had a big chill, suppose this Irishman got drunk before Heatter interviewed him? So, we went to see Heatter and lo and behold, Heatter said he would interview him and then we got still more scared. So, we rented a room in the downtown Athletic Club and we put Ryan in there with a day and night guard for ten days.

Meanwhile, our spirits rose again. We could see those books just going out in carloads. Then my promoter friend said, "Look, there should be a follow-up on a big thing like this here interview. It'll be heard all over the country... national network. I think folks that are the market for this book are the doctors, the physicians. I suggest that we pitch the last $500 that we have in the treasury on a postal card shower, which will go to every physician east of the Rocky Mountains. On this postal card we'll say "Hear all about Alcoholics Anonymous on Gabriel Heatter's Program - spend $3.50 for the book Alcoholics Anonymous, sure-cure for alcoholism." So, we spent the last $500 on the postal card shower and mailed them out.

They managed to keep Ryan sober although he since hasn't made it. All the drunks had their ears glued to the radio. The group market in Alcoholics Anonymous was already saturated because you see, we had 49 stockholders and they'd all gotten a book free, then we had 28 guys with stories and they all got a free book. So we had run out of the AA books. But we could see the book moving out in carloads to these doctors and their patients. Sure enough, Ryan is interviewed. Heatter pulled out the old tremolo stop and we could see the book orders coming back in carloads.

Well, we just couldn't wait to go down to old Post Office Box 658, Church Street Annex, the address printed in the back of the old books. We hung at it for about three days and then my friends Hank and Ruthie Hock and I went over and we looked in Box 658. It wasn't a locked box; you just looked through the glass. We could see that there were a few of these postal cards. I had a terrible sinking sensation. But my friend the promoter said "Bill, they can't put all those cards in the box, they've got bags full of it out there." We go to the clerk and he brings out 12 lousy postal cards, 10 of them were completely illegible, written by doctors, druggists, and monkeys? We had exactly two orders for the book Alcoholics Anonymous and we were absolutely and utterly stone-broke.

The Sheriff then moved in on the office, poor Mr. Blackwell wondered what to do for money and felt like taking the book over at that very opportune moment, the house which Lois and I lived in was foreclosed and we and our furniture were set out on the street. Such was the state of the book Alcoholics Anonymous and the state of grace the Wilson's were in in the summer of 1939. Moreover, a great cry went up from the drunks, "What about our $4,500?" Even Charlie (Towns) who was pretty well off was a little uneasy about the note for $2,500. What would we do? What could we do? We put our goods in storage on the cuff; we couldn't even pay the drayman. An AA lent us his summer camp, another AA lent us his car, and the folks around New York began to pass the hat for groceries for the Wilson's and supplied us with $50 per month. So, we had a lot of discontented stockholders, $50 bucks a month, a summer camp and an automobile with which to revive the failing fortunes of the book Alcoholics Anonymous.

We began to shop around from one magazine to another asking if they would give us some publicity, nobody bit and it looked like the whole dump was going to be foreclosed; book, office, Wilson's, everything. One of the boys in New York happened to be a little bit prosperous at the time and he had a fashionable clothing business on Fifth Avenue, which we learned was mostly on mortgage, having drunk nearly all of it up. His name was Bert Taylor.

I went up to Bert one day and I said "Bert, there is a promise of an article in Liberty Magazine, I just got it today but it won't come out until next September. It's going to be called 'Alcoholics and God' and will be printed by Fulton Oursler the editor of Liberty Magazine. Bert, when that piece is printed, these books will go out in carload lots. We need 1,000 bucks to get us through the summer."

Bert asked, "Well, are you sure that the article is going to be printed?"

"Oh yes," I said, "that's final."

He said, "O.K., I haven't got the dough but there's this man down in Baltimore, Mr. Cochran, he's a customer of mine, he buys his pants in here. Let me call him up."

Bert gets on long-distance with Mr. Cochran in Baltimore, a very wealthy man, and says to him "Mr. Cochran, from time to time I mentioned this alcoholic fellowship to which I belong. Our fellowship has just come out with a magnificent new textbook, a sure cure for alcoholism. Mr. Cochran, this is something we think every public library in America should have, and Mr. Cochran, the retail price of the book is $3.50. Mr. Cochran, if you'll just buy a couple of thousand of those books and put them in the large libraries, of course we would sell them for that purpose at a considerable discount.

"Mr. Cochran, some publicity will come out next fall about this new book Alcoholics Anonymous, but in the meantime, these books are moving slowly and we need, say, $1,000 to tide us over. Would you loan the Works Publishing Company this?"

Mr. Cochran asked what the balance sheet of the Works Publishing Company looked like and after he learned what it looked like he said, "No thanks."

So Bert then said, "Now Mr. Cochran, you know me. Would you loan the money to me on the credit of my business?"

"Why certainly," Mr. Cochran said, "send me down your note."

So Bert hocked the business that a year or two later was to go broke anyway and saved the book Alcoholics Anonymous. The $1,000 lasted until the Liberty article came out. Eight hundred inquiries came in as a result of that, we moved a few books and we barely squeaked through the year 1939. In all this period we heard nothing from John D. Rockefeller when all of a sudden, in about February 1940, Mr. Richardson came to a trustees meeting of the Foundation and announced that he had great news. We were told that Mr. Rockefeller, whom we had not heard from since 1937, had been watching us all this time with immense interest. Moreover, Mr. Rockefeller wanted to give this fellowship a dinner to which he would invite his friends to see the beginnings of this new and promising start.

Mr. Richardson produced the invitation list. Listed were the President of Chase Bank, Wendell Wilkie, and all kinds of very prominent people, many of them extremely rich. I mean, after a quick look at the list I figured it would add up to a couple of billion dollars. So, we felt maybe at least, you know, there would be some money in sight.

So, the dinner came, and we got Harry Emerson Fosdick who had reviewed the AA book and he gave us a wonderful plug. Dr. Kennedy came and spoke on the medical attitudes. He'd seen a patient of his, a very hopeless gal (Marty Mann) recover. I got up, talked about life among the "anonymie," and the bankers assembled 75 strong and in great wealth, sat at the tables with the alcoholics. The bankers had come probably for some sort of command performance and they were a little suspicious that perhaps this was another prohibition deal, but they warmed up under the influence of the alcoholics.

Mr. Ryan, the hero of the Heatter episode and still sober, was asked at his table by a distinguished banker, "Why, Mr. Ryan, we presumed you were in the banking business."

Ryan says, "Not at all sir, I just got out of Great Stone Asylum."

Well, that intrigued the bankers and they were all warming up. Unfortunately, Mr. Rockefeller couldn't get to the dinner. He was quite sick that night so he sent his son, a wonderful gent, Nelson Rockefeller, in his place instead. After the show was over and everyone was in fine form, we were all ready again for the big touch. Nelson Rockefeller got up and speaking for his father said, "My father sends word that he is so sorry that he cannot be here tonight, but is so glad that so many of his friends can see the beginnings of this great and wonderful thing. Something that affected his life more than almost anything that had crossed his path."

A stupendous plug that was! Then Nelson said, "Gentlemen, this is a work that proceeds on good will. It requires no money."

Whereupon, the two billion dollars got up and walked out. That was a terrific letdown, but we weren't let down for too long.

Again, the hand of Providence had intervened. Right after dinner, Mr. Rockefeller asked that the talks and pamphlets be published. He approached the rather defunct Works Publishing Company and said he would like to buy 400 books to send to all of the bankers who had come to the dinner and to those who had not. Seeing that this was for a good purpose, we let him have the books cheap. He bought them cheaper than anybody has since. We sold 400 books to John D. Rockefeller Jr. for one buck apiece to send to his banker friends. He sent out the books and pamphlets and with it, he wrote a personal letter and signed every doggone one of them. In this letter he stated how glad he was that his friends had been able to see the great beginning of what he thought would be a wonderful thing, how deeply it had affected him and then he added (unfortunately) "Gentlemen, this is a work of goodwill. It needs little, if any, money. I am giving these good people $1,000."

So, the bankers all received Mr. Rockefeller's letter and counted it up on the cuff. Well, if John D. is giving $1,000, me with only a few million should send these boys about $10! One who had an alcoholic relative in tow sent us $300. So, with Mr. Rockefeller's $1,000 plus the solicitation of all the rest of these bankers, we got together the princely sum of $3,000 which was the first outside contribution of the Alcoholic Foundation.

The $3,000 was divided equally between Smithy and me so that we could keep going somehow. We solicited that dinner list for five years and got about $3,000 a year for five years. At the end of that time, we were able to say to Mr. Rockefeller, "We don't need any more money. The book income is helping to support our office, the groups are contributing to fill in and the royalties are taking care of Dr. Bob and Bill Wilson."

Now you see Mr. Rockefeller's decision not to give us money was a blessing. He gave of himself. He gave of himself when he was under public ridicule for his views about alcohol. He said to the whole world "this is good." The story went out on the wires all over the world. People ran into the bookstores to get the new book and boy, we really began to get some book orders. An awful lot of inquiries came into the little office at Vessy Street. The book money began to pay Ruth. We hired one more to help. There was Ruthie, another gal and I. And then came Jack Alexander with his terrific article in the Saturday Evening Post. Then an immense lot of inquiries… 6,000 or 7,000 of them. Alcoholics Anonymous had become a national institution.

Such is the story of the preparation of the book "Alcoholics Anonymous" and of its subsequent effect you all have some notion. The proceeds of that book have repeatedly saved the office in New York. But, it isn't the money that has come out of it that matters; it is the message that it carried. That transcended the mountains and the sea and is even at this moment, lighting candles in dark caverns and on distant beaches.

This article is a transcript of the talk given by Bill Wilson in Dallas, TX. The actual recording is available at http://sponsormagazine.info/reader.html.

Early Recovery Rates

In great angst and superiority, old timers complain that we are doing things wrong - that in the beginning, AA had a 75% success rate. Today various current Recovery rates run between 5% and 35% (depending on the source or the viewpoint of the speaker).

The first question that is raised in this argument is how the statistics on an anonymous Recovery group were collected. Various numbers and percentages are thrown about regarding the number represented by this growth. But how do we draw numbers from simple requests from the New York office.

We have to assume:

That the voluntary responses were accurate (would anyone in Recovery fudge numbers, make their numbers larger to show how well they were doing, or report low end so as not to appear prideful?);

That all of the groups responded;

That the changing population within the group would relfect accurate numbers, likely to change within days of mailing a response to New York;

That existing groups would remain in existence (and if a group died, did they report that as well?);

That all new groups were reporting;

It must also be remembered that early AA was not like the current fellowship.

Members could only be admitted to the fellowship after a medical detox. The first time someone wanted to join who had not gone through the medical detox was a source of great conflict.

Early members were almost exclusively older, white, professional males. These were the "upper crust" of society the Oxford Group attracted. When the first women came to get sober, it was controversial. The first African-American was a transvestite drug addict who wanted to get sober and single-handedly kicked down the door so that many minorities were able to join the fellowship, although he himself did not stay sober.

Before going to the first meeting, you had to have a Sponsor and have done the work of what we would now call the first six steps.

So the early success rate is counting only people who;

Were male (later joined by a few women);

Were white;

Were from the upper classes;

Had gone through a medical detox;

Who knew "someone who knew someone" to locate and get into a meeting (and there were only two meetings anywhere at the time - Akron and New York);

Were Protestant Christian, or willing to become one (most early Oxford Group members were Episcopal, Lutheran, or Methodist);

Had already admitted their alcoholism;

Had found their personal Higher Power or concept of God;

Had already turned their life over to the care of that concept of God;

Had detailed their previous misdeeds and actions in an Inventory;

Had shared that Inventory with their Sponsor;

Had come to see their own defects in what had gone wrong in their life.

At that point, they were admitted to their first meeting, on their knees in Prayer to have their defects removed, and subject to the approval of the existing members of the group.

Of the people who had jumped through all these hoops, they then say 75% stayed sober or showed significant improvement from their first meeting. The real number of people who failed to reach the point of getting to a group may never be known.

Bill Wilson wrote with some concern how fear of losing what they found had prevented them from the kind of outreach AA now takes for granted. Today, meetings are available to anyone who looks, or has someone who cares enough to provide them with a meeting time and location. New people can find AA in the phone book; they can be directed to a meeting by a doctor, a judge, or a clergyman; or they may simply find AA through friends or family members who are already sober.

Bill kept track of the people whose stories appear in the First Edition of the book Alcoholics Anonymous, and noted the fate of those whose stories had appeared in the first edition of the Big Book.

In addition to Dr. Bob's story, thirty-two additional personal accounts of Recovery were published. Of these, twenty-one members went back out. Seven died drunk, but the others made it back for a second chance at Recovery.

Hank Parkhurst, the man who made it possible for the book to appear, was one of those who died drunk.

The lesson of the book has been that anyone, anywhere, who is willing to follow the directions, can find and keep sobriety.

When time came for a Second Edition, the stories in the back were changed partially to eliminate the stories of those who relapsed - they could not know what part of their story had opened the door to those relapses and didn't want to condemn others to the same path. The second edition also became open to more stories from women and minorities.

"Following the directions" is more than just a pass through the Twelve Steps, but it incorporates into our daily life the lessons and principles found in the Steps. We achieve that by repetition and constantly looking at how the tools we have been given can be used over and over again.

Bill and Bob reviewed the progress of their groups and reviewed their success rate. Different sources gave results from 5% to 35% actually remaining sober. Current medical tracking indicates from 31% to 37% of AAs attending maintain long-term sobriety, and the survey figures from AA's World Service give similar results.

But even those numbers defy the terminal nature of alcoholism over the previous history of mankind. The Twelve Step system, if followed, proved to provide the first substantial success for any system of finding and maintaining long-term sobriety.

And, again, how are those number generated? When you go to an AA meeting, do you check in with anyone or report to the New York office to inform them that you are attending?

It should also be remembered that with the exception of those few with significant religious or spiritual experiences, as indicated by Dr. Jung, there had been no system of getting anyone sober, and alcoholics had been doomed to a prolonged, agonizing death by the dissipation of the body and spirit alcoholism created, or the violent death alcoholics can bring upon themselves through their actions during drinking episodes.

It keeps us aware that anyone getting, and remaining sober, is a miracle by all spiritual and religious standards, and a "deviation" from previous expectations by scientific standards.

It should always keep us grateful.

Stories in Different Editions

There have been various stories about why different stories are included in the back of the Big Book.

In the frist edition there were thirty-two stories, in addition to The Doctor's Nightmare (Dr. Bob's story). Of these stories, twenty-one relapsed. Seven of them died drunk. The rest made it back and found sobriety that carried them through the rest of their lives.

When the time came for a Second Edtion, the decision was made to not re-share the stories of people who had relapsed. There was a fear that something in their story made their relapse possible.

So new stories were chosen and in those stories the examples of a wider spectrum of people in Recovery became possible.

When time came for a Third Edition, the diversity of stories was increased.

And the Fourth Edition, the current edition at this writing, it was in a different world. In addtion to Alcoholics Anonymous there were over sixty other programs using the 12-Step system for Recovery from various substances and behaviors. Citing the 'singleness of purpose' references to drugs and problems other than alcoholism were either deleted or revised.

For example, "Doctor, Addict, Alcoholic" became "Physician Heal Thyself." The author's reference to his problem with drugs, in addition to alcohol, was not deleted but the title eliminated the reference to the non-alcohol specific nature of his story.

References to 'sedatives' or 'pep pills' were not eliminated from Bill or Dr. Bob's personal stories.

Why some members of the fellowship may object to this seeming restriction of the definition, was best explained by one speaker. She said:

"I have problems other than alcohol, but when I am speaking an at AA meeting, I restrict my references to alcohol. That does not mean I deny the wider scope of what is necessary for my Recovery, but it means I will never be responsible for an alcoholic leaving his or her first meeting saying to themself 'I don't belong in AA - I never smoked crack.'

"Singleness of purpose keeps our story focused, but one to one we must be honest with all of what our needs for Recovery include. That is why we talk with our Sponsor and our companions on the road of happy destiny."

The First 25 AA Groups

1. *Ohio: Akron (June/July 1935)*

2. *New York City (Fall of 1935)*

3. *Ohio: Cleveland - Abby G. Group (May 11, 1939)*

4. *New Jersey: The New Jersey Group (May 14, 1939)*

5. *Connecticut: Greenwich Blythewood Sanitarium (June 1939)*

6. *Illinois: Chicago (September 13, 1939)*

7. *Ohio: Cleveland – Borton Group (November 16, 1939)*

8. *Ohio: Cleveland – Orchard Grove (November 20, 1939)*

9. *Washington, D.C. (December 1939)*

10. *California: San Francisco (December 1939)*

11. *California: Los Angeles (December 19, 1939)*

12. *New York: Orangeburg - Rockland State Hospital (December 1939)*

13. *Michigan: Detroit (December 1939)*

14. *Pennsylvania: Philadelphia (February 13, 1940)*

15. *Texas: Houston (March 15, 1940)*

16. *Arkansas: Little Rock (April 19, 1940)*

17. *Indiana: Evansville (April 23, 1940)*

18. *Ohio: Cleveland – West 50th Street Group (May 8, 1940)*

19. *Virginia: Richmond (June 6, 1940)*

20. *Maryland: Baltimore (June 16, 1940)*

21. *Ohio: Dayton (July 8, 1940)*

22. *Ohio: Cleveland – Berea (August 27, 1940)*

23. *Ohio: Cleveland – Westlake (September 20, 1940)*

24. *Ohio: Toledo (September 1940)*

25. *Ohio: Youngstown (September 1940)*

Before AA

The Washingtonians

During the early 19th Century, six drunks from a bar in Baltimore, MD decided they would go to a local Temperance lecture and heckle the speaker from the audience. After the lecture, they returned to the bar and discovered that they could stop their own drinking if they talked with each other about the reasons they felt they drank.

People moved away and started new groups in other cities. Visitors became impressed with the success of the new non-drinkers and carried the idea to still more groups that were started. By 1842, a large network of these meetings existed across the US and they decided to have a day of celebration. Letters went out declaring:

a) The groups would be known as the Washingtonians (named for Martha Washington, known for her temperance leanings) and

b) on George Washington's birthday (February 22, 1842) they would hold a national day of celebration. Groups were encouraged to host a picnic with speakers and general fellowship.

The speaker at the Springfield, IL meeting was a young Abraham Lincoln, who is recorded as saying:

"If we take habitual drunkards as a class, their heads and their hearts will bear an advantageous comparison with those of any other class. There seems ever to have been a proneness in the brilliant and warm-blooded to fall in to this vice. The demon of intemperance ever seems to have delighted in sucking the blood of genius and generosity."   *Abraham Lincoln,*
to the Washington Temperance Society,
Springfield, Illinois, 22 February 1842

But the rising popularity of the Washingtonians attracted the wider Temperance movement and they stopped being a society of drunks helping other drunks stay sober, and became a society lecturing on the evils of alcohol and later, other evils.

Founded on the success of the original Washingtonian group, the new Washingtonians crusaded in the war of Temperance on King Alcohol. Their popularity grew until, in 1852, they claimed to have five million people to have signed the Pledge, but you did not have to be an alcoholic to sign the Pledge. A Pledge was simply a paper that said you did not support the manufacture, sale, distribution, or use of alcohol. School children and others signed, but a block of five million could have a great deal of political importance.

The Washingtonians expanded beyond alcohol, to spread themselves to the issues of slavery, pro and con; the gold standard, pro and con; and the admission of Texas to the Union, pro and con.

They argued in their meetings, their public lectures flourished, then declined when the public tired of the public arguments. All of the good that could have been done was destroyed by their lack of unity. By 1861, at the start of the Civil War, they were gone. You could not find a Washingtonian group. They had died away.

We will never know how many alcoholics were lost because we do not know how many of the five million were actually alcoholics, but all the good they had done was swept away with the failure of that early fellowship.

Bill Wilson did not know about the Washingtonians when AA was first forming. He came to the conclusion the Washingtonians failed because of their lack of unity and lack of focus. The groups competed with each other for members. They debated issues in public, and divided along the pros and cons of those issues.

The Emmanuel Movement

In 1906, the Emmanuel Episcopal Church, under the direction of Dr. Elwood Worcester and Dr. Samuel McComb, began a new ministry to combine psychiatry and spirituality in the treatment of a dreaded disease of the time – tuberculosis. Tuberculosis (or TB) was rampant and had the same emotional impact on families and neighbors as AIDS had in the late 20th Century. This group was dubbed The Emmanuel Movement

Victims of the disease were shunned, isolated, and abandoned. Fear of contracting the disease dictated public policy and private conduct. The victims were generally left to die on their own.

But the Emmanuel movement taught that with a combination of psychiatry and their focus on faith, it was possible to live a life and be restored to the maximum productivity possible, even with the disease.

When they met with success with their "class" for victims of TB, they opened their class to "emotional problems" and a significant portion of the people who attended (some estimates say 80%) were alcoholic. The combination of spirituality and psychiatry proved to be effective in getting these newcomers sober and help them remain sober using the movements method.

The Jacoby Club

To their credit, and unlike the failed Washingtonian movement of the mid-19th Century, the Emmanuel movement did not try to put all its eggs in one basket and created a new sub-group specifically for alcoholics.

This new group was dubbed "The Jacoby Club" under the patronage of rubber merchant Ernest Jacoby, with weekly "Men Meeting Men" group sessions for alcoholics in the church basement.

It was members of the Jacoby Club who told the businessman mentioned in the Big Book (Rowland Hazard) that there was nothing they had to offer that would help him. It was their suggestion that Rowland enter real psychiatric therapy with a real therapist if he hoped to ever find and maintain sobriety.

The Jacoby Club continued until 1989, but the availability of Alcoholics Anonymous, made its weekly sessions unnecessary.

The Oxford Group

Frank Buchman, an Episcopal minister from the United States and serving at a boy's school in Keswick England, had a conversion experience and began a group he dubbed "A Century Christian Fellowship." Under his leadership, the group took teams of like-minded believers to China, Africa, India, and the United States. The group functioned as they imagined believers lived in the 1st Century. They received no salaries, held no positions, and were dependent on their fellowship for food, shelter, and transportation. Fortunately, Oxford Group members were very well situated and were seldom lacking for accommodations.

While a group of the First Century Christian Fellowship travelled in South Africa, a reporter asked a train porter how to find them. The man responded, "Oh, you mean the Oxford Group," indicating the luggage which had Oxford stenciled on all the bags. The reporter used that name to refer to the group and it stuck.

The group was unlike other forms of evangelism in that it targeted and directed its efforts to the "up and outers," the elites and wealthy of society. It made use of publicity regarding its prominent converts, and was caricatured as a "Salvation Army for snobs." Buchman's message did not challenge the status quo and thus aided the Group's popularity among the well-to-do. Buchman made the cover of Time Magazine as "Cultist Frank Buchman: God is a Millionaire" in 1936. For a U.S. headquarters, he built a multimillion-dollar establishment on Michigan's Macinac Island, with room for 1,000 visitors. From Caux to London's Berkeley Square to New York's Westchester County layouts, Buchman and his followers had the best. In response to criticism, Buchman had an answer, "Isn't God a millionaire?"

Buchman became a favorite of highly-placed men and women and frequently held audiences with presidents, kings, and world leaders. After meeting with Buchman, Mahatma Gandhi told reporters "people need to listen to this man. He has the first great idea to come out of the West."

After a meeting with Adolph Hitler, who Buchman had hoped to convert, the Oxford Group received negative publicity as Nazi sympathizers. The Oxford University demanded they stop calling themselves "the Oxford Group" and the name was changed to "Moral Re-Armament," the MRA.

With the death of Frank Buchman in 1961, the group lost much of its reputation on the world stage, although it still exists under the name Initiatives of Change (www.us.iofc.org/).

Members of what would become AA were members of the Oxford Group and we owe much of our structure and methods to that earlier group.

Members of the Oxford Group were given several sets of guidelines to be used in their personal spirituality.

The Four Absolutes

The Oxford Group taught a focus on a personal relationship to God through an effort to achieve Four Absolutes.

Absolute Purity

Absolute Honesty

Absolute Unselfishness

Absolute Love

While perfection was not likely, the need to struggle in that direction was still necessary.

The Five Cs

The Oxford Group also taught "Five Cs" to illustrate their program of spiritual growth.

> *Confidence*
>
> *Confession*
>
> *Conviction*
>
> *Conversion*
>
> *Continuance*

The Practices

Members of the Oxford Group had several daily practices that they used to maintain their focus and their growth.

> *Quiet Time – a period of quiet meditation, reflection, and prayer, usually every morning.*
>
> *Guidance – the process of praying, meditating, and when you felt your prayer had been answered with "Guidance" or direction for your actions, you checked your Guidance with other people, lest your Ego deceive you into inappropriate action.*

AA has continued stressing the practices of daily quiet time for prayer and meditation, but successful members also report some sort of 'checking' also be used, either through meetings or one-on-one discussions with a Sponsor or other members.

A Short History of the Oxford Group

The original name of the group was "The First Century Christianity Association." It was founded in 1927 by Frank Buchman, a American Lutheran minister at Oxford University in England.

The structure of the organization was completely voluntary. They did not have paid positions for speakers, preachers, or staff, but were dependent on the generosity of members and friends to provide for costs of organization, transportation, food, lodging and facilities for public events. This principle of avoiding paid positions served the group well and allowed missions to visit nations around the world.

Membership was composed of mostly upper class people. While most missionary movements are aimed at the "Down and Out", the focus of this organization was for the "Up and Out".

Local groups affiliated with the "OG" would host 'house parties' in the homes of individual members. They did occasionally rent public venues for larger events.

The group was dubbed The Oxford Group by a South African reporter. When he went to a train station to interview members of the First Century Christianity Association, the porter handling the group's luggage said, "You mean the Oxford group". He was referring to the group's luggage, all clearly marked with "Oxford Group" stencil on each case. The reporter used the name and it became the popular way of identifying the new fellowship.

Changes in the Oxford Group Name

"People need to listen to this man (Buchanan). He has the first great idea to come out of the West."

- Mohandas Gandhi

Frank Buchman met with the highest levels of governments and members of the 'upper classes'. Presidents, Prime Ministers, Kings and wealthy families attended his public talks. Buchman was followed by the press reporting on his public and private meetings with world leaders.

After an attempt by Buchman to convert Adolph Hitler resulted in bad publicity. Oxford University objected to the implied association between the university and Buchman's Group. They demanded Buchman stop using the name "Oxford Group". The First Century Christianity Association became "Moral Re-Armament" in 1939.

Rowland Hazard, the man who had been treated by Carl Jung in Switzerland, came to join the Oxford Group for his own spiritual process. He later introduced Ebbie Thacher to the Oxford Group meetings and methods.

Ebbie then carried the group's teachings to Bill Wilson. Bill Wilson is recognized as a co-founder of Alcoholics Anonymous and began attending the Oxford Group with his wife, Lois in 1938.

Bill Wilson, after a failed business trip to Akron, Ohio, connected Dr. Robert Smith ("Dr. Bob") through fellow Oxford Group member Henrietta Seiberling on Mother's Day, 1939.

After one relapse, Dr. Bob got sober and remained sober using the Oxford Group fellowship and teachings. Both Bill and Bob continued their active participation in the Oxford Groups until the separation of Alcoholics Anonymous as an independent organization in 1939.

When the writing of the Big Book, Alcoholics Anonymous, began all members of what would become the AA fellowship were still participants of the Oxford Group meetings.

In the early twenty-first century "Moral Re-Armament" was renamed "Initiatives of Change" and can be reached today through ioc.org. It lists the creation of Alcoholics Anonymous as a major accomplishment in its history.

sponsormagazine.info

Birth of the Big Book

The only meetings were in New York (under the direction of Bill Wilson) and Akron, OH (under the tutelage of Dr. Bob Smith). Correspondence between the meetings developed three primary ideas to spread the word.

The Big Book was created by a vote of the young fellowship while it was still identified as part of the Oxford Group and after discussions with sober alcoholics in that fellowship.

In 1938, the "alcoholic squad" wanted to find a way to share their message to other alcoholics seeking sobriety. Three options were considered.

a) AA Missionaries

b) AA Facilities (hospitals, etc.)

c) AA Book.

Option a) would include paid "missionaries" to carry the word of their system of Recovery from city to city. It was voted down because the newly sober drunks had not listened to any other type of missionary effort to get them sober. It would also create a paid, "professional" class of AAs who would be perceived as setting themselves above the common drunks they were trying to help. This option was not chosen.

Option b) would include a new hospital that would offer counseling, medical detox, and financial services, taking in drunks at one end and sending recovered alcoholics out into the community with their new, spiritual foundation to repair the damage they had done to their families and communities.

But a new hospital would restrict the Recovery effort to those who could afford another hospital, and most of the drunks at the level where our founders began their recoveries were not at a point where they no longer had those resources. A hospital would also create a new danger with positions, names of letterheads, budgets, and public prestige. Option b) was not chosen.

Option c) would mean the publication of a book to outline the AA process and would include stories of the members. Option c) was chosen.

Big Book Development

Bill Wilson fancied himself a writer. When the question of a book for the young fellowship came up, he began work on his own story, which would, of course, open the book.

The first man Bill helped get sober in New York was a businessman named Hank Parkhurst. Hank was running a car polish company out of New Jersey and had, among his skills from an erratic background, the knowledge of how to "package" a book. This means to coordinate a writer, an editor, a typesetter, a printer, a bindery, and a distributor to produce a book from the beginning until it was available for people to buy at newsstands.

When Hank saw what Bill had written he sat down and wrote out an outline of what needed to be in the book and in what order. He then made his secretary at the auto polish office available to Bill to type up what Bill wrote out in longhand.

Hank then kept after Bill to complete the manuscript while encouraging many other members of the fellowship to write out their own stories (the beginning of the personal stories at the back of each edition of the book).

While the book was being written, Bill and Hank tried to drum up interest in the book with publishers. They did receive an offer from Harper & Row to publish the book, and were offered an advance against royalties of $1500.

The offer convinced Bill and Hank that there was real potential in the sale of the book. Fifteen hundred dollars was more than most working people made in a year. The two began to develop a plan to publish the book themselves to allow control over what was published and to keep all the income for themselves.

While Bill was still writing, he and Hank created Works Publishing, Inc., and sold stock in the new company.

The "stock" consisted of a pad of blank stock certificates purchased from a local stationery store and on which they wrote "Works Publishing, Inc." and valued the stock at $25 each.

Many members purchased stock by paying in installments as low as 50¢ per month.

The Multilith Big Book

When the manuscript was finished, Hank thought he had a way to make some money off the unpublished book. He had 400 copies reproduced in a cheap, water-based printing system called "Multilith." His plan was to raise cash by selling these copies of the manuscript for $3.50 each, with a promise that the buyer would get a copy of the hardcover as soon as it was published.

No one bought a single copy of the manuscript.

So, in January 1939, the decision was made to circulate these copies to the fellowship for review. Every sober member of the program, their wives (and husbands, because women were getting sober by now), and any professional willing to comment on the book, received a copy. Those professionals included doctors, ministers, business professionals, and spouses of sober members.

The 400 copies went out in January and in less than 60 days they received almost half of the copies back with suggestions for change. But many of the suggestions were the same.

It should be understood that among the fellowship in those early Oxford Group were many "traveling men." Traveling salesman was a common profession, so men who had gotten sober in New York or Akron were responding from wherever they were on the road.

Responses and edits came from beyond New York and Akron, thanks to these traveling men. Copies were returned from Boston, Chicago, Detroit, St. Louis, Baltimore, and more.

A pattern developed that surprised the authors. Although the dozens of responders were separated in time and space, their comments shared the same ideas in the same sections of the original manuscript.

The decision was made to record all these changes in one copy of the Multilith edition, and despite the lack of direct communication between the members making comment, they came to the same conclusions at the same point.

This proved to be the beginning of what was later called "group conscience," but the changes to the document were recorded in one copy, which can still be found in the AA World Service Office archives. The changes to these few sections were so intense that the typesetter was unable to read the manuscript when the time came to cast the lead type for publication.

The most significant comment appears to be from Bill's personal psychiatrist, who suggested the original finger-wagging-in-your-face tone of Bill's first draft be changed to a simpler, invitational manner.

"You" and "You must" became "we" and a description of "what we did." It was possible for the drunk seeking Recovery to go through the book without feeling attacked. They were able to choose to do what the people in the book did, or not, with knowledge of the result if they refused to do what was required.

Not one copy of the book was sold. The $3.50 cost was exorbitant. At that time, a steak breakfast was 35¢, a movie matinee was 20¢, a lunch with two hotdogs and a cup of soda was 10¢, and a week in a reputable rooming house with your own bed and breakfast and dinner for seven days was $3.50.

With the unsold copies of the manuscript sitting in the New Jersey office, the decision was made to send out copies to everyone active in the program at that time. Those trying to get sober, their wives, interested doctors, ministers, and anyone else interested was invited to review the manuscript and make comments.

Within 60 days, the comments came in and focused on the language. Bill Wilson's therapist, Dr. Harry Tiebout, made the successful argument that the tone of the volume was too threatening. The manuscript was changed from the harsh direction of "You must do this" to the invitation to try "what we have done."

The idea "if you want what we have you can do the things we have done," or "do the work and get the result" became standard in AA presentation.

Hank Parkhurst negotiated with Cornwall Printers in Cornwall, NY to typeset, print, and bind the book Alcoholics Anonymous in their "down" time, and the printer allowed Hank to pick up copies of the bound book on a cash basis. Cornwall warehoused the book and did not release anything that was not paid for before it left the shop.

Despite his importance to the early fellowship, Hank did not stay sober. He endured years of relapse and Recovery and finally died drunk.

Opening the 'God' Door

Everyone involved in the Oxford Group before the separation into Alcoholics Anonymous was a Christian. They were all white, mostly male and predominatly Episcopalian, Lutheran or Methodist. Catholics were actually barred from attending Oxford Group meetings by their own church archdioceses. Some local Bishops went so far as threatening excommunication to Catholics who participated in Oxford Group 'public confession'.

If there were any other religions involved in those early days, they kept a low profile – we have found no evidence of early non-Christian participation.

When the idea of a book was circulated, a small but vocal minority within the program wanted an inclusion for people who were not within the identified religion of the first generation of Recoverees. Some were Jews, some were Buddhist, others were Atheists. Over time even more participation would come from Muslims, Buddhists, Sikhs, 'Red Road' (followers of American native religion) and people who could not define their spiritual path at all.

Modern research has shown that the 'path' leading to the many 12-Step Programs today actually began in an 18th Century Delaware native program requiring abstinence from alcohol through a focus on spiritual principles and the continued 19th Century native prophet sobriety movements.

With the inclusion of "As We Understood Him" into the Steps, the authors of the Big Book allowed people to face their problem as alcholics first and determine their spiritual path later. In the Traditions, a decade later, it was expanded in the Third Tradition - "The only requirement for membership was the desire to stop drinking."

Today there are 12-Step Programs that require adherence to a specific religion, or a specific allegience to not being in a religion. They are not in conflict with mainstream Alcoholics Anonymous, but may misrepresent the 12-Step Recovery program as only functioning through a specific religion.

The protection in current membership and the open door policy of our Program was started with the additions to the wording of the Steps – "as we understood Him."

Separation from the Oxford Group

In 1938, Clarence Snyder, a low-bottom alcoholic from Cleveland, OH, arrived in Akron to get sober with Dr. Bob and his Oxford Group "alcoholic squad." His sister's children used Bill Wilson's brother-in-law as their pediatrician, and it was his discussion of Bill's success with his alcohol problem that encouraged Clarence's family to send him to Akron.

Clarence became sober with Dr. Bob and eventually was able to return to Akron, where another man getting sober with Dr. Bob allowed Clarence to stay in his home in Cleveland. Clarence arrived in time to receive a Multilith copy of the Big Book manuscript.

When he returned to Cleveland, he tried to organize a new group, but found that most of the alcoholics he encountered were Catholics, and the local archdiocese had declared that the Oxford Group was not appropriate for Catholics. In fact, some Catholics who attended the Oxford Group were threatened with excommunication.

When he returned to Cleveland, Clarence wanted to form a new group but found that the men he encountered who wanted to get sober were Catholic. The local Catholic archdiocese had threatened excommunication for members who attended Oxford Group meetings.

The archdiocese for Akron had not made that same determination so Clarence loaded his group of drunks into some cars and headed down to Akron each Wednesday for their Oxford Group meeting with Dr. Bob.

During this time, the friction between the Akron Oxford Group and the growing, recovering community was increasing. One man told Dr. Bob "You are glorying in your sin – my tobacco is every bit the sin your alcohol is."

Dr. Bob's response was simple; "Your tobacco will not send you to the prison, the madhouse, or the gutter."

Clarence had discussed his growing resentment at the resistance of the Oxford group's more conservative members low opinion of the alcoholics they found in their midst.

On May 10th, shortly after his talk with Dr. Bob, who was his Sponsor, the tension was very high and Clarence decided he'd had enough. He announced, "Tomorrow night, in Cleveland, we will have the first meeting not associated with the Oxford Group. It will be based on this book, Alcoholics Anonymous, and we will study what is in this book!"

In one move, Clarence established AA as a separate fellowship, and the focus on a Big Book study. The following night, Thursday, March 18, 1939, the first AA meeting was held in Cleveland.

Clarence also changed the meaning of "Sponsor" to what we use today. Originally, a "Sponsor" was the man who agreed to cosign your detox bill at St.

Thomas Hospital in Akron, who then agreed to work with you on, what we would now call, the "first Six Steps," and then took the new man to his first Oxford Group meeting.

There was no open meeting list for the Oxford Group and you had to "know someone" to get in. The Sponsor was ensuring that if you broke or stole something, he would be responsible.

Clarence changed the definition of Sponsor to mean one man (or woman, now that women were getting sober, too) with some experience in the program working with a newcomer.

This system worked to grow Cleveland meetings at a rate which surprised Bill and Bob. At the end of 1939, there was one meeting in Akron, New York City and one meeting, and Cleveland had three meetings. In the first few months of 1940, two additional meetings formed in Cleveland.

Clarence was abrasive, actively disliked the Traditions, always introduced himself with his last name, and introduced himself frequently as "the man who founded AA."

But he has been slighted in some AA hisotries. He deserves recognition for his contributions for shaping our meetings, book studies, and Sponsorship as they are now enjoyed by the world wide fellowship.

Evolution of Sponsorship

We to recognize recognize the significant guidance Clarence Snyder of Cleveland, OH, provided the model for what we now call Sponsorship.

In the Oxford Group, your Sponsor was the man who cosigned for your admission into medical detox. Drunks were notorious for not paying their bills and without a cosigner, the hospital would not admit them for alcoholism. Remember, at this time alcoholism was not a recognized disease and most admissions were for "gastric distress."

The Sponsor then worked with the new man on what we would now call the first Six Steps. According to Clarence S., their first responsibility was helping the new man find his faith as a Christian.

This means that before the new man10 went to his first meeting, he had to be in a hospital detox with a Sponsor visiting to guide him and quiet time with Prayer and Meditation had been established. He worked with a Sponsor successfully to admit his own alcoholism, turned his life and will over to his new understanding of God or a Higher Power, made Inventory of his past, shared it with his Sponsor, and became willing to have his defects removed.

You could not simply "go to a meeting." There was no meeting guide. You had to know someone who knew where a meeting was being held.. The Sponsor also took responsibility for the man he brought to the meeting. If the new man broke or stole something, it was for the Sponsor to set it right.

The new man entered his first meeting of the fellowship on his knees, praying with the group to have his defects removed. It was also common in Akron for the "old men" of the group to take the newcomer upstairs to confirm that this candidate was an actual "member" of the group.

Clarence was responsible for changing this definition of Sponsor to a much simpler "someone who is ahead of you in the program and willing to show you what they had done," which is what we think of a Sponsor to be now.

With Clarence's influence, the Cleveland Plain Dealer newspaper ran articles on Alcoholics Anonymous (written by a member of Clarence's group), the archdiocese approved the non-Oxford Group fellowship as appropriate for Catholics, and the Cleveland Fellowship grew at a rate that surprised Bill and Bob.

In 1938, there were two groups; one in Akron and one in New York. In 1939, there were five; three groups formed quickly in Cleveland without Bill or Bob to guide them. And with Clarence's push, the new form of focusing on the Steps and the use of the Big Book for new members was introduced.

By January of 1940, two more groups had formed in Cleveland and as another landmark, the Cleveland Service Committee was the first service structure designed to serve AA.

When the Saturday Evening Post article by Jack Alexander appeared in 1941, it was estimated there were 400 members in the three cities (or traveling across the country for their jobs with one of those three cities as their base) who

10 Early members of what would become AA were all men. The story and process for women was later found to be the same as for men.

could count a year of sobriety or more. Immediately after the appearance of the article, the membership jumped from 400 to over 6,000.

The new groups were founded on the Big Book for use as a group study focus and personal work on the Steps. There were so many new people that there were not enough Sponsors to serve everyone, and several of the fellowships began "Newcomer" or "Beginner" classes to introduce the new people to the tools of the program, the use of the Big Book, the Steps, and getting into the new life.

The Recovery Reader is intended to follow that trail of shared education, and study.

Explosive Growth

In 1940, a reporter for the Saturday Evening Post was assigned the story to investigate Alcoholics Anonymous. The author, Jack Alexander, was a muckraker who had just exposed the corruption in the mineworker's union and fully expected to find another major scam in progress.

He attended a few meetings and shortly became an avid supporter of AA. His article appeared in the March 17, 1941 issue of the Saturday Evening Post, one of the most popular magazines of the era.

As a result of the article, the membership of AA exploded from approximately 400 at the time the article appeared, to over 6,000 in just a few weeks.

There were so many new members; there were not enough Sponsors to work with the new members. The "Class" was developed in several different areas at about the same time. Committees formed to establish local service offices around the country, and many independent groups issued their own Recovery oriented materials, such as 24 Hours a Day, the Eye Opener, Stools and Bottles, and more than a dozen beginner class outlines.

Much of the material for this class had been taken from the 1940s writings of the Akron Group, the Cleveland Service Committee, and the beginners' classes documented in many cities.

Hundreds of new groups were founded by individual alcoholics who ordered a copy of the book Alcoholics Anonymous from the New York service office, now dubbed the WSO (World Service Office), who proceeded to get sober and seek out other alcoholics to work with.

Recovery Reader – Second Edition

Big Book Names & Dates

FROM THE FIRST 188 PAGES OF THE BIG BOOK

Preface 2nd Ed

xv – Bill Wilson & Dr. Bob during a talk between a NY stockbroker & Akron physician (they first met on 5/12/35)

xvi – Ebby Thacher alcoholic friend in contact with Oxford Group

xvi – Dr. Silkworth (named) NY specialist in alcoholism

xvi – Bill Wilson The broker

xvi – Dr. Bob the Akron physician

xvii – Bill Dotson AA#3 (sober date was 6/26/35, Bill Wilson & Dr. Bob first visited him on 6/28/35)

xvii-xviii - Dr. Harry Emerson Fosdick (named) noted clergyman

xviii – Fulton Oursler (named) editor of Liberty

xviii – John Rockefeller Jr. (named) gave dinner

xviii – Jack Alexander (named) wrote Saturday Evening Post article

xix – Traditions all Twelve Traditions mentioned

xx – Recovery rate from 1939-1955 Of alcoholics who came to AA & really tried, 50% got sober at once & remained that way; 25% sobered up after some relapses, and among the remainder, those who stayed on with AA showed improvement

Doctor's Opinion

(was page 1 in the first edition of the Big Book)

xxv-xxxii Dr. William D. Silkworth well known doctor (worked at Towns Hospital, N.Y.C.)

xxv – Bill Wilson patient he regarded as hopeless

xxvii – Nine years experience Dr. Silkworth had nine years of experience with alcoholics & drug addicts when he wrote this

xxvii – Bill Wilson one of the leading contributors of this book

xxxi – Hank Parkhurst man brought in to be treated for chronic alcoholism

xxxi – Fitz Mayo another case, had hid in a barn

Bill's Story - Bill Wilson

1 – Winchester Cathedral Bill Wilson has a spiritual experience ("Here I stood on the edge of the abyss into which thousands were falling that very day. A feeling of despair settled down on me - where was He - why did He not come - and suddenly in that moment of darkness, He was there. I felt an all-enveloping, comforting, powerful presence. Tears stood in my eyes, and as I looked about, I saw on the faces of others nearby, that they too had glimpsed the great reality.")

1 – Thomas Thetcher an old tombstone (the name of the Hampshire Grenadier)

1 – a special token Upon leaving France the men of his [Bill Wilson's] battery paid him special honor. His letter of January 3, 1919, read: "Quite a touching thing happened yesterday. The men presented Captain Sackville and me each with a watch, chain and ring. The whole battery was lined up, and I tell you it was equal to promotion and decoration by J. J. Pershing himself! Coming as it did from a clear sky, it was quite overwhelming. Wouldn't have changed insignia with a brigadier general. It means so much more than promotion. Insofar as I know, we are the only people in the regiment who have been so honored. I'm sure you will be as happy and proud as I am."

4 – Penick & Ford XYZ-32 (stock) (Penick & Ford is a corn products company, it went from 52 to 32 in 1 day)

4 – Dick Johnson friend in Montreal (worked at Greenshields & Co., a brokerage house)

4 – 1930 By the following spring

4 – Macy's wife (Lois) work in dept. store

5 – A. Wheeler & F. Winans 1932 formed group to buy bender - chance vanished

5 – written sweet promises Promise followed empty promise. On October 20, 1928, Bill wrote in the family Bible, the most sacred place he knew: 'To my beloved wife that has endured so much, let this stand as evidence of my pledge to you that I have finished with drink forever.' By Thanksgiving Day of that year he had written, 'My strength is renewed a thousandfold in my love for you,' In January 1929, he added, 'To tell you once more that I am finished with it. I love you.' None of those promises, however, carried the anguish Bill expressed in an undated letter to Lois: 'I have failed again this day. That I should continue to even try to do right in the grand manner is perhaps a great foolishness. Righteousness simply does not seem to be in me. Nobody wishes it more than I. Yet no one flouts it more often.' Again, he wrote a promise to his wife in the family Bible: 'Finally and for a lifetime, thank God for your love.' The promise was dated September 3, 1930. Like those that had preceded it, it was not kept. That was the last of the Bible promises.

6-7 – doctor came with sedative, next day drinking gin & sedative

7 – early spring 1934 I was forty pounds under weight

7 – Dr. L. Strong & Dr. Emily brother in-law (husband of sister Dorothy) & mother put him in Towns Hospital

7 – Dr. Silkworth met kind doctor explained ill, body & mind

7 – Summer, 1934 After a time I returned to the hospital

8 – 11/11/34 Armistice Day 1934

8-12 – Ebby Thacher old school friend

9 – Shep C,Rowland H,Cebra G two? (three) men appeared in court (Shep Cornell, Rowland Hazzard & Cebra Graves) August 1934

9 – chartered an airplane January 1929, from Albany

N.Y. to newly opened Manchester Vt. 10 Fayette Griffith (Bill's) grandfather 10 Winchester Cathedral (see page 1) 12 the Cathedral Winchester Cathedral (see page 1)

13 – 12/11/34 At the hospital I was separated from alcohol for the last time (Bill is admitted to the hospital at 2:38PM and he is 39 years old)

13 – Ebby & Shep Cornell schoolmate visited at hosp with friend

14 – Dr. Silkworth friend, the doctor

14 – 12/14/34 God's impact on Bill is sudden & profound, he calls Silky & describes what just happened, this spiritual experience as THE result of the work he did on pages 13 & 14 were all done when Bill had 3 days of sobriety or less!

14 – Ebby friend emphasized

16 – Bill C. committed suicide in Bill & Lois's home after having stolen & sold about $700 worth of their clothes and luggage (a lawyer, stayed with them almost a year, died 1936)

16 – 36 years sober, age 75 Bill W., co-founder of AA, died January 24,1971

There Is A Solution

21 – mostly from Bill's story Here is the fellow who has been puzzling you..

26 – Rowland Hazard certain American Business man -treated by Dr. Carl Jung (1931) & joined the Oxford Group in February 1934

26 – Freud & Adler consulted best known American psychiatrists (Freud was sick & Adler was booked up so Rowland ended up working with Jung)

26 – Dr. Carl Jung (named) European psychiatrist

28 – William James (named)American psychologist who wrote "Varieties of Religious Experience"

More About Alcoholism

32-3 – A man of thirty (On page 123 of Richard Peabody's 1931 book "The Common Sense of Drinking", Peabody briefly mentions an unknown man who gave up drinking until he had made his fortune five years later. Resuming "moderate" drinking, he was soon back in his

alcoholic difficulties, losing his money in two or three years and dying of alcoholism a few years after that. This anecdotal account was probably the germ idea for this story)

35-7 – Ralph Furlong a friend we shall call Jim (Ralph is the author of the story "Another Prodigal Son" which only appeared in the first edition of the Big Book)

37-8 – jay walker story

39-43 – Harry Brick Fred

43 – Dr. Percy Poliak staff member world-renowned hospital (Bellevue Hospital, N.Y.)

We Agnostics

50 – Alfred E. Smith "celebrated American statesman" (four time governor of New York and unsuccessful first Roman Catholic presidential candidate.)

51 – Wright brothers (named) first successful flight 1903

51 – Professor Langley Samuel P. Langley, flying machine landed in Potomac - 1903 project for War Dept.

52 – Wright brothers (named) built a machine that could fly

55 – people who proved that man could never fly

56 – Fitz Mayo the minister's son

56 – Bill Wilson approached by an alcoholic

How It Works

No References

Into Action

76 – Book of James 2:20, 26 Faith without works is dead

79 – man we know was remarried

80 – Oxford Group member he accepted sum of money from business rival - explained in church

Working With Others

101 – Eskimo running away from drinking to Greenland Ice cap

To Wives

No References

Family Afterward

124 – Henry Ford (named)

133 – one of the many doctors

135 – Earl Treat one of our friends is a heavy smoker and coffee drinker

To Employers

(chapter was written by Hank Parkhurst)

136 – Hank Parkhurst member who spent life in world of big business

136 – Mr. B.

137 – one of the best salesmen

137 – man who hung himself

138 – Frank Winans? officer of one of largest banks in America

138 – Bob E. or Rowland H.? an executive of the same bank

140 – Dr. Edward Cowles? Chicago doctor with spinal fluid theory of alcoholics (see www.eskimo.com/~burked/history/cowles.html)

141 – Standard Oil New Jersey "if my company" (that Hank Parkhurst worked for)

148 – vice-president of large industrial concern

149 – Honor Dealers Co. I own a little company (an automobile polish distributorship (see page 246 & 248)

149-50 – Bill Wilson & Jim Burwell two alcoholic employees

Vision For You

151 – Bill's former Higher Power King Alcohol

151 – Four Horsemen (named) Terror, Bewilderment, Frustration, Despair - Revelations 6:2-8 war, famine, pestilence, and death personified the four plagues of mankind

153 – Bill Wilson one of our numbers made a journey

153 – Akron, OH a certain western city

153 – National Rubber Machinery business (of that trip) involved in proxy fight

154 – Akron, Ohio in a strange place (had to have that one)

154 – The Merry Man Tavern an attractive bar

154 – Mayflower Hotel paced a hotel lobby

154 – Reverend Walter Tunks clergyman he phoned (Rector of St. Paul's Episcopal Church in Akron)

155 – "the old Episcopal Church" church selected at random

155 – Dr. Bob resident near nadir of alcoholic despair

155 – AMA convention went on a roaring bender (Traymore Hotel in Atlantic City, NJ)

156 – around 6/17/35 He (Dr. Bob) has not had a drink since. (It is generally stated that Dr. Bob's sobriety date and the founding date of AA is 6/10/35, but recent facts around Dr. Bob's last drink indicate that this date is closer to a week or so later.)

156 – Mrs. Hall/Akron City Hosp head nurse of local hospital

156-8 – Bill Dotson real corker, none too promising, future AA, lawyer

158 – 6/26/35 He (Bill Dotson) never drank again.

158 – Ernie Galbraith - Akron devil-may-care young fellow

159 – Bill Wilson our friend of the hotel lobby incident

159 – Dr. Bob, Bill D, Ernie G leaving behind his first acquaintance, the lawyer and the devil-may-care chap

159 – Archie T, Bill/Bob G (Salesman), Bill Van H, Dr. Bob, Charlie S, Dick S (AA#7), Ernie G, Harry Z, Jim S (Writer), Joe D (AA #5), Marie B, May B & Tom L/Jim L, Paul S, Ralph F, Wally G, Walter B - all 17 have stories in 1st edition. Additionally, Phil S (AA#5), Bill V, J.D.H., Bob E, Ken A were sober by 1937. Some may go with p.161. A year and 6 months later these 3 succeeded with 7 more (puts this early 1937)

160 – T. Henry & Clarace Williams One man and his wife

161 – Cleveland, OH. community 30 miles away

161 – Lloyd T, Clarence S, Charlie J. (see names from pg. 159) has 15 fellows of AA

161 – New York eastern city

162 – Towns Hospital, NYC well known hospital for treatment of alcohol & drugs

162 – Bill Wilson member there 6 years ago

162 – Dr. Silkworth doctor in attendance

162 – eastern city NYC

162 – western friends Ohio

162 – New York, Akron/Cleveland our two large centers

163 – Hank Parkhurst AA member living in a large community (Montclair, NJ)

163 – Dr. Howard prominent psychiatrist (of Montclair, NJ/Chief Psychiatrist for the State of NJ)

163 – Dr. Russell Blaisdell chief psychiatrist of a large public hospital (Rockland State Hospital in NY)

Doctor Bob's Nightmare - Dr. Bob Smith

171 – Sister Ignatia (named) At St. Thomas Hospital, Dr. Bob was well assisted beginning in August 1939 (along with Dr. Bob's office girl Lillian)

171 – St. Johnsbury, VT. I was born (8/8/1879) in a small New England village

171 – Judge & Mrs. Walter Perrin Smith Dr. Bob's father & mother

172 – St. Johnsbury Academy Dr. Bob graduates from high school 1898

172 – Dartmouth College one of the best colleges in the country (in Hanover, N.H., graduated 1902)

173 – Univ. of Michigan entering one of the largest universities in the country (1905)

174 – Rush Medical Univ. another of the leading universities of the country (near Chicago, Ill., received medical degree 1910)

174 – Akron, OH. western city

174 – 1912 I opened an office downtown

174-5 local sanitarium

175 – Scylla and Charybdis (named) (mythology: Strait of Messing-Big rock with monster (Scylla) one side, whirlpool (Charybdis) on other. Odysseus managed to navigate through translated: "between a rock & a hard place"

175 – 1/16/19 - 12/5/33 Eighteenth Amendment (Prohibition)

176 – ? hide out in one of the clubs

176 – ? registering at a hotel

176 – Anne Smith my wife (Anne & Dr. Bob went out together for 17 years before they were married)

177 – Wallace Beery/Tugboat Annie (named)play or movie involving a drinking man

178 – Oxford Group crowd of people -their poise, health and happiness (Dr. Bob got involved with the O.G. in 1933 & separated himself from them Nov. or Dec. 1939)

179 – Henrietta Seiberling a lady called up my wife

179 – 5/12/35 We entered her house at exactly five o'clock

179 – AMA Convention meeting of a national. society (Traymore Hotel in Atlantic City, NJ; June 10-14, Monday-Friday, 1935)

179 – nurse Lily/Cuyahoga Falls I woke up at a friend's house, town near home

179 – Bill Wilson my newly made friend

179 – Bill Wilson meets a friend of hers 181 11/16/50 Dr. Bob died on 11/16/50, he was 55 years old, he had 20 years sober

Principles of Recovery

The steps from pages 59 & 60 of the Big Book.

Step One – Surrender. (Capitulation to hopelessness.)

Step Two – Hope. (the Second Step is the mirror image or opposite of step 1. In step 1 we admit that alcohol is our Higher Power, and that our lives are unmanageable. In the Second Step, we find a different Higher Power who we hope will bring about a return to sanity in the management of our lives.)

Step Three – Commitment. (The key word in step 3 is decision.)

Step Four – Honesty. (An Inventory of self.)

Step Five – Truth. (Candid confession to God and another human being.)

Step Six – Willingness. (Choosing to abandon defects of character.)

Step Seven – Humility. (Standing naked before God, with nothing to hide, and asking that our flaws—in His eyes—be removed.)

Step Eight – Reflection. (Who have we harmed? Are we ready to make amends?)

Step Nine – Amendment. (Making direct amends/restitution/correction, etc.)

Step Ten – Vigilance. (Exercising self-discovery, honesty, abandonment, Humility, reflection, and amendment on a momentary, daily, and periodic basis.)

Step Eleven – Attunement. (Becoming as one with our Father.)

Step Twelve – Service. (Awakening into sober usefulness.)

You may have good reason to believe the above distillation could be improved upon. Do it! The purpose of this activity is to sharpen up our thinking about the nature of AA Recovery. Honest inquiry and loving debate are essential to deep learning.

Principles of the TRADITIONS: Perhaps you should take a shot at these if you wish. Let us know what you come up with.

And Down to Business. Now for the fun. We have uncovered 36 instances of the word principle in the Big Book. From these we have discovered 31 principles of AA Recovery. You may have noticed that in eight instances we are talking specifically about "spiritual principles."

But the "principles" addressed thus far are but a few of the principles that should guide our lives. For example:

Patience, tolerance, understanding, and love are the watchwords.   *Page 118*

These are the four additional principles we once affectionately called PLUT (Patience, Love, Understanding, and Tolerance).

You are going to have an exciting time identifying AA's principles, in the literataure and in your daily life. It is suggested that you and some friends start with the first printed page in the Big Book, and that you each read a paragraph out loud, then ask each other if the paragraph contains any basic action guidelines for Recovery from alcoholism. If it does, write them down and discuss how to take those actions with your Sponsor.

Awakening to Principles

Here in Southern California most AA groups read the first 77 lines of Chapter 5, How It Works, at the beginning of their meetings. While reading the 12 Steps one encounters...

Step Twelve – Having had a spiritual awakening as the result of these steps, we tried to carry this message to alcoholics, and to practice these principles in all our affairs.   *page 60*

Some of us have asked, "What are these principles?" Anticipating this to be anything but a trivial question, we searched the Big Book for the word principle. It must be important to the program of Recovery because it is used 36 times. Appendix II displays all 36 references.

Definition of Principle. Thus aroused, we have explored. The next thing we did was to investigate the definition of principle in our dictionary. Definitions were extracted from Webster's New International Dictionary, Second Edition, published in 1935. It should be a reliable source for word usage as understood over 50 years ago by the authors of the Big Book, Alcoholics Anonymous, which was first published in April, 1939.

Principle, n fr ...Latin principium beginning, foundation...

2. *A source, or origin; that from which anything proceeds; fundamental substance or energy; primordial; ultimate basis or cause....*

4. *A fundamental truth; a comprehensive law or doctrine from which others are derived, or on which others are founded; a general truth; an elementary proposition or fundamental assumption; a maxim; an axiom; a postulate.*

5. *A settled rule of action; a governing law of conduct; an opinion, attitude or belief which exercises a directing influence on the life and behavior; a rule (usually a right rule) of conduct consistently directing one's actions...*

One might distill these definitions of principle down to basic rules of action. However, some of our members are opposed to rules, so we adopted the following short definition:

"a principle is a basic action guideline"

Searching the Big Book on the word "Principle," what are the principles of the AA program of Recovery? Five of the 36 uses of the word principle are clearly statements of principles: Numbers 1 through 36 below refer to the order in which the statement appears)

22) *The first principle of success is that you should never be angry.*   *Page 111*

Although we alcoholics are not saints, it seems the authors of the Big Book thought that our spouses should be. It is obvious that this principle is avoiding anger.

28) *Another principle we observe carefully is that we do not relate intimate experiences of another person unless we are sure he would approve.*

Page 125

This principle urges us to respect the privacy of others, especially fellow members of AA.

29) *Giving, rather than getting, will become the guiding principle.*   *page 128,*

We practice service of others rather than self-service.

36 References to Principles

"PRINCIPLES" IN THE BIG BOOK

Your new courage, good nature and lack of self-consciousness will do wonders for you socially. The same principle applies in dealing with the children.

Page 115

Our relationships with others will be vastly improved when we display courage and good nature, just as when we do not display self-consciousness.

Five additional examples make direct reference to the steps and traditions of AA as being principles:

The Steps of AA are principles (and a listing of these appears soon):

- Step Twelve. Having had a spiritual awakening as the result of these steps, we tried to carry this message to alcoholics, and to practice these principles in all our affairs...   Page 60

- No one among us has been able to maintain anything like perfect adherence to these principles.   Page 60

- The principles we have set down are guides to progress. We claim spiritual progress rather than spiritual perfection.   Page 60

Traditions are Principles:

- As we discovered the principles by which the individual alcoholic could live, so we had to evolve principles by which the AA groups and AA as a whole could survive and function effectively.   Page xix

- Though none of these principles had the force of rules or laws, they had become so widely accepted by 1950 that they were confirmed by our first International Conference held at Cleveland.   Page xix

Thus far we may have uncovered 31 of AA's principles. Four were the easy uses of the word principle in examples 22, 28, 29, and 36. Three more were found in 25, and there are the 12 Steps and 12 Traditions, each being a principle.

The Word "Principle" in the Big Book:

1 & 2) As we discovered the principles by which the individual alcoholic could live, so we had to evolve principles by which the AA groups and AA as a whole could survive and function effectively.   Page xix

3) Though none of these principles had the force of rules or laws, they had become so widely accepted by 1950 that they were confirmed by our first International Conference held at Cleveland.   Page xix

4) The basic principles of the AA program, it appears, hold good for individuals with many different life-styles, just as the program has brought Recovery to those of many different nationalities.

5) My friend had emphasized the absolute necessity of demonstrating these principles in all my affairs.   Page 14

6) We feel elimination of our drinking is but a beginning. A much more important demonstration of our principles lies before us in our respective homes, occupations and affairs.   Page 19

7) Quite as important was the discovery that spiritual principles would solve all my problems.   Page 42

8) That was great news to us, for we had assumed we could not make use of spiritual principles unless we accepted many things on faith which seemed difficult to believe.   Page 47

9) Step Twelve. Having had a spiritual awakening as the result of these steps, we tried to carry this message to alcoholics, and to practice these principles in all our affairs...   Page 60

10) No one among us has been able to maintain anything like perfect adherence to these principles.   Page 60

11) The principles we have set down are guides to progress. We claim spiritual progress rather than spiritual perfection.   Page 60

12) We listed people, institutions or principles with whom we were angry. We asked ourselves why we were angry.   Page 64

13) Although these reparations take innumerable forms, there are some general principles which we find guiding.   Page 79

14) *Unless one's family expresses a desire to live upon spiritual principles we think we ought not to urge them.* Page 83

15) *If not members of religious bodies, we sometimes select and memorize a few set Prayers which emphasize the principles we have been discussing.* Page 87

16) *The main thing is that he be willing to believe in a Power greater than himself and that he live by spiritual principles.* Page 93

17) *When dealing with such a person, you had better use everyday language to describe spiritual principles.* Page 93

18) *We are dealing only with general principles common to most denominations.* Page 93

19) *Should they accept and practice spiritual principles, there is a much better chance that the head of the family will recover.* Page 97

21) *When your prospect has made such reparation as he can to his family, and has thoroughly explained to them the new principles by which he is living, he should proceed to put those principles into action at home.*
Page 98

22) *The first principle of success is that you should never be angry.* Page 111

23) *If you act upon these principles, your husband may stop or moderate.*
Page 112

24) *The same principles which apply to husband number one should be practiced.* Page 112

25) *Your new courage, good nature and lack of self-consciousness will do wonders for you socially. The same principle applies in dealing with the children.* Page 115

26) *Now we try to put spiritual principles to work in every department of our lives...* Page 116

27) *Though it is entirely separate from Alcoholics Anonymous, it uses the general principles of the AA program as a guide for husbands, wives, relatives, friends, and others close to alcoholics.* Page 121, footnote

28) *Another principle we observe carefully is that we do not relate intimate experiences of another person unless we are sure he would approve.*
Page 125

30) Whether the family has spiritual convictions or not, they may do well to examine the principles by which the alcoholic member is trying to live.

Page 130

31) They can hardly fail to approve these simple principles, though the head of the house still fails somewhat in practicing them. *Page 130*

32) Without much ado, he accepted the principles and procedure that had helped us. *Page 139*

33) The use of spiritual principles in such cases was not so well understood as it is now. *Page 156*

34) Twelve—Anonymity is the spiritual foundation of all our Traditions, ever reminding us to place principles before personalities."

Appendix I, page 564

35) & 36) "There is a principle which is a bar against all information, which is proof against all arguments and which cannot fail to keep a man in everlasting ignorance— that principle is contempt prior to investigation."— Herbert Spencer

Appendix II, page 570

Grief and Amends

As a member of the human race, you will be required to pass through your own trials related to loss. As a Sponsor you will be asked to help your Sponsee through the human ordeal of suffering loss. It is your experience that will make you valuable to helping someone stay sober while going through the grief associated with such losess. Theories or stories you have heard about how other people successfully processed Grief might be helpful to some degree, but it will always be experience that proves to be of the greatest value.

When death is expected and we have time to prepare, the actual event will come as a shock and we will know the difference between what we thought it would be like, and the reality. When death is unexpected we need help to find our footing after the shock knocks us off balance.

Escape from Old Patterns

People in Recovery drank and used drugs to escape from feeling. With the gift of Sobriety comes the return of human feelings, which we must learn to integrate into our new, healthy lives. There is no way to turn on Good Feelings and turn off Bad Feelings – we feel or we are numb. We must feel love and joy with the same capacity we can feel anger or grief. Most alcoholics and addicts are newcomers to successfully living with these feelings, and sometimes we are thrown into new rounds of emotion to which we must adjust without advance warning.

When you are asked for help beyond you own life and Recovery experience, you must admit that fact and work with the person to help him find someone with the experience they need.

Grief is the normal reaction to loss. Sometimes it is the loss of a person close to us, sometimes it is something else. We grieve over pets, missed opportunities or the fantasy which must be surrendered to move deeper into a healthy, functional human being. Denying grief can offer a temporary benefit but is not something for prolonged indulgence; no one is qualified to tell someone how long they should spend in any stage of grief.

Grief hurts. No one can tell someone else what they are not to feel. Each person will have his or her own reactions and must discover their process to get through the grief.

You will hear it said that the depth of grief is directly related to how much we loved, or at least cared about, the thing which was lost. This usually means that the loss of a parent or spouse will be a much deeper experience compared to the passing of an acquaintance with whom we shared a class many years ago. The loss of a child is almost impossible to describe and is best shared with someone else who has lost a child. The death of a beloved pet may strike one person deeply, and may not effect another person at all.

There are excellent books on grief, which can be helpful, particularly when used to prepare for a forthcoming death.

We tend to fall back to complete self absorption at the time of crisis, whether it is a death we have expected after a long period of illness, or something unexpected such as an accident or a criminal act. We return to our old pattern of making everything our drama, rather than accept it as part of our life. And our Ego makes us think that everything around the loss we are grieving is about ourselves - the old, familiar "me, me, me."

Service for Healing

When confronting Grief, one of the best tools is the same tool that allows us to get through the new awareness of our past, our damage to other people and the need to make things better –Service. When we face a loss, it serves us to comfort the other people who share that loss.

For example, when a parent or other family member dies, there are brothers and sisters, aunts and uncles, in-laws and friends of that person we grieve. By providing comfort to others, we take our minds off of our own pain and loss to provide the same compassionate understanding we need.

Frequently in Recovery, our healing comes by giving away the very thing we feel we are lacking. When we need encouragement, it helps us to encourage others. When we need understanding for some confusion or wrong ideas that have created a problem, we must offer forgiveness and understanding for someone else going through that same problem. When we need love, we love others more. When we feel we need to matter to other people, we need to recognize how important people around us are to us, and then communicate that fact while they are able to hear us and know how we feel.

Amends and Grief

Sometimes in the Amends process you will have a name that represents something or someone who is gone. Some people say it is enough to visit a grave to speak your apologies, or to write a letter.

But we are also taught that this is a Program of Action and processing Grief may mix in with our amends. What Action can you take that would have been accepted as an amends with the person or organiation to whom you owed amends?

If you owed money, how will the amount of that debt you owed go to benefit something that the lost name would approve?

If you owed a repair other than money, how could that be carried out in the name of the lost person or organization for a cause or an action.

If you had to restore an object but the person who was to receive it is not longer available, to what appropriate person, organization or location can the object be returned.

Death is unavoidable, but it does not mark the end of the object of our Grief's effect on our lives.

Twelve Warnings

The book Alcoholics Anonymous contains a series of propositions and proposals, the successful outcome of these depends upon the actions of the reader.

The book directs us as to what we must start doing, what we must stop doing, what happens when we fulfill the propositions and proposals and what will happen if we fail to fulfill them.

These are the Twelve Warnings as to what will happen if we fail to heed the directions:

1. For if an alcoholic failed to perfect and enlarge his spiritual life through work and self-sacrifice for others, he could not survive the certain trials and low spots ahead. Page 14

2. The feeling of having shared in a common peril is one element in the powerful cement which binds us. But that in itself would never have held us together as we are now joined. Page 17

3. Above everything, we alcoholics must be rid of this selfishness, we must, or it kills us! God makes that possible. Page 62

4. Though our decision (Third Step) was a vital and crucial Step, it could have little permanent effect unless at once followed by a strenuous effort to face and be rid of, the things in our lives which had been blocking us. Page 64

5. It is plain that a life, which includes deep resentment, leads only to futility and unhappiness. To the precise extent that we permit these, do we squander the hours that might have been worth while. But with the alcoholic, whose hope is the maintenance and growth of a spiritual experience, this business of resentment is infinitely grave. We found that it is fatal. For when harboring such feelings we

---

11 This list was submitted through several correspondents and websites, but we have not been able to confirm the original source.

shut ourselves off from the sunlight of the spirit. The insanity of alcohol returns and with us to drink is to die. Page 66

6. *Concerning sex. Suppose we fall short of the chosen ideal and stumble? Does this mean we are going to get drunk? Some people tell us so. But this is only a half-truth. It depends on us and our motives. If we are sorry for what we have done, and have the honest desire to let God take us to better things, we believe we will be forgiven and will have learned a lesson. If we are not sorry, and our conduct continues to harm others, we are quite sure to drink. We are not theorizing. These are facts about our experience.* Page 70

7. *If we skip this vital Step (5), we may not overcome drinking. Time after time newcomers have tried to keep to themselves certain facts about their lives. Trying to avoid this humbling experience, they have turned to easier methods. Almost invariably they got drunk.* Page 72

8. *We must lose our fear of creditors no matter how far we have to go, for we are liable to drink if we are afraid to face them.* Page 78

9. *We feel that a man is unthinking when he says that sobriety is enough.* Page 82

10. *It is easy to let up on the spiritual program of action and rest on our laurels. We are headed for trouble if we do, for alcohol is a subtle foe.* Page 85

11. *Our rule is not to avoid a place where there is drinking, if we have a legitimate reason for being there. That includes bars, nightclubs, dances, receptions, weddings, even plain ordinary whoopee parties. To a person who has had experience with an alcoholic, this may seem like tempting Providence, but it isn't. You will note that we made an important qualification. Therefore, ask yourself on each occasion, "Have I a good social, business, or personal reason for going to this place? Or am I expecting to steal a little vicarious pleasure from the atmosphere of such places?" If you have answered these questions satisfactorily, you need have no apprehension. Go or stay away, whichever seems best. But be sure you are on solid spiritual ground before you start and that your motive in going is thoroughly good. Do not think of what you will get out of the occasion. Think of what you can bring to it. But if you are shaky, you had better work with another alcoholic instead!* Page 101

12. *The head of the house ought to remember that he is mainly to blame for what befell his home. He can scarcely square the account in his lifetime. But he must see the danger of over-concentration on financial success. Although financial Recovery is on the way for many of us, we found we could not place money first. For us, material well-being always followed spiritual progress, it never preceded.*

Page 127)

Thirty Eight Musts

Frequently you will hear it said in meetings: "There are no musts in this program."

This is not supported by the body of the texts.

1. *"It must be done if any results are to be expected.*   Page 99

2. *"We must try to repair the damage immediately lest we pay the penalty by a spree."*   Page 99

3. *"It must be on a better basis, since the former did not work."*   Page 99

4. *"Yes, there is a long period of reconstruction ahead. We must take the lead."*   Page 83

5. *"We must remember that ten or twenty years of drunkenness would make a skeptic out of anyone."*   Page 83

6. *"Those of us belonging to a religious denomination which requires confession must, and of course, will want to go to the properly appointed authority whose duty it is to receive it."*   Page 74

7. *"The rule is we must be hard on ourself, but always considerate of others."*   Page 74

8. *"But we must not use this as a mere excuse to postpone."*   Page 75

9. *"But we must go further and that means more action."*   Page 85

10. *"Every day is a day when we must carry the vision of God's will into all of our activities."*   Page 85

11. *"These are thoughts which must go with us constantly."*   Page 85

12. *"If we have obtained permission, have consulted with others, asked God to help and the drastic step is indicated we must not shrink."*   Page 80

13. *"I must turn in all things to the Father of Light who presides over us all."*   Page 14

14. *"Above everything, we alcoholics mus t be rid of this selfishness. We must, or it kills us!"* Page 62

15. *"The man must decide for himself."* Page 144

16. *"To watch people recover, to see them help others, to watch loneliness vanish, to see a fellowship grow up about you, to have a host of friends - this is an experience you must not miss."* Page 89

17. *"If we are planning to stop drinking, there must be no reservation of any kind"* Page 33

18. *"We must not shrink at anything."* Page 79

19. *"But we must be careful not to drift into worry, remorse or morbid reflection, for that would diminish our usefulness to others."* Page 86

20. *"He must redouble his spiritual activities if he expects to survive."* Page 120

21. *"I know I must get along without liquor, but how can I?"* Page 152

22. *"He must decide for himself whether he wants to go on"* Page 95

23. *"If he is to find God, the desire must come from within."* Page 95

24. *"Though they knew they must help other alcoholics if they would remain sober, that motive became secondary."* Page 159,

25. *"Both saw that they must keep spiritually active."* Page 156

26. *"That is where our work must be done."* Page 130

27. *"Certainly he must keep sober, for there will be no home if he doesn't."* Page 82

28. *"He should understand that he must undergo a change of heart."* Page 143

29. *"Whatever our ideal turns out to be, we must be willing to grow toward it."* Page 69

30. *"We must be willing to make amends where we have done harm"* Page 69

31. *"We had to face the fact that we must find a spiritual basis of life - or else."* Page 44

32. *"We must lose our fear of creditors no matter how far we have to go, for we are liable to drink if we are afraid to face them."* Page 78

33. *"To be vital, faith must be accompanied by self-sacrifice and unselfish, constructive action."* Page 93

34. *"His defense must come from a Higher Power."* Page 43

35. *"We saw that these resentments must be mastered."* Page 66

36. *"For he knows he must be honest if he would live at all."*   *Page 146*

37. *"We must be entirely honest with somebody if we expect to live long or happily in this world."*   *Page 73*

But Remember...

38. *"When the man is presented with this volume it is best that no one tell him he must abide by its suggestions."*   *Page 144*

109 Promises

How many promises await us as we trudge this road of happy destiny? Some folks think they are limited to those following the Ninth Step on page 83. There are 20 there (not the 12 often mentioned). But you will find promises for each step and in many other places as well. We are sure you want to know what they are.

Thanks to Buddy T. at About.com we were referred to the Big Book Comes Alive website, which lists their version of 147 Big Book promises. We have not yet added from their list to ours the missing promises that meet our promise criteria.

However, there is a price to pay for reading on. You must contact us with additional promises from inside the front cover through page 164. Here are well over 100 presented as of today:

Promises of Step Two

1) *There is a solution. Almost none of us liked the self-searching, the leveling of our pride, the confession of short-comings which the process requires for its successful consummation. But we saw that it really worked in others, and we had come to believe in the hopelessness and futility of life as we had been living it. When, therefore, we were approached by those in whom the problem had been solved, there was nothing left for us but to pick up the simple kit of spiritual tools laid at our feet.*

2) *We have found much of heaven and*

3) *we have been rocketed into a fourth dimension of existence of which we had not even dreamed.*

4) *The great fact is just this, and nothing less: That we have had deep and effective spiritual experiences which have*

revolutionized our whole attitude toward life, toward our fellows and toward God's universe.

5) *The central fact of our lives today is the absolute certainty that our Creator has entered into our hearts and lives in a way which is indeed miraculous.*

6) *He has commenced to accomplish those things for us which we could never do by ourselves.*   *Page 25*

7) *Here and there, once in a while, alcoholics have had what are called vital spiritual experiences. To me these occurrences are phenomena. They appear to be in the nature of huge emotional displacements and rearrangements.*

8) *Ideas, emotions, and attitudes which were once the guiding forces of the lives of these men are suddenly cast to one side,*

9) *and a completely new set of conceptions and motives begin to dominate them.*   *Page 27:*

10) *We, in our turn, sought the same escape with all the desperation of drowning men. What seemed at first a flimsy reed, has proved to be the loving and powerful hand of God.*

11) *A new life has been given us or, if you prefer, "a design for living" that really works.*   *Page 28*

Much to our relief, we discovered we did not need to consider another's conception of God.

12) *Our own conception, however inadequate, was sufficient to make the approach*

13) *and to effect a contact with Him.*

14) *As soon as we admitted the possible existence of a Creative Intelligence, a Spirit of the Universe underlying the totality of things, we began to be possessed of a new sense of power and direction, provided we took other simple steps.*

15) *We found that God does not make too hard terms with those who seek Him.*

16) *To us, the Realm of Spirit is broad, roomy, all inclusive; never exclusive or forbidding to those who earnestly seek.*

17) *It is open, we believe, to all men.*   *Page 46*

18) *Do not let any prejudice you may have against spiritual terms deter you from honestly asking yourself what they mean to you. At the start, this was all we needed to commence spiritual growth, to effect our first conscious relation with God as we understood Him.*

19) *Afterward, we found ourselves accepting many things which then seemed entirely out of reach.*

20) *That was growth, but if we wished to grow we had to begin somewhere. So we used our own conception, however limited it was. We needed to ask ourselves but one short question. "Do I now believe, or am I even willing to believe, that there is a Power greater than myself?" As soon as a man can say that he does believe, or is willing to believe, we emphatically assure him that he is on his way.*

21) *It has been repeatedly proven among us that upon this simple cornerstone a wonderfully effective spiritual structure can be built.*   *Page 47*

22) *Faced with alcoholic destruction, we soon became as open minded on spiritual matters as we had tried to be on other questions. In this respect alcohol was a great persuader.*

23) *It finally beat us into a state of reasonableness. Sometimes this was a tedious process; we hope no one else will be prejudiced for as long as some of us were.*   *Page 48*

24) *Here are thousands of men and women, worldly indeed. They flatly declare that since they have come to believe in a Power greater than themselves, to take a certain attitude toward the Power, and to do certain simple things, there has been a revolutionary change in their way of living and thinking.*

25) *In the face of collapse and despair, in the face of the total failure of their human resources, they found that a new power, peace, happiness, and sense of direction flowed into them.*

26) *This happened soon after they whole-heartedly met a few simple requirements. Once confused and baffled by the seeming*

futility of existence, they show the underlying reasons why they were making heavy going of life. Leaving aside the drink question, they tell why living was so unsatisfactory. They show how the change came over them. When many hundreds of people are able to say that the consciousness of the Presence of God is today the most important fact of their lives, they present a powerful reason why one should have faith. Page 50

27) *We finally saw that faith in some kind of God was a part of our make-up, just as much as the feeling we have for a friend. Sometimes we had to search fearlessly, but He was there. He was as much a fact as we were. We found the Great Reality deep down within us. In the last analysis it is only there that He may be found. It was so with us.* Page 55

28) *Even so has God restored us all to our right minds. To this man, the revelation was sudden. Some of us grow into it more slowly.*

29) *But He has come to all who have honestly sought Him.*

30) *When we drew near to Him He disclosed Himself to us!*

Contributed by Joe Mc.
Page 57

Promises of Step Three

31) *When we sincerely took such a position, all sort of remarkable things followed.*

32) *We had a new Employer.*

33) *He provided what we needed, if we kept close to Him and performed His work well.*

34) *Established on such a footing we became less and less interested in ourselves, our little plans and designs.*

35) *More and more we became interested in seeing what we could contribute to life.*

36) *As we felt new power flow in,*

37) *as we enjoyed peace of mind,*

38) *as we discovered we could face life successfully,*

39) as we became conscious of His presence,

40) we began to lose our fear of today, tomorrow or the hereafter.

41) We were reborn.

42) an effect, sometimes a very great one, was felt at once.
Contributed by Kay G. and Jon T.
Page 63

43) At once, we commence to outgrow fear.
Contributed by Kay G.
Page 68

43a) We have begun to learn tolerance, patience and good will toward all men, even our enemies, for we look on them as sick people. Contributed by Tom T. of Omaha.
Page 70

Promises of Step Five

Once we have taken this step, withholding nothing,

44) we are delighted.

45) We can look the world in the eye.

46) We can be alone at perfect peace and ease.

47) Our fears fall from us.

48) We begin to feel the nearness of our Creator.

49) We may have had certain spiritual beliefs, but now we begin to have a spiritual experience.

50) The feeling that the drink problem has disappeared will often come strongly.

51) We feel we are on the Broad Highway, walking hand in hand with the Spirit of the Universe. Page 75

Promises of Step Eight

52) If our manner is calm, frank, and open, we will be gratified with the result.

53) In nine cases out of ten the unexpected happens. Sometimes the man we are calling upon admits his own faults,

54) *so feuds of years standing melt away in an hour.*

55) *Rarely do we fail to make satisfactory progress. Our*

56) *former enemies sometimes praise what we are doing and wish us well.*

57) *Occasionally, they will offer assistance.*   *Page 78*

Promises of Step Nine

If we are painstaking about this phase of our development,

58) *we will be amazed before we are half way through.*

59) *We are going to know a new freedom*

60) *and a new happiness.*

61) *We will not regret the past*

62) *nor wish to shut the door on it.*

63) *We will comprehend the word serenity and*

64) *we will know peace.*

65) *No matter how far down the scale we have gone, we will see how our experience can benefit others.*

66) *That feeling of uselessness (will disappear)*

67) *and self-pity will disappear.*

68) *We will lose interest in selfish things and*

69) *(We will) gain interest in our fellows.*

70) *Self-seeking will slip away.*

71) *Our whole attitude and outlook upon life will change.*

72) *Fear of people (will leave us) and*

73) *(fear) of economic insecurity will leave us.*

74) *We will intuitively know how to handle situations which used to baffle us.*

75) *We will suddenly realize that God is doing for us what we could not do for ourselves.*

76) *Are these extravagant promises? We think not. They are being fulfilled among us—sometimes quickly, sometimes slowly.*

77) They will always materialize if we work for them.   Page 83

Promises of Step Ten

64) And we have ceased fighting anything or anyone — even alcohol.

65) For by this time sanity will have returned.

66) We will seldom be interested in liquor.

67) If tempted, we recoil from it as from a hot flame.

68) We react sanely and normally, and

69) we will find that this has happened automatically.

70 We will see that our new attitude toward liquor has been given us without any thought or effort on our part. It just comes! That is the miracle of it.

71) We are not fighting it,

72) neither are we avoiding temptation.

73) We feel as though we had been places in a position of neutrality—safe and protected.

74) We have not even sworn off. Instead, the problem has been removed. It does not exist for us.

75) We are neither cocky nor are we afraid.

76) That is our experience. That is how we react so long as we keep in fit spiritual condition.   Page 84

Promises of Step Eleven

On awakening let us think about the twenty-four hours ahead. We consider our plans for the day. Before we begin, we ask God to direct our thinking, especially asking that it be divorced from self-pity, dishonest or self-seeking motives. Under these conditions

77) we can employ our mental faculties with assurance, for after all God gave us brains to use.

78) Our thought-life will be placed on a much higher plane when our thinking is cleared of wrong motives.

79) In thinking about our day we may face indecision. We may not be able to determine which course to take. Here we ask God for inspiration, an intuitive thought or a decision. We relax and take it easy. We don't struggle. We are often surprised how the right answers come after we have tried this for a while.

Page 86

80) What used to be the hunch or the occasional inspiration gradually becomes a working part of the mind.

81) Being still inexperienced and having just made conscious contact with God, it is not probable that we are going to be inspired at all times. We might pay for this presumption in all sorts of absurd actions and ideas. Nevertheless, we find that our thinking will, as time passes, be more and more on the plane of inspiration.

82) We come to rely upon it.

83) We are careful never to pray for our own selfish ends. Many of us have wasted a lot of time doing that and it doesn't work. You can easily see why.

As we go through the day we pause, when agitated or doubtful, and ask for the right thought or action. We constantly remind ourselves we are no longer running the show, humbly saying to ourselves many times each day "Thy will be done."

84) We are then in much less danger of excitement,

85) fear,

86) anger,

87) worry,

88) self-pity,

89) or foolish decisions.

90) We become much more efficient.

91 We do not tire so easily, for we are not burning up energy foolishly as we did when we were trying to arrange life to suit ourselves.

92) *It works—it really does.* *Page 87*

93) *Practical experience shows that nothing will so much insure immunity from drinking as intensive work with other alcoholics. It works when other activities fail.*

94) *You can help when no one else can.*

95) *You can secure their confidence when others fail.*

96) *Life will take on new meaning.*

97) *To watch people recover, to see them help others, to watch loneliness vanish, to see a fellowship grow up about you, to have a host of friends—this is an experience you must not miss. We know you will not want to miss it. Frequent contact with newcomers and with each other is the bright spot of our lives.* *Page 97*

Promises of Step Twelve

98) *Both you and the new man must walk day by day in the path of spiritual progress. If you persist, remarkable things will happen.* *Contributed by Kate O.*

99) *When we look back, we realize that the things which came to us when we put ourselves in God's hands were better than anything we could have planned.* *Contributed by Kate O.*

100) *Follow the dictates of a Higher Power and you will presently live in a new and wonderful world, no matter what your present circumstances!* *Contributed by Beth*

101) *Assuming we are spiritually fit, we can do all sorts of things alcoholics are not supposed to do.* *Contributed by Kate O.* *Page 100*

102) *Your job now is to be at the place where you may be of maximum helpfulness to others, so never hesitate to go anywhere if you can be helpful. You should not hesitate to visit the most sordid spot on earth on such an errand. Keep on the firing line of life with these motives and God will keep you unharmed.* *Contributed by Beth*

103) The power of God goes deep!   *Contributed by Kate O.*
Page 102

104) But sometimes you must start life anew. We know women who have done it. If such women adopt a spiritual way of life their road will be smoother.   *Contributed by Kate O.*
Page 114

105) How much better life is when lived on a spiritual plane.
Contributed by Kate O.
Big Book page 116

106) These work-outs should be regarded as part of your education, for thus you will be learning to live.

107) You will make mistakes, but if you are in earnest they will not drag you down.

108) Instead, you will capitalize them.

109) A better way of life will emerge when they are overcome.
Contributed by Kate O.

The Most Dangerous Part of the Alcoholic Brain

a Talk by Dr. Harry T. Tiebout

Dr. Tiebout

Throughout the conference approved literature issued by AA's World Service Office tells us that we have great friends in the non-alcoholic community. We are also told to seek and use the professional services of the medical professionals available to us.

Bill Wilson, the primary author of the Big Book followed his own advice and had a psychiatrist, Dr. Harry T. Tiebout, who, through Bill's sessions with him, specialized in the field of Alcoholism and Recovery for the remaining years of his professional career.

Dr. Tiebout published in professional journals and presented additional papers on his findings related to the mind of the alcoholic at early International Conventions of the fellowship. At the 1960 Inernational in Long Beach he presented a talk12 on the most insidious aspect of the alcoholic brain in Recovery.

Dr. Tiebout repeatedly stressed that the reduction of the Ego was a prerequisite to success in Recovery. The state of being humble is desired, but is not under the

---

[12] The original recording will be hosted at the http://sponsormagazine.info site for those who prefer to hear Dr. Tiebout make this presentation in his own words and in his own voice. It will also be posted to archive.org for long term availability.

mind's ability to bring about. He said, "You can no more will yourself to be humble than you can pull yourself up by your own bootstraps."

As illustrations Dr. Tiebout presented several case histories where someone in Recovery, who was respected by his local fellowship for his or her Recovery, fell victim to the most dangerous part of the Alcoholic's brain - the self-healing Ego.

In one case he cited a man with several years Recovery who was invited to speak at an event. He said he would do it but, owing to his long sobriety, he insisted that he go on as the last speaker. It was a minor point and the event placed him in the desired position. But from such a simple position, feeling that his presentation would be of particular value to the audience, the man's Ego reasserted itself. Within two years the man had relapses and died as a direct result of his alcoholism.

A patient of Dr. Tiebout said she did not like people with resurrected Egos. The comment disturbed Dr. Tiebout, prompting him to ask, "How do you view such people?" "To be honest," the patient said, "I look down on those people." The doctor considered the response, then asked, "If you are looking down on them, in what position does that put you?"

The patient became uncomfortable. "It means I am above them, I guess," she admitted meekly. He said that with that admission, she was beginning to take an inventory that might be more than the list of words. She was having a first hand contact with humility and was, he felt, beginning to feel some truths about herself.

In a third case he was present at a meeting in New England where the speaker announced that he was the "humblest man in the room" and was confused when this prompted a hearty horse-laugh from the crowd. He did not see the source of their amusement at first.

This kind of Ego-blindness is, of course, the source of profound trouble. Its presence can be denied with the utmost sincerity. It takes considerable digging and large doses of honesty before the inner self can be reached. In its quietly stubborn way, it can ruin our best intentions.

The sad truth is that the Ego is always more visible in others, than in ourselves. We can delight in puncturing the pomposities of others. We can recognize the wisdom of deflating inflated egos, but all too often the target is someone else. When it is ourselves, our aim can be notoriously bad. We can laugh with the saying of Chinese philosopher Lao Tse who had this gem to offer: "He who feels pricked must have been a bubble."

The Ego can be seen as the driving force that seeks to dominate and feel comfortable only when it is able to maintain a non-underdog position. It may recoil at any display of "big-shotism," but down inside where the feelings count it can be as touchy as a sore thumb.

It is not an accident that the members of Dr. Tiebout's specialty are called "head shrinkers."

The doctor then explored the ability to detect evidence which shows that the ego has gone. That evidence can be summed in one of two words. Humbleness and Humility. Assured the Ego has departed, the mind treats the two as synonyms and fails to see the difference between the two states, nor the need of active contact with a Higher Power to maintain the reduced Ego condition.

The problem is 'How does one feel when one feels Humble?" The answer to that question, he said, was identifying the state of being 'up' and the state of being 'down'.

When one is 'up', one is cheerful, positive, and animated. A person in such a state may be up on his toes, in high gear, or perhaps 'up and at 'em'. He is all for action, charges in, and makes improvements. Getting somewhere. And is rendered accurately uneasy whenever his perceived advances are in any way impeded.

Perhaps more than he knows, he seeks to make life a pink cloud. In a deep sense, he lives off hope. An insistent force drives him, telling him his ship will come in and his worries will be over. For him, surrender is a completely shattering experience, impossible to contemplate. It means renouncing the will to live. The force that keeps him going.

The person in the 'up' state seldom questions its validity. It seems the epitome of health and well being.

'Down' on the other hand, is the exact opposite. In the state of being down the individual is not gay, lacks energy, drive, finds life a dreary bore. Such phrases as down in the mouth or down in the dumps successfully picture the 'down' frame of mind. It is a state of mind that is voided and smacks little of health.

In keeping with most everyone else, for years Dr. Tiebout viewed the 'up' state with kindly eyes, and the 'down' one to be the enemy of mankind. In AA and in life a whole new series of facts were forced upon him.

The 'pink cloud' is an 'up' state if ever there was one, yet clearly not an entirely healthy one. Even more confusing, Humbleness and Humility, which were certainly part of a 'down' state, were essential to sobriety.

And finally, to his surprise, he came to realize that being sober meant being sober minded, with no trace of being 'up'.

There were incontrovertible facts that seemed to fly in the face of all logic. In fact they were, and some sense had to be, made out of Humbleness and Humility.

The question was how can one lose the up state without plunging into a down, which is crippling and surely a miserable form of existence. The answer to that question lies in direct admission of the fact that the word 'down' does not have to mean down and out. It can also mean 'down to earth'. This down is a very healthy one, too.

The down to earth individual has his feet on the ground. He can spot the pink cloud for the element it is, and can distrust the airy, insubstantial quality. The man with his feet on the ground is a solid citizen, going nowhere, interested in nothing spectacular, but able to live each 24 hours as a contributing member of the human race.

Here is a very different down from the depressed, unhappy sort of down which formerly had been envisioned. Here is a down that stood for substance, for lasting values. A down which should not be deplored. This kind of down meant health and real well being. Not the ephemeral kind, which lifts the individual slightly off this earth. 'Down' could mean being Humble and free from a lot of giddy notions about ourselves. It could mean the end of Ego and all the unrest associated with that part of our nature.

In a very deep and profound sense, down could mean that we were able to accept ourselves for what we are. No longer do we have to be up, looking with scarcely concealed loathing. We are down, we can look up, maybe even to a deity who has never looked down on us.

We can now talk about Humbleness. In the light of our discussion of the up and down states we can realize that Humbleness is the down state which puts it in the right place for our daily life. Whenever the individual stands on Earth, rather than plunging on through to the lower regions, the individual is 'down' but his or her feet are on solid ground.

False fears of what will happen to him or her when they drop from the high state vanishes. As experience is gained we receive the comforting realization that we can let lesser gods fight among themselves.

All we need to do is stay where we are and learn to live.

The Ego in the genuinely humble person is in abeyance, for the moment at any rate. It is accurate to say that true humility is the real evidence that the Ego has gone or is no longer influencing the individual's thoughts or feelings.

The next question is now clear. How can this down-to-earth state of mind, which is the real source of Humbleness, be induced and then maintained.

Hitting bottom is the key. It brings the individual into contact with the Earth, usually with a resounding 'whack'. The use of the word bottom suggests exactly where the hitting is applied. For the fortunate he has been spanked into some measure of sense. The whole of engineering the individual so he hits a bottom is a fascinating matter about which to conjecture.

Dr. Tiebout admitted that the individual members of the Program have been through the mill and seen many others through the same rough time. Any extended discussion of hitting bottom and its role in producing sobriety is wasted time – nothing he had to say will match your first hand experiences to the nature of the forces within which try to produce a breakthrough leading to hitting bottom and surrender.

There he moved into the trickiest problem of maintaining the sober person.

A considerable portion of his practice was devoted to helping members develop a capacity to stay humble or down on Earth. It is one thing to knock a person off his pedestal. It is a much more difficult task to keep him from climbing right back on again.

Out of my experience, three points seem to be of pertinence to this audience.

The first is to recognize that the ability to remain on Earth is not under the conrol of the will. It is just as impossible to will yourself to be humble as it is to lift yourself by your bootstraps. The very effort to will humbleness is, in itself, an act of sheer arrogance. It is a test to dictate how one should feel. One can only hope for the desired feelings to come along. One cannot just order them to be present as feelings have an independence which must be respected.

The second point of consideration is that people have forces within them which can carry us 'up', off Earth so subtly and so quickly that we are totally unaware that anything has happened. The climb back on the pedestal can go completely unnoticed. The old timer who insisted on a preferred position could still have thought himself an AA, and be convincing to himself and others.

The member who claimed to be the 'Humblest person in the room' had a choice and conspired with the returned Ego, but was totally innocent of the fact. His Ego said he should flatly assert his Humbleness, and he could believe he was quite honest. Even if it was quite inaccurate.

The problem of the unnoticed return of the Ego is widespread. The individual who enters into AA after hitting bottom has his own experience which provides him with a genuine feeling of humility. Then a tragic thing often happens. The memory lingers but the humility slowly seeps away.

We can discover the damage created by our unrestrained Ego, work our Steps, work our Program, and devote ourselves to Service, then realize we have achieved a level of Humility. Which is a realization of which we become proud. That pride then opens the door for Ego to find its way back to its pedestal. Having accepted the beating it has recevied, the Ego whispers its way back in as it builds a new takeover of the sober alcoholic's brain. It's self-healing capacity will remain a threat as the AA member progresses into longer and longer terms of Sobriety.

The third point Dr. Tiebout stressed was the problem of remaining Humble. He considered the actual ways and means by which Humbleness is preserved. Obviously no foolproof formula exists. The pitfalls are many. It means Twelve Step work, reporting Inventories, and improving our contact with a Higher Power, are all helpful and may be depended on in most instances.

However, the unwary individual may get trapped in ways which he least suspects.

This article is drawn from the talk given by Dr. Tiebout in Long Beach, CA in 1960. The actual recording is available at http://sponsormagazine.info/reader.html.

Gossip and The 13th Step

Many people talk about the "Thirteenth Step" - the predatory sexual manipulation of a newcomer.

Recovery requires trust. When trust is breached, resentments rise and all the other principles are out the window, and often times Sobriety goes with it. That is why it is so important that no member should ever breach another member's confidence... and especially the ability to trust guidance from the more responsible members of their groups.

This applies as well to any and all gossiping between members about what another member has said or done.

This particularly applies to "The Thirteenth Step" – advances leading to financial or sexual abuse of members, especially newcomers. Newcomers are in a vulnerable position and predators may take advantage of them.

Probably more members lose their Sobriety for this single reason, than all others combined. This means newcomers and those with long term Recovery. It may over guilt of actions they knew were not appropiate, it may be because of damage that was done during the 'relationship', or as a result of the resentments and gossip that run through the local fellowship. It can lead to relapse, damage and sometimes criminal charges.

Newcomers are vulnerable, naive, confused, and fearful. They are looking for any bit of acceptance or comfort that will fill that emptiness they find in their gutA breach of trust can cause a resentment that could mean their Sobriety or their Life.

Newcomers are the life blood of our fellowships and must be protected from the predators among us..We do this to protect the newcomer, and to protect our own Sobriety.

Conflict in AA Histories

WITH ONE CASE STUDY

It does not seem possible to have a large community without the development of myth structures. Myths are created to fill a personal need, to create an explanation or to teach a lesson.

The fellowship of Alcoholics Anonymous is large and has spread around the world. The estimates place membership in the millions, though people argue over the exact number. It has been accepted by followers of almost all of the religions and philosophical beliefs.

In their journey people have tried to explain things they have not understood and have been limited to their own life story and personal experiences to create those explanations. Some of these explanations have been importing ideas and sayings from other sources, some have been completely fabricated, often with good intention.

The problems happen when people create conflicting stories and then try to elevate the version they have been told over the versions other people have been told. Dr. Ernie Kurtz, author of "Not God," the first comprehensive study of the history of Alcoholics Anonymous, addressed this in a YouTube video. The specific video is called "Ernie Kurtz on Researching AA History" (https://youtu.be/2-IyzinVRq8).

In that talk Dr. Kurtz explains we cannot find the whole truth - we have to accept that people have reasons for believing the version they tell, and it is seldom the result of a desire to sabotage or damage someone else or those other people's beliefs.

Dr. William White, who has inherited the mantle of keeper of historical reserach for alcohol and drug Recovery, described it simply:

> *"When I began writing a book in the early 1990s on the history of addiction treatment and Recovery in America, several people directed me to Ernie Kurtz as the authoritative source. I had no way of knowing that what I expected to be a brief consultation on the history of AA would evolve into a prolonged mentorship, multiple professional collaborations, and an enduring friendship. Through these years, Ernie Kurtz communicated a number of*

crucial lessons to me about researching and writing history. He repeatedly challenged me to:

Tell the story chronologically (do not confuse your reader).

Tell the story in context (let your reader know what else is going on around the event you are profiling).

Present the historical evidence (sources)—all the evidence.

Separate statements of fact from conjecture and opinion.

Tell the story from multiple perspectives.

Localize and personalize the story.

Stay connected to your readers—keep them wanting to turn the page to find out what happens next (for an elaboration of these, see White, 2004).

I will try to be faithful to these guidelines in telling Ernie's own story.

http://www.williamwhitepapers.com/ernie_kurtz/

To illustrate this idea I want to address one specific example of this problem and attempt to follow Dr. Kurtz' suggestions with a well known conflict in AA history.

Once Case Study

At the point where the Big Book had been written and was about to be released, there was a new member gertting sober and living with Dr. Bob in Akron, Ohio. His name was Clarence Snyder and many believe he should been given much more credit for the founding of AA and particularly for its growth as an independent organization from the Oxford Group.

Clarence Snyder's sobriety date is February 11, 1938. He is listed as one of the first forty people to get sober using the AA/12-Step system. His story was one of those included in the first edition of the Big Book ("The Home Brewmeister"), also published in the second and third editions. He was present in the early meetings in Akron when the unnamed group was still a part of the Oxford Group.

In 1939 Clarence returned home and had a problem organizing a new group. The men he knew who wanted to get sober were Catholics and the local Diocese had forbidden its members from attending Oxford Group meetings. The Diocese in

Akron had made that declaration13, so Clarence organized a weekly caravan from Cleveland to Akron for the Wednesday night meeting.

There was some complaining about making the journey, since there were more men in the cars making the journey than there were local people in the Akron meeting they attended. Clarence had to remind them about the problem with their church, which some people reported had threatened excommunication, and the grumbling died out.

But in the Akron meeting there was a growing conflict with the Oxford Group about the 'alcoholic squad', the 'type' of man they were bringing into people's homes (recovering alcoholics from all social levels), and the focus on alcoholism. Some members of the Oxford Group complained that these people were 'glorying in their sin'.

The Big Book had just been printed, and the 'Multilith edition' was still in circulation. On the night of May 10, 1939, during one of these argumentative meetings, Clarence announced that he would host a new meeting in Cleveland on the following night. The new meeting would not be affiliated with the Oxford Group and they would use the book Alcoholics Anonymous as their focus.

Members of the Oxford Group objected and called friends in Cleveland to prevent that first meeting. But Clarence, in a single action, created the new unaffiliated group, named it Alcoholics Anonymous after the book, and laid the foundation for the AA saying "All you need to start a new meeting is a coffee pot and a resentment." This meeting was also the first to form without the personal presences of Bill Wilson or Dr. Bob.

At the end of 1939 two more groups had formed in Cleveland. Meetings would form in the the following year in Detroit, Chicago, Boston, Baltimore, and a dozen other cities.

Clarence also wrote the first guide on , the Cleveland meetings created the first 'service board' which released the first literature based on the sermons of a preacher connected to Clarence.

But Clarence does not receive credit for much of what he did in the Cleveland area in the later literature of AA. The sudden growth in Cleveland is acknowledged but Clarence's name is seldom mentioned.

---

13 Clarence was later abel to get the local Bishop's blessing on the non-Oxford Group approach found in AA

It was not the only conflict within the early fellowship. Akron members complained that the New York fellowship and the New York members claimed that the Akron fellowship was unrealistic.

When the time came for the first international convention of representatives of the growing Alcoholics Anonymous, the conflict prevented either New York or Akron from hosting the historic gathering.

Cleveland served as the neutral ground for this first major gathering of the fellowship.

This is not to say there is no controversy with Clarence's role in the growth of Alcoholics Anonymous. Clarence himself seemed to enjoy the attention he received from making statements that outraged the people who were far from the Cleveland area, and his followers in Cleveland were vocal in their support.

For example, Clarence would introduce himself as "the man who founded AA" or make no comment when someone else made the claim. He is recognized as one of the first forty people to get long term sobriety and he did create the first meeting to be free of Oxford Group constraints. He called his group 'Alcoholics Anonymous', but it was named after the book. The name 'Alcoholics Anonymous' was established before the writing of the book following the first institutional meeting in New Jersey, credited to an alcoholic patient named Joe Worther, and it was being used by Rev. Shoemaker of the Calvary Mission immediately after that.

Clarence was very specifric in his dislike of Bill Wilson and anything he did. In particular, Clarence disliked the Traditions Bill proposed and was vocal about his resistance to adopting them. It is also said that he felt Dr. Bob never should have agreed to presenting them.

Clarence seemed to enjoy the controversy he created and was recorded several times making fun of the Traditions and anyone who approached Recovery in any way different from his own approach. He introduced himself with his full name, mocked anonymity and ridiculed anything Bill presented.

But it should also be said that there are rumors that Bill Wilson may have had an affair with Clarence's wife Grace. These stories were also told by Grace herself, according to some of her Sponsees. While AA does not encourage acting on resentments, it might make Clarence's opposition understandable.

Clarence's followers in the Cleveland area meetings encouraged the positions championed by the man who brought Recovery to Cleveland, and who did so many good things for the growth of the fellowship.

And he was to have a significant supporter after a sad episode in New York.

Hank Parkhurst Goes to Cleveland

Within a few months of the publication of the Big Book, Hank Parkhurst, the man who was pivotal in getting the book completed, relapsed. Hank had hoped the Big Book would create a cash flow, which he needed. His auto polish business, which employed Bill Wilson and Jimmie Burwell, was failing. His secretary took Bill Wilson's handwritten sheets and typed them.

Hank put together the 'Multilith' edition to raise money, but it did not succeed. Instead this set of copies of the original manuscript became the source of comment from the fellowship, which shaped the final verson of the Big Book, but did not produce any income.

The publication of the Big Book, given as April 1, 1939, was another disappointment. The book did not sell. One woman bought one copy on the condition that members in Akron and New York autograph the frontpiece14, but the expected cashflow did not materialize.

Hank began drinking after the publication of the book, and became an active opponent of Bill Wilson. He went to Cleveland while drinking and fed more information to Clarence Snyder, which fed Clarence's public pronouncements against Bill.

For example, John D. Rockefeller provided a $5,000 account with a New York bank. This account was not accessible to Bill or Bob, directly, and was administered by a local clergyman, but it was to be used to provide support for the early fellowship. This took the form of a stipend for Bill and Bob and $3,000 was used to pay off Dr. Bob's mortgage. The whole amount was repaid as one of the first obligations of the AA service structure.

But Hank told Clarence that Bill and Bob had stolen $40,000 from the account, and Clarence repeated the accusation. Over time the amount became even more inflated, and it was great fodder to feed the controversy.

Hank returned to New Jersey and made it back to the program, temporarily. He relapsed again and died in January of 1954. Lois Wilson said that he was drinking at the time, and there is also evidence of prescription drug abuse.

---

14 This copy is now in the archives at the New York offices of Alcoholics Anonymous.

Clarence After Hank

When Hank Parkhurst returned to New Jersey, Clarence continued his opposition to Bill Wilson. This led to an angry exchange of letters with the Alcoholic Foundation (precursor of the AA World Service Organization) and Clarence's resignation from the Cleveland Service Board in 1944. This incident has been used by anti-AA voices on the Internet.

Clarence, however, became a respected 'elder statesman' of AA's early days and a sought-after speaker at meetings and events until his death in 1984. In particular his work modeling the creation of local AA meetings, his guidance in creating the foundations of modern , and his adherence to a strictly Christian interpretation of AA, remain points of appreciation in many areas.

Some of Clarence's talks were recorded and can be heard through xa-speakers.org on the internet.

But Clarence's followers continued to play a part in maintaining a darker view of AA's early days, and Bill Wilson in particular.

For example, it was widely circulated that Bill Wilson's philandering caused local groups to create a protective squad to keep Wilson away from the local woman when he was in town to speak.. Dr. Ernie Kurtz reported that his research showed that none of the cities where such squads had been formed knew anything about the story. Bill Wilson had come to town, spoke and left without the local flower of womenhood being threatened.

But the story continues to circulate.

At this point Dr. Kurtz chose to make a point about attempts at getting to the 'real' story in any historical research. When you encounter this kind of 'two story' conflict, it becomes an effort to understand that each side of the story has a reason for its proponents to tell the tale the way they do. He suggested that all sides of a story be told and the job of an historian is to share what he found.

Recovery Rate = 1

If you stay around AA for any length of time, you will start to hear statistics. People will say only a certain number of drunks get sober and stay sober. Sometimes you will hear 1-in-50, or 1-in-17, or 1 in 5. Other numbers are spread around.

Or you will hear numbers for the fellowship. There are five million people involved in Alcoholics Anonymous. Or twelve million. Or one hundred million.

The question comes up - where do these number come from?

Are these from treatment centers or from the actual 12-Step fellowship?

Are the numbers from insurance companies?

Are the numbers from someone with a very specific bias for, or against, 12-Step Recovery?

Did you ever have to report your membership to anyone?

Did you have to reveal how long you have been sober?

There is a number for people coming into the fellowship to know. It is the only number that really matters.

One.

You.

The statistics of Recovery reduce down to the only Recovery that matters - yours.

Be the one. It doesn't matter one-in-how-many…just be the one.

More Than Words

WHAT THE WORDS MEAN

More Than Words is one of those documents you find on the internet that does not carry identification of the source and status. We are making the call to share the information exactly as it was made available. We make no claims on authorship and there is no copyright showing. The Recovery Reader is released through Creative Commons to be shared with the fellowship.

If you are the copyright owner or have more information on when and where this series of resources was produced or used, please get in touch with us at Sponsormagazine@gmail.com.

Big Book Seminar 1991

MORE THAN WORDS

12 Steps of Alcoholics Anonymous:
Are you sure you know what those words mean?

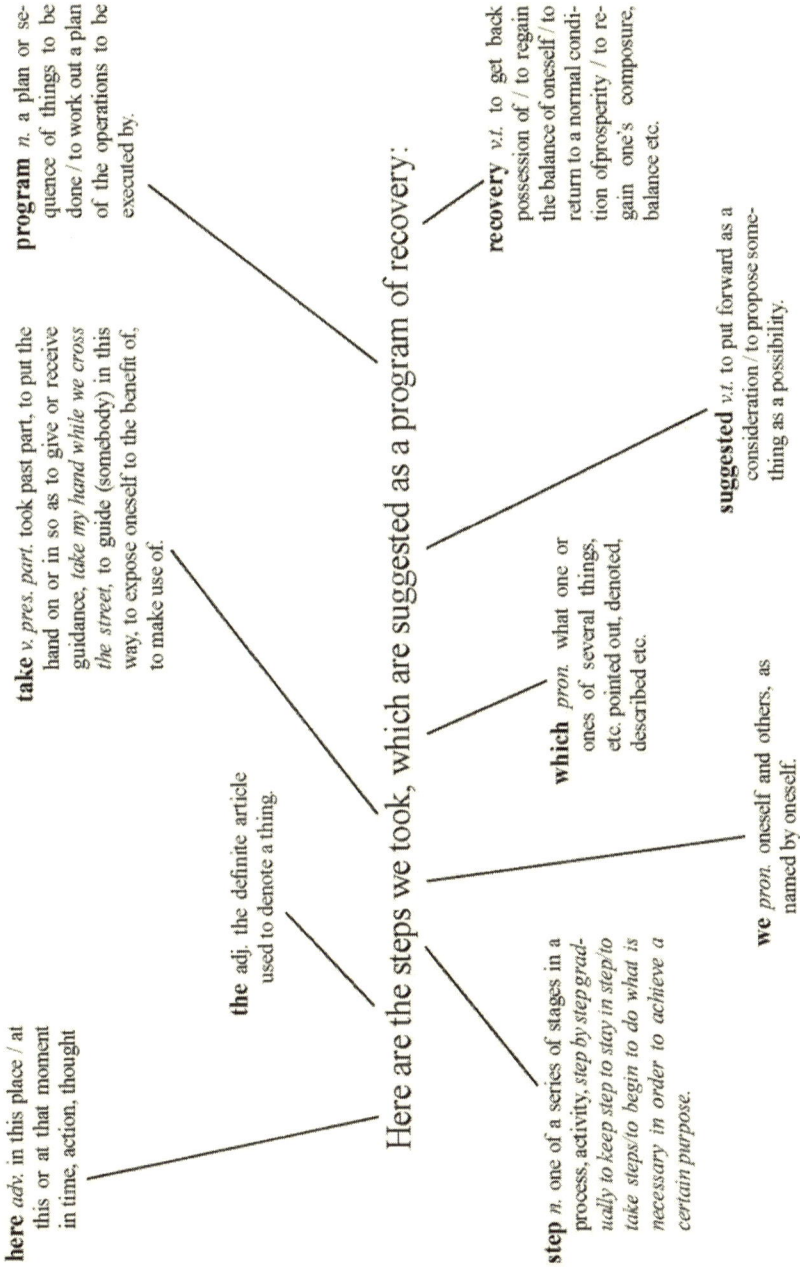

program *n.* a plan or sequence of things to be done / to work out a plan of the operations to be executed by.

recovery *v.t.* to get back possession of / / to regain the balance of oneself / to return to a normal condition of prosperity / to regain one's composure, balance etc.

take *v. pres. part.* took past part. to put the hand on or in so as to give or receive guidance, *take my hand while we cross the street*, to guide (somebody) in this way, to expose oneself to the benefit of, to make use of.

suggested *v.t.* to put forward as a consideration / to propose something as a possibility.

Here are the steps we took, which are suggested as a program of recovery:

which *pron.* what one or ones of several things, etc. pointed out, denoted, described etc.

the adj. the definite article used to denote a thing.

we *pron.* oneself and others, as named by oneself.

here *adv.* in this place / at this or at that moment in time, action, thought

step *n.* one of a series of stages in a process, activity, *step by step gradually to keep step to stay in step/to take steps/to begin to do what is necessary in order to achieve a certain purpose.*

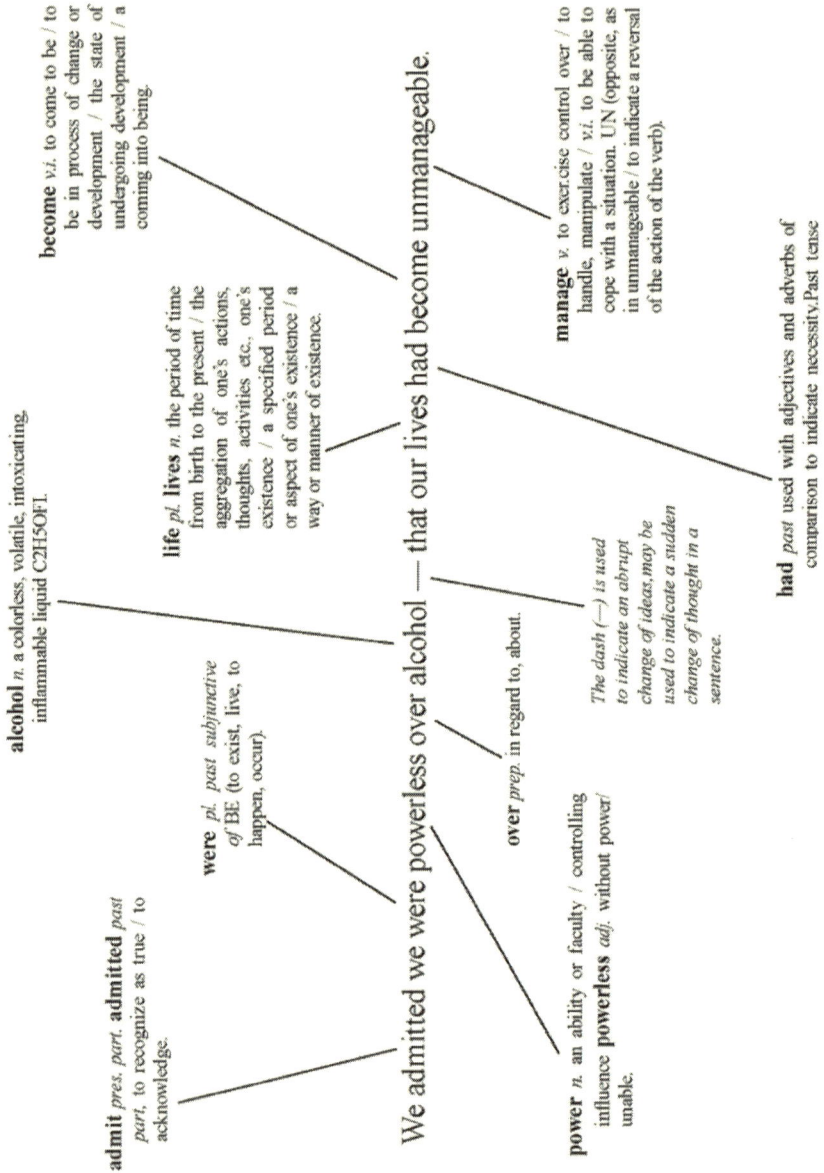

become *v.i.* to come to be / to be in process of change or development / the state of undergoing development / a coming into being.

manage *v.* to exercise control over / to handle, manipulate / *v.i.* to be able to cope with a situation. UN (opposite, as in unmanageable/ to indicate a reversal of the action of the verb).

life *pl.* **lives** *n.* the period of time from birth to the present / the aggregation of one's actions, thoughts, activities etc., one's existence / a specified period or aspect of one's existence / a way or manner of existence.

alcohol *n.* a colorless, volatile, intoxicating, inflammable liquid C_2H_5OH.

had *past* used with adjectives and adverbs of comparison to indicate necessity. Past tense

were *pl. past subjunctive of* BE (to exist, live, to happen, occur).

The dash (—) is used to indicate an abrupt change of ideas, may be used to indicate a sudden change of thought in a sentence.

over *prep.* in regard to, about.

admit *pres. part.* **admitted** *past part.* to recognize as true / to acknowledge.

power *n.* an ability or faculty / controlling influence **powerless** *adj.* without power/ unable.

We admitted we were powerless over alcohol — that our lives had become unmanageable.

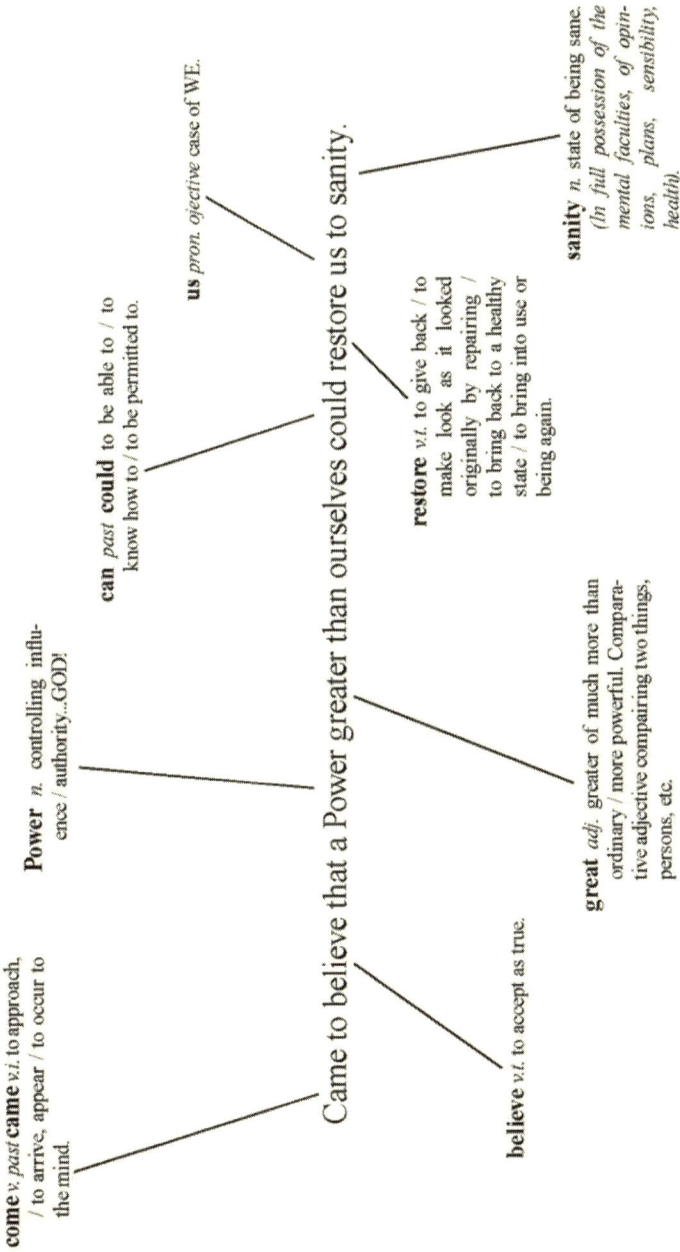

Came to believe that a Power greater than ourselves could restore us to sanity.

come *v. past* **came** *v.i.* to approach, / to arrive, appear / to occur to the mind.

believe *v.t.* to accept as true.

Power *n.* controlling influence / authority...GOD!

great *adj.* greater of much more than ordinary / more powerful. Comparative adjective comparing two things, persons, etc.

can *past* **could** to be able to / to know how to / to be permitted to.

restore *v.t.* to give back / to make look as it looked originally by repairing / to bring back to a healthy state / to bring into use or being again.

us *pron. ojective* case of WE.

sanity *n.* state of being sane. *(in full possession of the mental faculties, of opinions, plans, sensibility, health).*

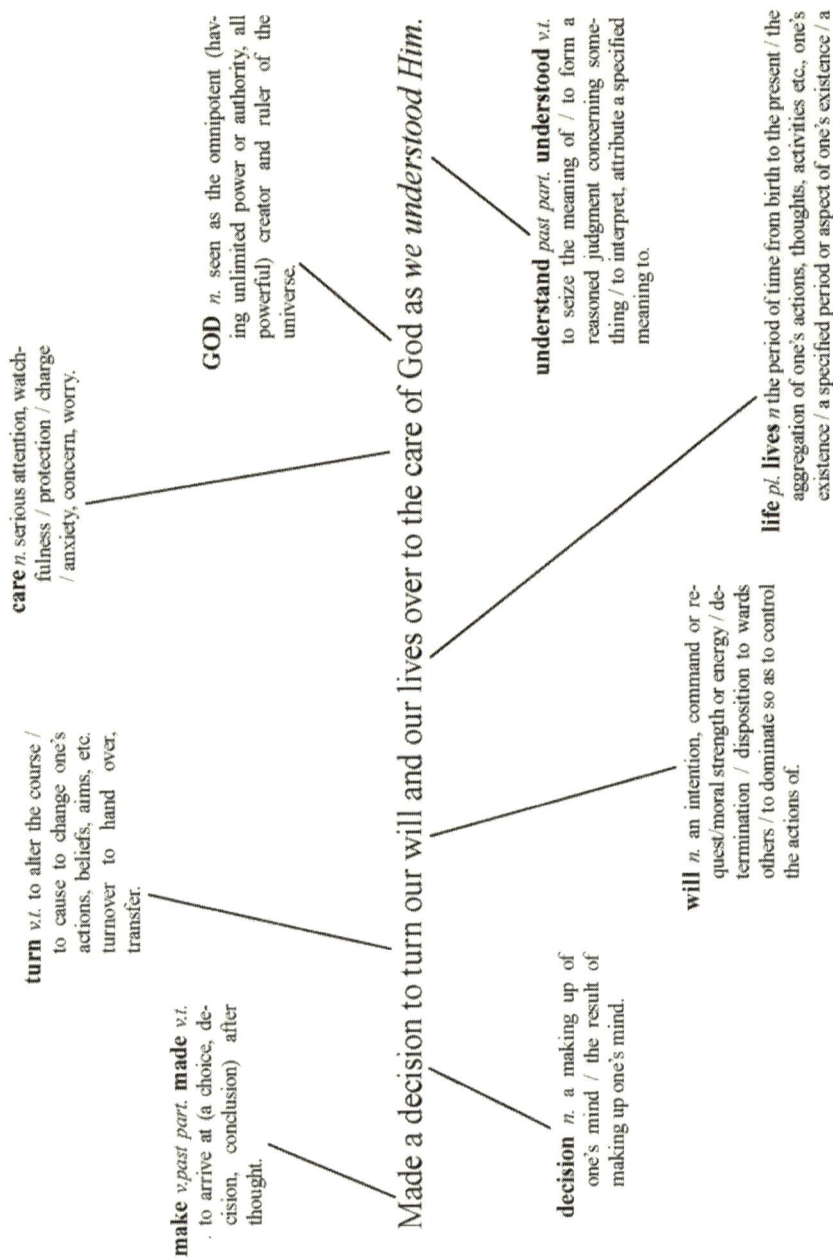

care *n.* serious attention, watchfulness / protection / charge / anxiety, concern, worry.

GOD *n.* seen as the omnipotent (having unlimited power or authority, all powerful) creator and ruler of the universe.

understand *past part.* **understood** *v.t.* to seize the meaning of / to form a reasoned judgment concerning something / to interpret, attribute a specified meaning to.

life *pl.* **lives** *n* the period of time from birth to the present / the aggregation of one's actions, thoughts, activities etc., one's existence / a specified period or aspect of one's existence / a

turn *v.t.* to alter the course / to cause to change one's actions, beliefs, aims, etc. turnover to hand over, transfer.

make *v.past part.* **made** *v.t.* to arrive at (a choice, decision, conclusion) after thought.

Made a decision to turn our will and our lives over to the care of God as *we understood Him.*

decision *n.* a making up of one's mind / the result of making up one's mind.

will *n.* an intention, command or request/moral strength or energy / determination / disposition to wards others / to dominate so as to control the actions of.

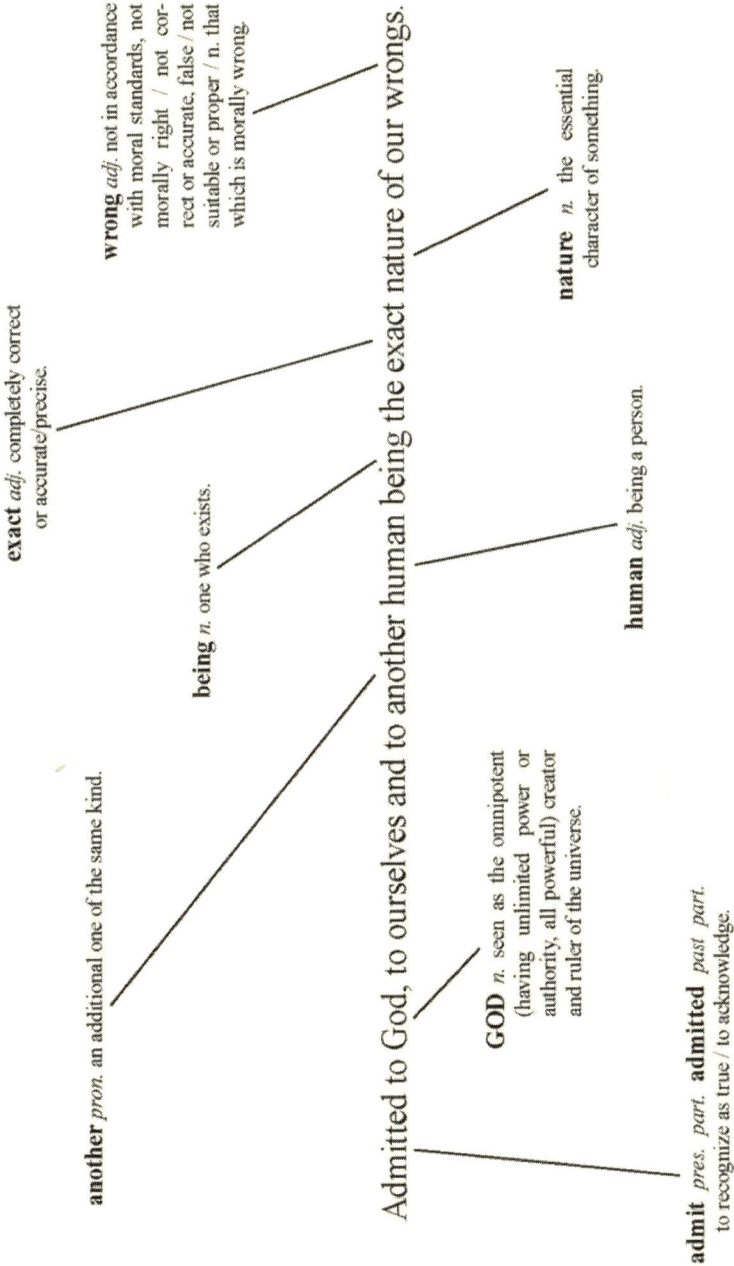

Admitted to God, to ourselves and to another human being the exact nature of our wrongs.

wrong *adj.* not in accordance with moral standards, not morally right / not correct or accurate, false / not suitable or proper / n. that which is morally wrong.

exact *adj.* completely correct or accurate/precise.

being *n.* one who exists.

nature *n.* the essential character of something.

human *adj.* being a person.

another *pron.* an additional one of the same kind.

GOD *n.* seen as the omnipotent (having unlimited power or authority, all powerful) creator and ruler of the universe.

admit *pres. part.* **admitted** *past part.* to recognize as true / to acknowledge.

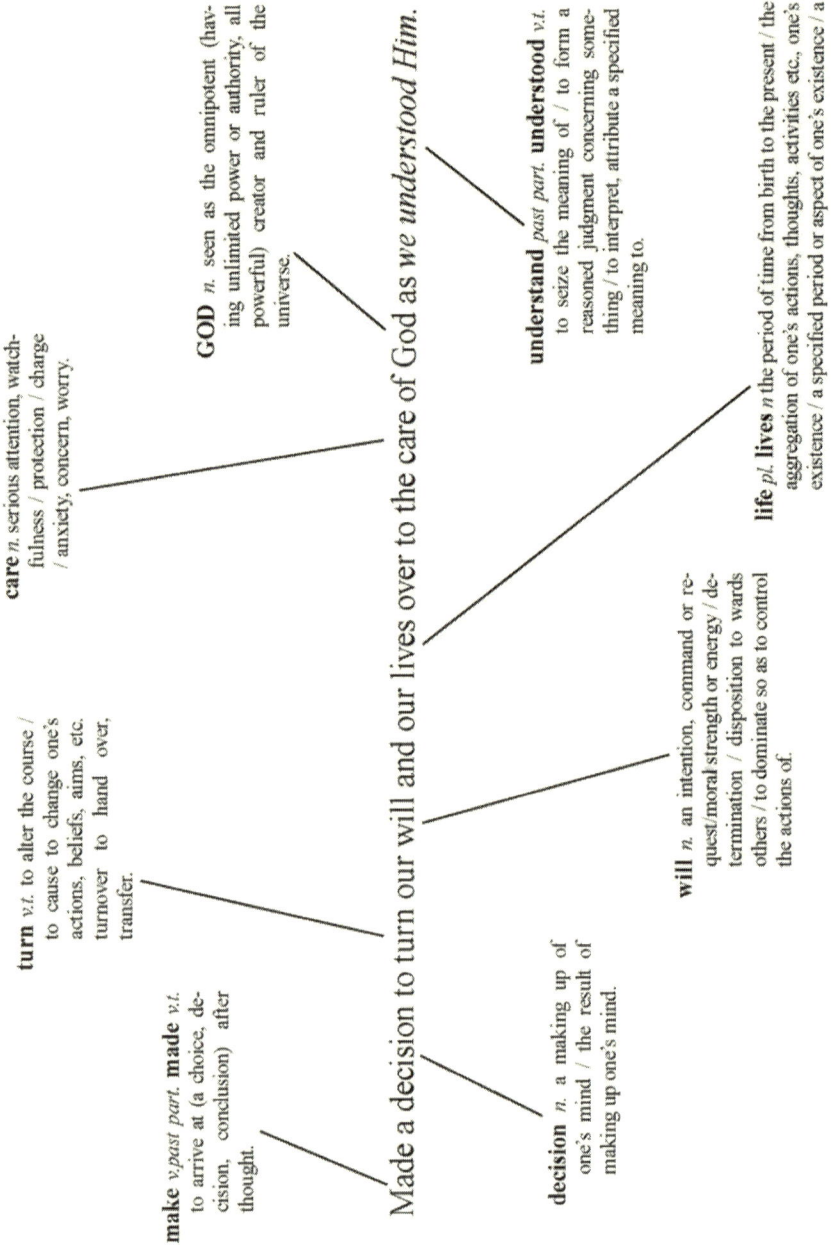

care *n.* serious attention, watchfulness / protection / charge / anxiety, concern, worry.

GOD *n.* seen as the omnipotent (having unlimited power or authority; all powerful) creator and ruler of the universe.

understand *past part.* **understood** *v.t.* to seize the meaning of / to form a reasoned judgment concerning something / to interpret, attribute a specified meaning to.

life *pl.* **lives** *n* the period of time from birth to the present / the aggregation of one's actions, thoughts, activities etc., one's existence / a specified period or aspect of one's existence / a

Made a decision to turn our will and our lives over to the care of God as *we understood Him.*

turn *v.t.* to alter the course / to cause to change one's actions, beliefs, aims, etc. turnover to hand over, transfer.

make *v.past part.* **made** *v.t.* to arrive at (a choice, decision, conclusion) after thought.

decision *n.* a making up of one's mind / the result of making up one's mind.

will *n.* an intention, command or request/moral strength or energy / determination / disposition to wards others / to dominate so as to control the actions of.

search adj. *searching* to go or look over or through in order to find something, gain information, etc.

moral *adj.* concerned with right and wrong and the distinctions between them.

of *prep.* originating or comming from.

inventory *n.* an itemized list / the making of such a list.

fear *n.* the instinctive emotion aroused by impending or seeming danger, pain or evil / **fearless** *adj.* having no fear.

Made a searching and fearless moral inventory of ourselves.

shortcoming *n.* a failure to reach an expected or desired standard of conduct or outcome.

defect *n.* a shortcoming, inadequacy / a fault, blemish.

character *n.* the total quality of a person's behavior, as revealed in his habits of thought and expression, his attitudes and interests, his actions, and his personal philosophy of life.

have *v.* to experience, undergo / let / to permit / to engage in some activity.

all *adj.* the whole quantity.

remove *pres.* to move from a place / to eliminate, to take out.

Were entirely ready to have God remove all these defects of character.

ready *adj.* a state fit for immediate action / in an emotional state adapted to a possible set of circumstances, willing / the state of being fit or poised for immediate action or use.

entirely *adj.* whole and complete, absolute / *adv.* wholly and completely.

shortcoming *n.* a failure to reach an expected or desired standard of conduct or outcome.

remove *pres.* eliminate, to move from a place / to take out.

him *pron.* GOD.

Humbly asked Him to remove our shortcomings.

ask *v.t.* to request / to make a request.

humble *adj.* **humbly** in a humble way / possessing or marked by the virtue of humility / humble oneself to perform an act of submission by way of apology or penitence.

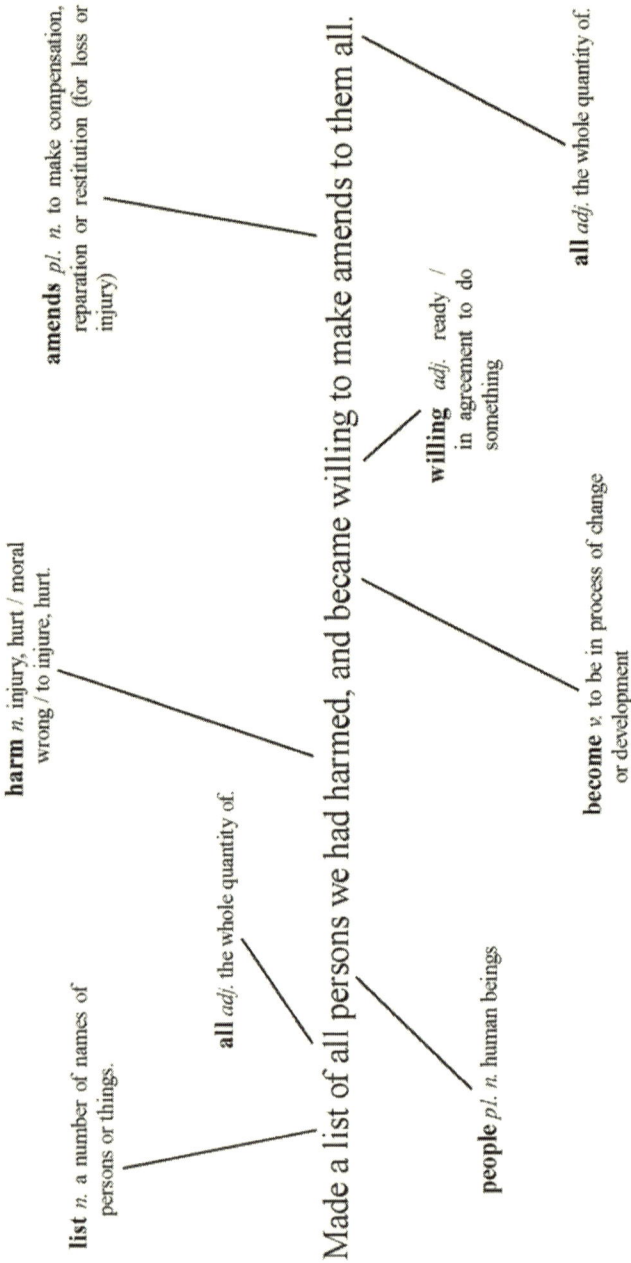

Made a list of all persons we had harmed, and became willing to make amends to them all.

amends *pl. n.* to make compensation, reparation or restitution (for loss or injury)

all *adj.* the whole quantity of.

willing *adj.* ready / in agreement to do something

become *v.* to be in process of change or development

harm *n.* injury, hurt / moral wrong / to injure, hurt.

all *adj.* the whole quantity of.

list *n.* a number of names of persons or things.

people *pl. n.* human beings

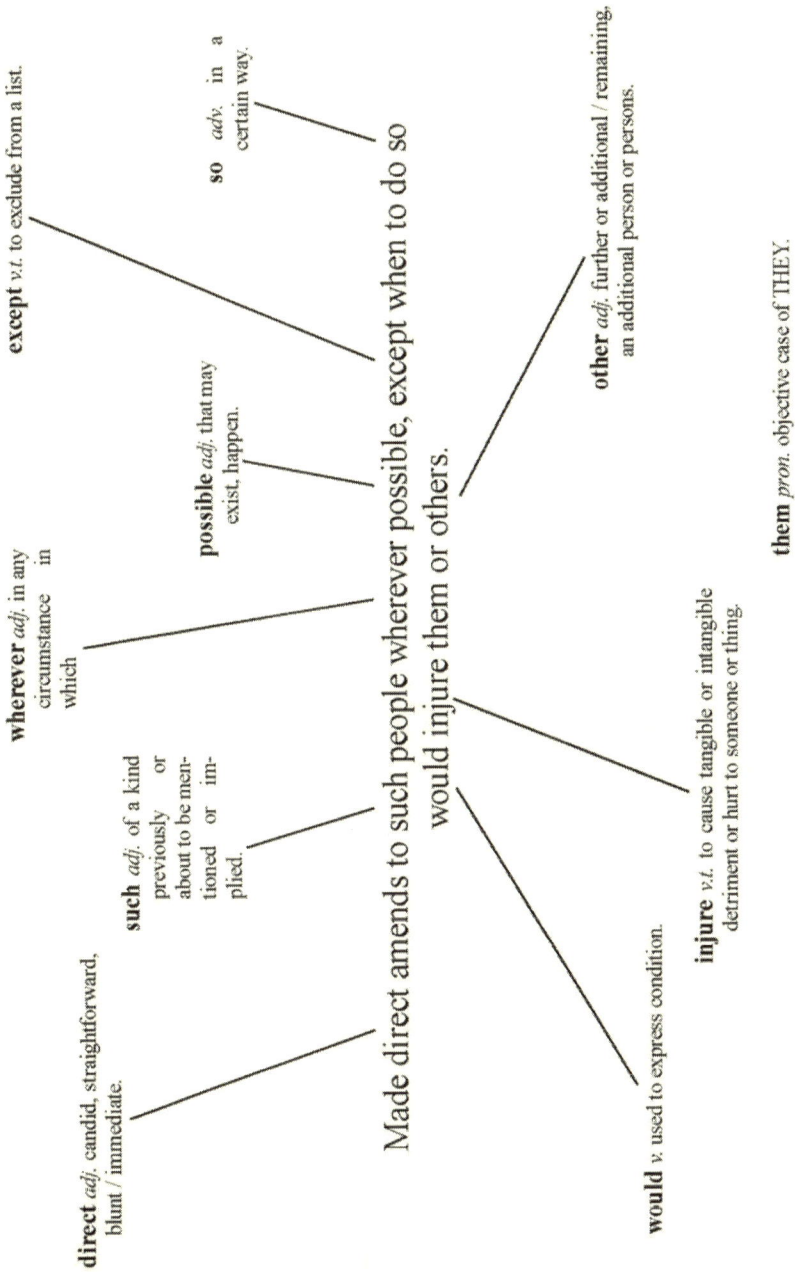

except *v.t.* to exclude from a list.

so *adv.* in a certain way.

possible *adj.* that may exist, happen.

wherever *adj.* in any circumstance in which

other *adj.* further or additional / remaining, an additional person or persons.

such *adj.* of a kind previously or about to be mentioned or implied.

direct *adj.* candid, straightforward, blunt / immediate.

Made direct amends to such people wherever possible, except when to do so would injure them or others.

injure *v.t.* to cause tangible or intangible detriment or hurt to someone or thing

would *v.* used to express condition.

them *pron.* objective case of THEY.

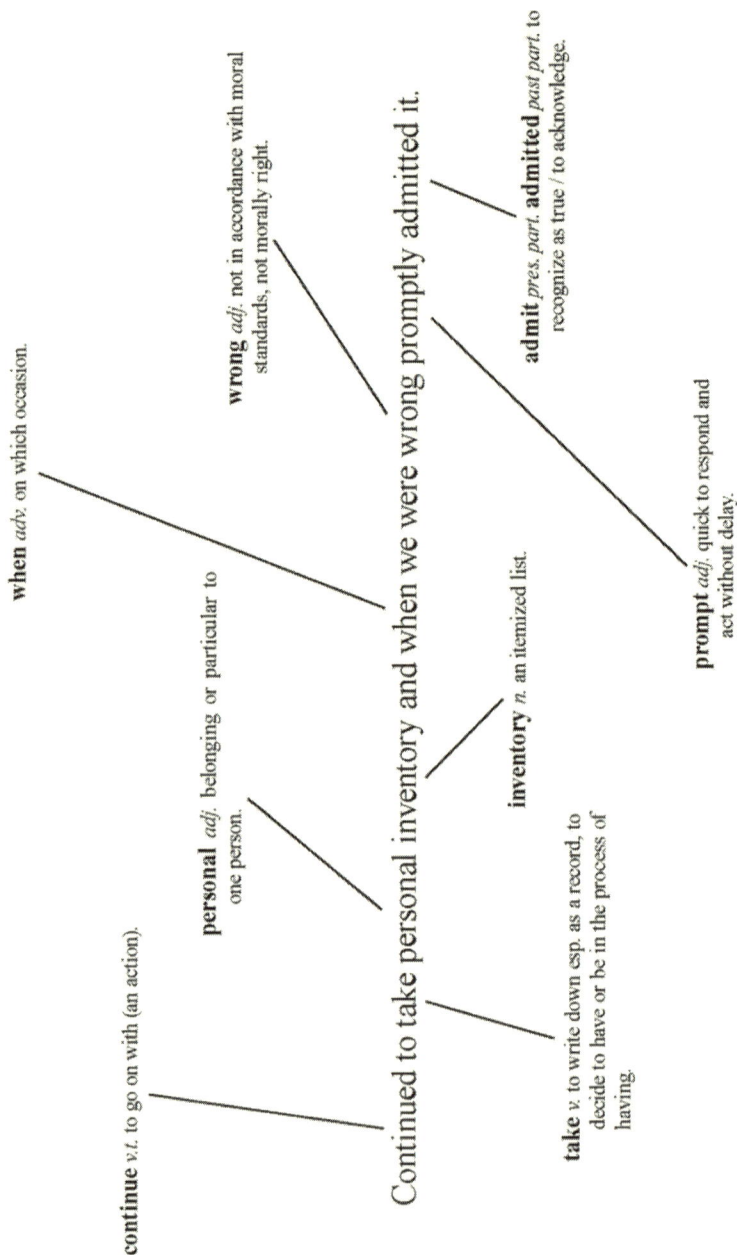

when *adv.* on which occasion.

wrong *adj.* not in accordance with moral standards, not morally right.

admit *pres. part.* **admitted** *past part.* to recognize as true / to acknowledge.

personal *adj.* belonging or particular to one person.

inventory *n.* an itemized list.

prompt *adj.* quick to respond and act without delay.

Continued to take personal inventory and when we were wrong promptly admitted it.

continue *v.t.* to go on with (an action).

take *v.* to write down esp. as a record, to decide to have or be in the process of having.

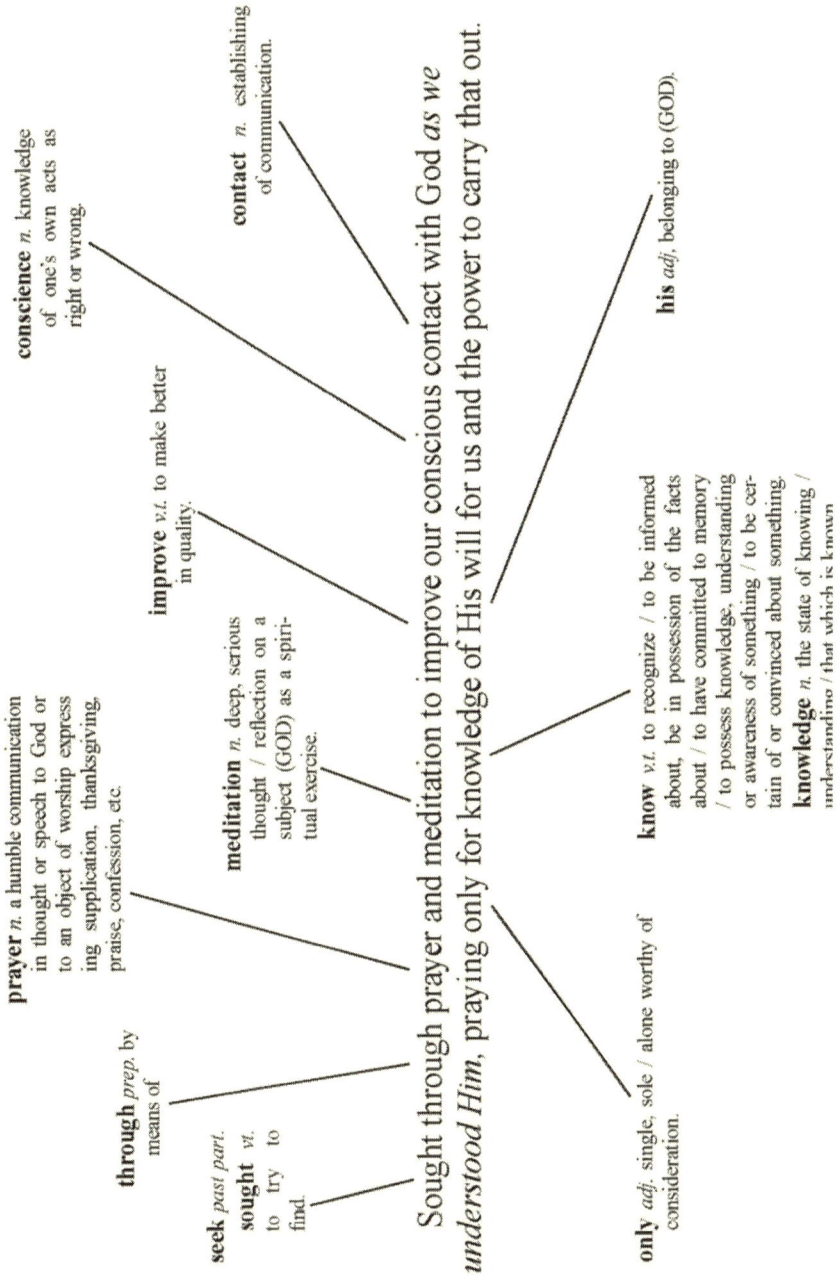

conscience *n.* knowledge of one's own acts as right or wrong.

contact *n.* establishing of communication.

his *adj.* belonging to (GOD).

improve *v.t.* to make better in quality.

prayer *n.* a humble communication in thought or speech to God or to an object of worship expressing supplication, thanksgiving, praise, confession, etc.

meditation *n.* deep, serious thought / reflection on a subject (GOD) as a spiritual exercise.

through *prep.* by means of

seek *past part.* **sought** *v.t.* to try to find.

Sought through prayer and meditation to improve our conscious contact with God *as we understood Him*, praying only for knowledge of His will for us and the power to carry that out.

only *adj.* single, sole / alone worthy of consideration.

know *v.t.* to recognize / to be informed about, be in possession of the facts about / to have committed to memory / to possess knowledge, understanding or awareness of something / to be certain of or convinced about something.

knowledge *n.* the state of knowing / understanding / that which is known

Having had a spiritual awakening as the result of these steps, we tried to carry this message to alcoholics and to practice these principles in all our affairs.

try *v.* to attempt to do / to test experimentally.

affair *n.* daily concerns.

principle *n.* a law of nature as formulated and accepted by the mind / the acceptance of moral law as a guide to behavior.

awakening *n.* a realization of circumstances / an arousal of interest or activity.

practice *v.* repeated performance or systematic exercise for the purpose of learning or acquiring proficiency.

spiritual *adj.* of, relating to, or concerned with the soul or spirit / the intelligent or immaterial part of man as distinguished from the body/the moral nature of a man I a supernatural being, usually regarded as invisible but as having the power to become visible at will/a specified mental or emotional attitude characterizing words, actions, opinions, etc.

message *n.* inspired revelation / ethical or spiritual teaching.

References

A few lists for quick access to additional information about, for, and by people in long term recovery.

Various Internet Sources

Dr. Robert Smith with Bill Wilson, the 'co-founders' of Alcoholics Anonymous

AA Chronology

This list has been drawn from many sources and is offered for general references.

July 22, 1877 – William Duncan Silkworth is born in Brooklyn, NY.

August 8, 1879 – Dr. Bob is born in St. Johnsbury, VT.

March 21, 1881 – Anne R., Dr. Bob's wife, is born.

January 2, 1889 – Sister Ignatia, is born in Ballyhane, Ireland.

August 15, 1890 – E M Jellinek, author of "The Disease Concept of Alcoholism" and the "Jellinek Curve is born ."

March 4, 1891 – Lois W. is born.

December 27, 1893 – Rev. Samuel Shoemaker is born.

November 26, 1895 – Bill W. is born in East Dorsett, VT.

March 25, 1898 – Jim B. ("The Vicious Cycle") is born.

October 15, 1904 – Marty M., early AA woman, is born in Chicago.

February 1908 – Bill makes boomerang.

January 25, 1915 – Dr. Bob marries Anne Ripley.

January 24, 1918 – Bill marries Lois Burnham in the Swedenborgen Church in Brookyn Heights, NY.

February 15, 1918 – Sue Smith Windows, Dr. Bob's adopted daughter, is born.

May 1919 – Bill returns home from service.

October 20, 1928 – Bill writes promise to Lois in family Bible to quit drinking. By Thanksgiving adds second promise.

January 1929 – Bill writes third promise in Bible to quit drinking.

September, 1930 – Bill writes 4th (last) promise in family Bible to quit drinking.

August 1934 – Rowland H. and Cebra persuade court to parole Ebby T. to them.

November 1934 – Ebby T. carries message to Bill.

November 11, 1934 – Armistice Day; Bill starts drinking after dry spell, beginning of Bill's last drunk.

December 1934 – Bill & Lois start attending Oxford Group meetings.

December 11, 1934 – Bill admitted to Towns Hosp for the 4th and last time (fall '33, '34 in summer, midsummer, and final admittance). Bill's last drink is one beer he brought with him to Towns.

December 12, 1934 – Bill has Spiritual Experience at Towns Hospital.

December 13 or 14, 1934 – Ebby visits Bill at hospital, brings William James's book, "Varieties of Religious Experience."

December 1934 to May 1935 – Bill works with alcoholics, but none of them get sober. Lois reminds him HE is sober.

April 1935 – Dr. Silkworth tells Bill to quit preaching at drunks & tell them of obsession & allergy.

May 11, 1935 – Bill W. makes calls from the Mayflower Hotel and is referred to Dr. Bob.

May 12, 1935 @ 5 pm – Bill W. meets Dr. Bob at the home of Henrietta Seiberling.

June 10, 1935 – The date that is celebrated as Dr. Bob's last drink and the official founding date of AA. There is some evidence that the founders, in trying to reconstruct the history, got the date wrong and it was actually June 17.

June 26, 1935 – Bill Dotson (AA #3) enters Akron's City Hospital for his last detox and his first day of sobriety.

June 28, 1935 – Dr. Bob and Bill Wilson visit Bill Dotson at Akron's City Hospital.

October 17, 1935 – Ebby T., Bill's Sponsor, moves in with Bill and Lois.

December 1955 – 'Man on the Bed' painting by Robert M. first appears in Grapevine. Painting originally called 'Came to Believe'.

March 1936 – AA has ten members staying sober. At end of 1936, AA has 15 members.

October 1936 – Bill C., a Canadian alchy staying at Bill's house, commits suicide using a gas stove.

November 1936 – Fitz M. leaves Towns Hospital to become 'AA #3 in NY', with Bill W. and Hank P.

January 15, 1937 – Fitz M. brings AA meetings to Washington, DC.

February 11, 1937 – First New Jersey meeting is held at the home of Hank P. ("The Unbeliever" in the first edition). Some sources report this as happening February 13, 1937.

September 13, 1937 – Florence R., 1st female in AA in NY.

November 1937 – Bill and Dr. Bob compare notes in Akron; count forty cases staying sober. The meeting of the Akron Group considers Bill's ideas for how to expand the movement ... a book, AA hospitals, paid missionaries. It passed by a majority of 2.

December 12, 1937 – Bill meets with Rockefeller Foundation and tries to get money.

December 13, 1937 – Rockland State Mental Hospital takes patients to meeting in New Jersey.

February 11, 1938 – Clarence S. ("Home Brewmeister" 1st -3rd edition) sobriety date.

March-May 1938 – Bill begins writing the book Alcoholics Anonymous. Works Publishing Inc. established to support writing and printing of book.

April 11, 1938 – The Alcoholic Foundation is formed as a trusteeship for AA (sometimes reported as May 1938).

May 1, 1939 – Bank forecloses on 182 Clinton Street. (Sometimes reported as April 26, 1939.)

June 16, 1938 – Jim Burwell, "The Vicious Cycle" in Big Book, has his last drink.

June 24, 1938 – Two Rockefeller associates tell the press about the Big Book "Not to bear any author's name but to be by 'Alcoholics Anonymous.'"

August 11, 1938 – Akron & NY members begin writing stories for Big Book.

July 15, 1938 –The first documented use of name Alcoholics Anonymous; AA archives letter from Bill to Willard Richardson.

July 18, 1938 – In letter to Dr. Richards at Johns Hopkins, Bill uses Alcoholics Anonymous as working title for Big Book & name for the fellowship.

September 21, 1938 – Bill W. & Hank P. form Works Publishing Co.

December 1938 – Twelve Steps is written.

January 1939 – 400 copies of manuscript of Big Book are circulated for comment, evaluation, and sale.

January 3, 1939 – First sale of Works Publishing Co. stock is recorded.

January 8, 1938 – New York AA splits from the Oxford Group.

February 1939 – Dr. Harry Tiebout, becomes the 1st psychiatrist to endorse AA and use it in his practice.

February 1939 – Dr. Howard of Montclair, NJ suggests swapping "you must" for "we ought" in the Big Book.

February 5, 1939 – Dr. Bob tells Ruth Hock in a letter that AA has "to get away from the Oxford Group atmosphere."

March 1, 1939 – Readers Digest fails to write article on AA.

April 1, 1939 – Publication date of Alcoholics Anonymous, AA's Big Book.

April 10, 1939 – The first ten copies of the Big Book arrive at the office Bill and Hank P. shared.

April 24, 1989 – Dr. Leonard Strong dies.

April 25, 1939 – Morgan R. is interviewed on Gabriel Heatter radio show.

April 26 or May 1, 1939 – Bank forecloses on 182 Clinton Street.

May 1939 – Lois W. Home Replacement Fund starts as Alcoholic Foundation.

May 6, 1939 – Clarence S. of Cleveland tells Dr. Bob, his Sponsor, he will not go back to Oxford Group meetings in Akron and will start an "AA" meeting in Cleveland.

May 10, 1939 – Clarence S. announces to the Akron Oxford Group members that the Cleveland members are starting a meeting in Cleveland and calling it Alcoholics Anonymous.

May 11, 1939 – First group to officially call itself Alcoholics Anonymous meets at Abby G.'s house in Cleveland (some sources say the 18th).

June 7, 1939 – Bill and Lois Wilson have an argument, the first of two times Bill almost slipped.

June 25, 1939 – The New York Times reviewer writes that the Big Book is "more soundly based psychologically than any other treatment I have ever come upon."

July 1939 – Warren C. joins AA Cleveland, causes debate because he was not hospitalized.

July 4, 1939 –The first AA meeting starts in Flatbush, NY.

July 14, 1939 – Dr. Tiebout gives Big Book to Marty M. who promptly throws it back at him.

August 1939 – Dr. Bob writes & may have signed article for Faith magazine.

August 16, 1939 – Dr. Bob and Sister Ignatia admit 1st alcoholic to St. Thomas Hospital, Akron, Ohio.

September 1, 1939 –The first AA group founded in Chicago by Earl T.

September 30, 1939 – Article appears in Liberty magazine, "Alcoholics and God" by Morris Markey.

October 1939 –The first central committee formed in Cleveland; 1st example AA rotation.

October 14, 1939 – Journal of American Medical Association gives Big Book unfavorable review.

October 21, 1939 – Cleveland Plain Dealer begins series of articles on AA by Elrick Davis.

November/December 1939 – Akron group withdraws from association with Oxford Group. Meetings moved from T. Henry & Clarence Williams to Dr. Bob and other members' homes.

November 13, 1939 – Bill wants to go to work at Towns Hosp, NY. Drunks want him to stay on as head of the movement.

November 21, 1939 – AA's in San Francisco hold 1st California AA meeting in the Clift Hotel.

November 26, 1939 – Dilworth Lupton gives sermon "Mr. X and Alcoholics Anonymous." It becomes one of first pamphlets on AA.

November 28, 1939 – Hank P. writes Bill advocating autonomy for all AA groups.

December 1939 – The first AA group in mental institution, Rockland State Hospital, NY.

December 1939 – The first home meeting in Los Angeles at Kaye M.'s house.

December 1939 – Matt Talbot Club has 88 members, uses wagons to collect old furniture to recondition & sell, not AA, uses AA program material, marks 1st effort reach alcoholics outside married middle-class catEgory.

December 6, 1939 – Bert the Tailor lends Works Publishing $1000.

January 4, 1940 – The first AA group formed in Detroit, Michigan.

January 10, 1940 – The first AA meeting not in a home meets at King School, Akron, Ohio.

February 1940 – The first AA clubhouse opens at 334-1/2 West 24th Street, NYC.

February 8, 1940 – Rockefeller dinner.

February 8, 1940 – Houston Press runs first of six anonymous articles on AA by Larry J.

February 28, 1940 – First organization meeting of Philadelphia AA is held at McCready Huston's room at 2209 Delancy Street.

March 1940 – Mort J. comes to LA from Denver; starts custom of reading Chapter 5 from the Big Book at Cecil Group.

March 7, 1940 – Bill and Lois visit the Philadelphia AA group. Any drunk who wants to get well is more than welcome at the AA meeting at 115 Newbury St., at 8 PM Wednesdays.

March 16, 1940 – Alcoholic Foundation & Works Publishing move from Newark to 30 Vesey St. in lower Manhattan. First headquarters of its own.

April 1, 1940 – Larry J. of Houston, writes "The Texas Prayer," used to open AA meetings in Texas.

April 16, 1940 – A sober Rollie H. catches the first opening day no-hitter in baseball history since 1909.

April 19, 1940 – The first AA group in Little Rock, Arkansas, is formed. First 'mail order' group.

April 22, 1940 – Bill and Hank transfer their Works Publishing stock to the Alcoholic Foundation.

April 23, 1940 – Dr. Bob writes the Trustees to refuse Big Book royalties, but Bill W. insists that Dr. Bob and Anne receive them.

April 24, 1940 – The first AA pamphlet, "AA," is published.

May 1, 1940 – Rollie H., of the Cleveland Indians, is first to break anonymity on national level.

May 4, 1940 – Sunday Star reports founding of first AA group in Washington, DC.

June 5, 1940 – Ebby Thacher takes a job at the NY World's Fair.

June 6, 1940 – The first AA Group in Richmond, VA, is formed.

June 15, 1940 – The first AA Group in Baltimore, MD, is formed.

June 18, 1940 – One hundred attend the first meeting in the first AA clubhouse at 334-1/2 West 24th St., New York City.

July 7, 1940 – Bill attends 1st Summer Session at School of Alcohol Studies at Yale University.

July 8, 1940 – The first AA Group is formed in Dayton, Ohio.

July 23, 1940 – Philly AAs send 10% of kitty to Alcoholic Foundation; sets precedent.

September 1940 – AA group is started in Toledo by Duke P. & others.

September 1940 – Journal of Nervous and Mental Diseases gives Big Book unfavorable review.

September 24, 1940 – Bill 12 steps Bobbie V., who later replaced Ruth Hock as his secretary in NY.

November 10, 1940 – The first AA group is formed in Minneapolis.

November 12, 1940 – The first AA meeting is held in Boston.

November 14, 1940 – Alcoholic Foundation publishes 1st AA Bulletin.

December 1940 – The first AA group is formed in St. Louis, Missouri.

December 1940 – Group is started in Ashtabula, Ohio due to Plain Dealer articles. AA Cleveland has about 30 groups.

December 1, 1940 – Chicago Daily Tribune begins a series of articles on AA by Nall Hamilton.

February 15, 1941 – Baltimore Sunday Sun reports that the city's first AA group, begun in June 1940, has grown from 3 to 40 members.

February 20, 1941 – The Toledo Blade publishes first of three articles on AA by Seymour Rothman.

March 1941 – Second printing of Big Book.

March 1941 – The first Prison AA Group is formed at San Quentin.

March 1, 1941 – Jack Alexander's Saturday Evening Post article is published and membership jumps from 2,000 to 8,000 by year's end.

March 7, 1941 – Boston newspaper reports that any drunk who wants can attend that city's first AA meeting.

March 9, 1941 – Wichita Beacon reports AA member from NY who wants to form a group in Wichita.

March 15, 1941 – The first AA group is formed in New Haven, Connecticut. Not reported in paper until Oct 1, 1941.

April 3, 1941 – The first AA meeting is held in Florida.

April 7, 1941 – Ruth Hock reports there are 1,500 letters asking for help as a result of the Saturday Evening Post Article by Jack Alexander.

April 11, 1941 – Bill and Lois finally find a home, Stepping Stones in New Bedford.

April 19, 1941 –The first AA group in the State of Washington is formed in Seattle.

May 1, 1941 –The first Wisconsin AA meeting is held at a hotel in Milwaukee.

May 2, 1941 – Jacksonville, FL newspaper reports the start of an AA group in Jacksonville.

May 3, 1941 – The first AA group in New Orleans, Louisiana, is formed (sometimes dated as May 2, 1943.)

May 3, 1941 – Democrat Chronicle in Rochester, NY, reports first annual AA dinner at Seneca hotel with 60 attending.

May 16, 1941 – Ruth Hock finds that Joe Worth (former publisher of the New Yorker) is credited in Hank Parkhurst's diaries with coming up with the name Alcoholics Anonymous, has a "wet brain."

June 7, 1941 – The first AA Group in St. Paul, Minnesota, is formed.

June 8, 1941 – Three AAs start a group in Kalamazoo, Michigan.

June 30, 1941 – Ruth Hock shows Bill Wilson the Serenity Prayer and it is adopted readily by AA.

July 10, 1941 – Texas newspaper publishes anonymous letter from founding member of Texas AA Group. (Larry J.)

July 20, 1941 – The first AA group is formed in Seattle, Washington.

August 1941 – The first meeting in Orange County, California is held in Anaheim.

August 19, 1941 – The first AA Meeting in Colorado is held in Denver.

September 13, 1941 – WHJP in Jacksonville, FL airs Spotlight on AA.

October 1, 1941 – Local news organizations report 1st AA Group in New Haven, CT.

October 6, 1941 – 900 dine at Cleveland dinner for Dr. Bob.

November 1941 – "First Mass AA Meeting" in Oklahoma City, 8 present.

December 11, 1941 – Dallas Morning News reports 1st AA group is formed in Dallas.

February 1 or 2, 1942 – Ruth Hock, AA's 1st paid secretary, resigns to get married.

May 17, 1942 – The Dayton Journal Herald publishes pictures of AA members wearing masks to protect their anonymity.

May 17, 1942 – New Haven, CT paper has article on AA. Picture shows faces of members sitting in a circle.

June 17, 1942 – New York AA groups Sponsor the first annual NY area meeting. Four hundred and twenty-four hear Dr. Silkworth and AA speakers.

June 19, 1942 – Columnist Earl Wilson reports that NYC Police Chief Valentine sent six policemen to AA and they sobered up. "There are fewer suicides in my files," he comments.

October 1942 – The first issue of Cleveland Central Bulletin is published.

January 1, 1943 – Columbus Dispatch reports 1st Anniversary of Columbus, Ohio Central Group.

January 19, 1943 – The first discussion for starting AA group in Toronto.

February 18, 1943 – During gas rationing in WWII, AAs are granted the right to use cars for 12th step work in emergency cases.

March 29, 1943 – The Charleston Mail, WV, reports on Bill W.'s talk at St. John's Parish House.

May 8, 1943 – Akron AA Group celebrates 8th anniversary with 500 present and sober.

July 23, 1943 – New Haven CT Register reports arrival of AAs to study with E. M. Jellinek.

July 24, 1943 – LA press reports formation of all-Mexican AA Group.

August 1, 1943 – Washington Times-Herald (DC) reports on AA clubhouse; to protect anonymity withholds address.

August 9, 1943 – LA groups announce 1000 members in 11 groups.

October 10, 1943 – 6 of 1st 9 AAs attend clubhouse anniversary in Toledo.

October 24, 1943 – Wilson starts 1st major AA tour, returns Jan 19, 1944.

November 28, 1943 – Bill guest speaker at San Quentin Penitentiary (sometimes dated Dec 2, 1943).

January 1944 – Dr. Harry Tiebout's first paper on the subject of Alcoholics Anonymous.

January 19, 1944 – Wilsons return from 1st major AA tour started in Oct 24 1943.

March 10, 1944 – New York Intergroup is established.

July 1944 – Bob writes article for Grapevine "On Cultivating Tolerance."

June 21, 1944 – The first Issue of the AA Grapevine is published.

October 1944 – First non-American branch started in Sydney, Australia by Father T. V. Dunlea & Rex.

October 2, 1944 – Marty M. founds National Committee Education Alcoholism, later becomes National Council on Alcoholism.

January 15, 1945 – The first AA meeting is held in Springfield, Missouri.

January 24, 1945 – The first black group is established in St. Louis.

March 5, 1945 – Time Magazine reports Detroit radio broadcasts of AA members (Archie T.).

June 11, 1945 – 2500 attend AA's 10th Anniversary in Cleveland, Ohio.

June 13, 1945 – Morgan R. makes a radio appearance for AA with large audience. He is kept under surveillance to make sure he doesn't drink.

October 3, 1945 – AA Grapevine is adopted as national publication of AA.

November 1945 – Bill's article called 'Those Goof Balls' is published in Grapevine.

December 20, 1945 – Rowland H. dies (he carried the Oxford Group message to Ebby).

January 1946 – Readers Digest does a story on AA.

March 1946 – The March of Time film is produced by NY AA office.

May 6, 1946 – The long form of the "Twelve Traditions" is published in the AA Grapevine.

September 1946 – Bill & Dr. Bob both publicly endorse National Committee Education Alcoholism founded by Marty M.

September 1946 – The first AA group in Mexico.

November 18, 1946 – The first Dublin Ireland group meets.

March 31, 1947 – The first AA group is formed in London, England.

September 18, 1947 – Dallas Central Office opens its doors.

October 13, 1947 – "The Melbourne Group" holds its first meeting in Australia.

November 1, 1947 – The first AA Group in Anchorage, Alaska.

January 1948 – The first AA meeting in Japan.

June 1948 – A subscription to the AA Grapevine is donated to the Beloit, Wisconsin Public Library by a local AA member.

September 1948 – Bob writes article for Grapevine on AA "Fundamentals – In Retrospect."

December 1948 – Dr. Bob's last major talk, in Detroit.

March 1949 – Dr. Bob considers idea of an AA conference premature.

March 11, 1949 – The Calix Society, an association of Roman Catholic alcoholics who are maintaining their sobriety through participation in Alcoholics Anonymous, is formed in Minneapolis by five Catholic AA members.

May 1949 – The first AA meetings in Scotland are held in Glasgow and Edinburgh.

June 1, 1949 – Anne Smith, Dr. Bob's wife, dies.

September 1949 – The first issue of Grapevine is published in "pocketbook" size.

November 15, 1949 – Bill W. suggests that groups devote Thanksgiving week to discussions of the 12 Traditions.

December 7, 1949 – Sister Ignatia receives Poverello Medal on behalf of AA.

April 1950 – Saturday Evening Post article "The Drunkard's Best Friend" by Jack Alexander appears.

May 1950 – Nell Wing becomes Bill W.'s secretary.

May 1951 – Al-Anon is founded by Lois W. and Anne B.

May 18, 1950 – Dr. Bob tells Bill "I reckon we ought to be buried like other folks" after hearing that local AAs want a huge memorial.

July 28-30, 1950 – The first AA International Convention is held in Cleveland, Ohio. Twelve Traditions are adopted. Dr. Bob makes last appearance at large AA gathering.

November 16, 1950 – Dr. Bob dies.

December 1950 – Grapevine article is signed by both Bill and Dr. Bob recommending the establishment of AA General Service Conference.

January 1951 – AA Grapevine publishes memorial issue for Dr. Bob.

February 1951 – Fortune magazine article about AA New York reprints in pamphlet form for many years.

March 1951 – American Weekly publishes memorial article for Dr. Bob.

March 22, 1951 – Dr. William Duncan Silkworth dies at Towns Hospital.

April 25, 1951 – AA's first General Service Conference is held.

October 1951 – Lasker Award is given to AA by American Public Health Association.

October 1951 – Sister Ignatia writes "Care of Alcoholics – St.Thomas Hospital & AA Started Movement Which Swept Country" article in "Hospital Progress," the journal of Catholic Hospital Association. In October 1954 – The "Alcoholic Foundation" is renamed the "General Service Board of AA."

November 21, 1952 – Willard Richardson, past Treasurer/Chairman of Alcoholic Foundation, dies.

January 21, 1954 – Hank P. who helped Bill start NY office dies in Pennington, New Jersey.

August 3, 1954 – Brinkley S. gets sober at Towns Hosp after 50th detox.

August 28, 1954 – "24 Hours a Day" is published by Richmond W.

September 17, 1954 – Bill D., AA #3 dies.

July 2-3, 1955 – 20th Anniversary Convention at St. Louis, MO. The Three Legacies of Recovery, Unity, and Service, is turned over to the movement by the old-timers. AA comes of Age.

October 1, 1957 – Book "AA Comes of Age" is published.

January 1958 – Bill writes article for Grapevine on "Emotional Sobriety."

April 1958 – The word "honest" is dropped from AA Preamble, "an honest desire to stop drinking."

February 23, 1959 – AA grants permission to "Recording for the Blind" to tape the Big Book.

April 3, 1960 – Fr. Ed Dowling, S.J., dies. He was Bill W.'s "spiritual Sponsor."

July 1-3, 1960 – 25th Anniversary of AA in Long Beach, CA.

July 11, 1960 – Time publishes article called "Passionately Anonymous" on the 25th Convention.

January 30, 1961 – Dr. Carl Jung answers Bill's letter with "Spiritus Contra Spiritum."

September, 1962 – The first appearance of Victor E. in Grapevine.

February 1963 – Harpers carries article critical of AA.

November 1, 1963 – Reverend Sam Shoemaker dies.

July 2, 1965 – The first copies of "Best of Bill" and Pocket-Sized "12 and 12" are sold.

July 2, 1965 – The first "La Vigne," Canadian Grapevine, is published.

July 2-4, 1965 – 30th Anniversary of AA in Toronto. Adopts "I Am Responsible."

July 16, 1965 – Frank Amos, AA Non-Alcoholic Trustee, dies.

September 19, 1965 – The Saturday Evening Post publishes article "Alcoholics Can Be Cured – Despite AA."

March 21, 1966 – Ebby dies.

April 1966 – Change in ratio of trustees of the General Service Board; now two-thirds (majority) are alcoholic.

April 1, 1966 – Sister Ignatia dies.

April 2, 1966 – Dr. Harry Tiebout dies.

November 9, 1966 – President Johnson appoints Marty M. to the 1st National Advisory Committee on Alcoholism.

February 19, 1967 – Father "John Doe" (Ralph P.), 1st Catholic Priest in AA dies.

October 9-11, 1969 – The first World Service meeting is held in New York with delegates from 14 countries.

April 1970 – GSO is moved to 468 Park Ave. South, NYC.

July 3-5, 1970 – 35th Anniversary of AA in Miami. "Declaration of Unity." Bill's last public appearance.

October 10, 1970 – Lois reads "Bills Last Message" at annual dinner in NY.

January 24, 1971 – Bill W. dies at Miami Beach, FL.

January 26, 1971 – New York Times publishes Bill's obituary on Page 1.

February 14, 1971 – AA groups worldwide hold memorial service for Bill W.

May 8, 1971 – Bill W. is buried in private ceremony, East Dorset, Vermont.

July 31, 1972 – Rollie H. dies sober in Washington, DC.

October 5-7, 1972 – 2nd World Service meeting is held in New York.

April 16, 1973 – Dr. Jack Norris presents President Nixon with the one millionth copy of the Big Book.

October 24, 1973 – Trustees' Archives Committee of AA at its first meeting

May 28, 1974 – The first World Service Meeting of AA outside North America is held in London.

July 4-6, 1975 – 40th Anniversary of AA in Denver. World's largest coffee server serves half million cups a day.

September 19, 1975 – Jack Alexander, author of original Saturday Evening Post article, dies.

December 10, 1975 – Birds of a Feather AA group for pilots is formed.

June 6, 1979 – AA gives the two millionth copy of the Big Book to Joseph Califano, then Secretary of Health, Education, and Welfare. It is presented by Lois Wilson, Bill's wife, in New York.

December 6, 1979 – Akron Beacon reports death of Henrietta Seiberling.

May 29, 1980 – "Dr. Bob and the Good Oldtimers" is published.

July 3-6, 1980 – 45th Anniversary of AA in New Orleans. First true marathon meeting is held.

July 3-6, 1980 – Gay AAs have own program at 40th AA Anniversary in New Orleans.

July 22, 1980 – Marty M. early AA woman and founder of NCADD dies.

August 1981 – Distribution of Alcoholics Anonymous passes 3 million.

December 1982 – Nell Wing retires from GSO after 35 years of service.

March 22, 1984 – Clarence S., "Home Brewmeister," dies.

December 5, 1985 – Dave B., founder of Montreal Group dies weeks before 50th anniversary. His story is added to the 4th Edition Big Book.

July 5-7, 1985 – 50th AA Anniversary in Montreal, Canada. Ruth Hock is given five millionth Big Book.

January 13, 1988 – Dr. Jack Norris Chairman/Trustee of AA for 27 years dies.

August 18, 1988 – The first Canadian National AA Convention in Halifax, Nova Scotia.

October 5, 1988 – Lois Burnam Wilson dies.

October 8, 1988 – Memorial Service for Lois W. at Stepping Stones, NY.

October 10, 1988 – Lois is buried next to Bill in East Dorset, Vermont.

April 30, 1989 – Film "My Name is Bill W." a Hallmark presentation is broadcast on ABC TV.

July 5-8, 1990 – 55th AA Anniversary in Seattle, WA. Nell Wing given ten millionth Big Book.

July 2, 1993 – 50 years of AA is celebrated in Canada.

Oct 28, 1994 – National Council on Alcoholism and Drug Dependence celebrates 50 years.

January 19, 1999 – Frank M., AA Archivist since 1983, dies peacefully in his sleep.

February 14, 2000 – William Y., "California Bill," dies in Winston-Salem, NC.

May 19, 2000 – Dr. Paul O., Big Book story "Doctor, Alcoholic, Addict" (renamed "Acceptance Was the Answer" in the 4th edition) dies at the age of 83.

June 2000 – More than 47,000 from 87 countries attend the opening meeting of the 65th AA Anniversary in Minneapolis, MN.

July 2, 2000 – Twenty millionth copy of Big Book is given to Al-Anon in Minneapolis, MN.

January 5, 2001 – Chuck C. from Houston dies sober in Texas at 38 years sober.

September 11, 2001 – 30 Vesey St, New York, location of AA's first office is destroyed during the World Trade Center attack.

Bibliography

This book is offered as a reference and a set of resources to be used in understanding the origins and applicaton of the Recovery process outlined through the Twelve Steps as introduced through Alcoholics Anonymous in 1938. This process is used by more than 60 identified 12-Step fellowships and an unknown number of private organizations for members limited by occupation, religion or other identifying factor. (For example, meetings only for Mormons, or Lawyers, or connected through another group or organization.)

This book cannot be, and is not intended to be, the only guide to Recovery, Steps or the Twelve Step system. There are many other books, excellent books, examining history and application of the Steps, and Recovery beyond the narrow confines of the Twelve Step process.

There are a few books we would like to recommend because of their value to the authors and editors of Recovery Reader. We hope that you might find other personal benefits from examining and learning from these particular titles.

Drunks and Other Poems of Recovery
BY JACK MCCARTHY

Jack is the author of the emotional poem "Drunks" that provides the anchor for this book, We want you to know poet Jack McC. as who he was. We missed him by a few days when we tried to reach him to tell him the decision had been made to move forward with the second edition of the book. His other works share the experience of Recovery with a rich, full-tilt run into life from the unlikely world of the "Poetry Slams" from around the country.

His website provides his life, his work and access to what he left us. He provided spirit to keep me going in the first edition and, we hope, remains much appreciated beyond the cirlce of people who were lucky enough to know him.

You can also enjoy his performance of "Be Careful What You Ask for" on Youtube:

https://youtu.be/xsTZohyFFJE

And you can get his work in print and other media through:

http://standupoet.net

Not God
BY DR. ERNIE KURTZ

This was a landmark work where the history of Alcoholics Anonymous was examined outside the restrictions of the service structure. This means it approached issues many people within the World Service Office would not have allowed to be explored, and does not make every portrait it paints flattering.

But Dr. Kurtz blazed a trail which many other writers, scholars and educators have followed.

He also provided helpful guidance in the creation, and now the revision, of Recovery Reader, and it is through his work we found a place to stand.

The Recovery Book, 2nd Edition
BY CAROLYN DOLD, DR. AL J. MOONEY, M.D., AND HOWARD EISENBERG

The Second Edition of Recovery has been released and is a serious historical updating of an early book showing the academic, medical and philosophical aspects of Recovery. This book provides physicians viewpoitns and experience with many decades actively involved with the problems of the individual in clarifying the problem of alcoholism and addiction through identification, treatment and life after treatment.

http://theRecoverybook.com/

Slaying the Dragon, 2nd Edition
BY WILLIAM WHITE

This is a book targeted at academic and professional communities, which contains a wealth of research on the histories of Recovery systems before the emergence of the Twelve Steps with rich documentation on the evolution of the movement in this country.

http://goo.gl/qx0wBo

The pre-aa history book
BY BOB S.

This is a detailed work, lovingly compiled to cover the area from the late 19th Century growth and decline of The Washingtonians, the psychological writings of Sigmund Freud and Karl Jung, through the Emmanuel Movement, the Jacobi Group and includes details on The Oxford groups. There is no print-on-demand copy available at this time and the downloaded PDF is free to share with whomever you choose.

The book is avaialable at:

https://dl.dropboxusercontent.com/u/102806363/PreAAx.pdf

Additional Book Recommendations

Recovery has invited personal reflections, histories and biographies from its earliest days. This list is incomplete, but mostly because authors have risen, gained popularity with the Recovering community, and gone. Their works were lost as publishing houses folded, or copyrights expired and the public no longer wanted to hear what they had to say.

But you would be amazed at what a variety of stories they tell of times, communities and, above all, the people who brought our Program to us. We enjoy the gifts these authors have given us. They allow us to enjoy how our Program arrived, changed and became what we know today.

From AA World Services

AA comes of Age - AA World Services

Dr Bob and the Good Old Timers - AA World Services

Language of the Heart - AA World Services

Lois Remembers AA World Services

Pass It On - Bill Wilson and the AA Message, AA World Services

World services offers a large number of conference approved writings in English and other languages.

from Other Publishers

AA Master Inventory - Dick B $25 to Purchase Read Free Online 2002 New Editions Available soon

A Simple Program **by** J Big Book rewritten in Modern Language

Alcoholics Anonymous Cult or Cure - Charles Buffe

Anne Smith's Journal - Dick B.

Beware the 1st Drink!! The Washingtonian Temperance Society and AA - by Bill Pittman, 1991 Blumberg Pittman

Bill W. and Mr. Wilson - Matthew J. Raphael (pseudonym) Highly recommended!!

Bill W. - Francis Hartigan

Bill W. - Robert Thomsen c.1975, Published by Harper & Row

Bill W., My First 40 Years, an Autobiography by the Cofounder of AA - Bill Pittman, Hazleden Publisher

But, for the Grace of God… Wally P., Bishop of Books

Changed by Grace: V. C. Kitchen, the Oxford Group, and AA - Glenn Chestnut, September 2006

Changed Lives: The Story of Alcoholics Anonymous - Dennis C. Morreim 1992

Children of the Healer, the Story of Dr. Bob's Kids - Sue Smith Windows, Hazelden

Conversion of Bill W - Dick B. www.dickb.com

Courage To Change: Shoemaker - Bill Pittman and Dick B., Hazelden

Diary of Two Motorcycle Hobos by Lois Wilson, Gratitude Press, This book was pulled from publication - scarce!!!

Ebby the Man who Sponsored Bill Wilson - Mel B., 1998 Hazelden

Getting Better Inside AA - Nan Robertson, 1988 Thomas Congan Books

Grateful to Have Been There - Nell Wing

How It Worked, the Story of Clarence H. Snyder - Mitchell K. Out of Print Read on Web

Mrs. Marty Mann : The First Lady of AA - Sally Brown Hazelden

My Name Is Bill: Bill Wilson: His Life and the Creation of Alcoholics Anonymous - Susan Cheever 2006

My Search for Bill W. - Mel B., 2000 Hazelden

New Wine - Mel B., 1991 Hazelden

Physician, Heal Thyself! - Dr. Earle M., CompCare Publishers

Practice These Principles/What is Oxford Group - Bill Pittman, Hazelden

Road to Fellowship: Role of the Emmanuel Movement / Jacoby Club and AA - Richard M. Dubiel, 2004

Silkworth: The Dr. Who Loved Drunks - Dale Mitchel-Hazleden 2002

Sister Ignatia: Angel of Alcoholics Anonymous by Mary Darrah, Loyola Univ Press)

That Amazing Grace - Dick B., Paradise Research Publications

The Higher Power of the Twelve-Step Program: For Believers & Non-believers - Glenn Chestnut 2001,

The Collected Ernie Kurtz - Bishop of Books

The Lois Wilson Story -When Love Is Not Enough - William G. Borchert, 2005

The Natural History of Alcoholism - George E. Valiant

The Roots of AA - Bill Pittman Hazelden - Out of Print - Original title: *AA The Way It Began*

The Soul of Sponsorship : The Friendship of Fr. Ed Dowling and Bill Wilson - Robert Fitzgerald

The Spirituality of Imperfection - Ernest Kurtz, Katherine Ketcham

The Steps We Took: A Teacher of the Twelve Steps Shares His Experience, Strength, and Hope - Joe McQ

There's More to Quitting Drinking than Quitting Drinking - Dr. Paul O., Sabrina Pub.

To Be Continued-AA World Bibliography - Charles Bishop and Bill Pittman, Bishop Books OUT OF PRINT

Turning Point AA Comprehensive History - Dick B. this Book covers all the bases. Oxford Akron

Twelve Step Sponsorship: How It Works - Hamilton B., Hazelden

Understanding the 12 Steps - Terrence T Gorski, Fireside/Parkside 1991

Women Pioneers in 12 Step Recovery - Charlotte Hunter

Internet Recommendations

In the 21st Century it would be irresponsible to publish this kind of book without references to the links that have become a serious part of our regular search for details and new resources.

And, as with books, there are some which become more valuable than others, and we would like to share the addresses of a few websites that have become our favorites.

Listing does not indicate any association, endorsement or approval by the authors of the individual sites.

xa-speakers.org

This is the website that became a serious channel of experience, strength and hope. The name of the site comes from the fact that they offer recorded talks from many fellowships; AA, NA, Al-Anon and others. The "x" of xa-speakers.org is a place-holder. Which ever -A you find valuable here, they will keep it available.

You can search the site by fellowship, name, event, or topic, and they usually have all the parts of multi-speaker events.

The site is free and there is a request to support it through a PayPal donation button, and applying the Seventh Tradition to help the site support its costs is a good thing.

silkworth.net

Named for Dr. Silkworth at Towns Hospital, this site has become a staple for students and researchers for twelve step history and process. It offers an in depth library, most of which can be downloaded and has been helpful in many papers and options in various media. The editors of this book use silkworth.net regularly for general and detailed docu-mentation.

hindsfoot.org

A site offering a scholarly tone and deep archive of material on AA, the Twelve Steps, and the internal and external history of people, events, organizations and attitudes surrounding the growth of the Program.

This is an excellent resource for any student or researcher, and also offers information of value to individuals with an interest in the process, or Sponsors looking to improve their usefulness to others.

anonpress.org

The anonpress.org site has been the source of study information, including various versions of the Second Edition (public domain) version of the book Alcoholics Anonymous. These versions include a red-cover and camo-cover vest-pocket edition with original Chapter Five manuscript version and directory to most service offices around the world; reproductions of the First Edtion (red and yellow cover); 'study editions' (hardback and paperback Second Editions with each page faced with a lined blank page for extensive annotation); an in-depth Concordance to the first 188 pages plus Appendix II; and a detailed index to the first 164 pages.

We recommend the free version of the index to the first 164 pages, which can be used through the online page and on that page there is a link to download a free version to your computer. (http://anonpress.org/bbindex/)

Additional Web Resources

aahistory.com

164andmore.com

thejaywalker.com

www.royy.com/concord.html

www.bigbookdictionary.com

barefootsworld.net/aahistory.html

whytehouse.com/big_book_search

Submit corrections, additions or deletions to Sponsormagazine@gmail.com

12 Step Fellowships

Anon Family Group Inc.
1600 Corporate Landing Parkway
Virginia Beach, VA 23454-5617
(757) 563-1600
al-anon.alateen.org

All Addicts Anonymous (AAA)
40 Wickstead Way
Thornhill, Ont L3T 5E4
Canada
Tel: (416) 657 7771
alladdictsanonymous.org

AA World Services, Inc.,
PO Box 459
New York, NY 10163
(212) 870-3400
aa.org

Adult Children of Alcoholics WSO (ACA)
PO Box 3216
Torrance, CA 90510 USA
(562) 595-7831
adultchildren.org

Cocaine Anonymous WSO (CA)
PO Box 492000
Los Angeles, CA 90049-8000
www.ca.org

Clutterers Anonymous World Service Organization (CLA WSO)
PO Box 91413
Los Angeles, CA 90009-1413
(310) 281-6064
sites.google.com/site/clutterersanonymous

Crystal Meth Anonymous (CMA)
CMA General Services
4470 W Sunset Blvd Ste 107 PMB 555
Los Angeles, CA 90027-6302
www.crystalmeth.org

Co-Dependents Anonymous Fellowship Services Office (CoDA)
PO Box 33577
Phoenix, AZ 85067-3577
coda.org

Co-Anon Family Groups World Services
PO Box 12722
Tucson, AZ 85732-2722
(520) 513-5028
co-anon.org

COSA - Codependents of Sex Addicts
ISO of COSA
PO Box 79908
Houston, TX 77279-9908
Fellowship-Wide Services
1550 NE Loop 410, Ste 118
San Antonio, TX 78209
slaafws.org

Debtors Anonymous General Service Office (DA)
PO Box 920888
Needham, MA 02492-0009
Toll Free: (800) 421-2383 - US Only (781) 453-2743

Depressed Anonymous
PO Box 17414
Louisville, KY 40217

Dual Recovery Anonymous
World Network Central Office
PO Box 8107
Prairie Village, Kansas 66208
draonline.org

Eating Addictions Anonymous (EAA) General Service Office
PO Box 8151
Silver Spring, MD 20907-8151
(202) 882-6528
eatingaddictionsanonymous.org

Emotions Anonymous International (EA)
PO Box 4245, St. Paul, MN 55104-0245
Phone: (651) 647-9712
emotionsanonymous.org/

Emotional Health Anonymous (EHA)
San Gabriel Valley Intergroup
PO Box 2081
San Gabriel, CA 91778
(626) 287-6260 PH

Families Anonymous (FA)
P O Box 3475
Culver City, CA 90231-3475
(800) 736-9805
FamiliesAnonymous.org

Food Addicts in Recovery Anonymous (FA)
400 W Cummings Park #1700
Woburn, MA 01801
(781) 931-6300
foodaddicts.org

Food Addicts Anonymous (FAA)
529 N W Prima Vista Blvd. #301 A
Port St. Lucie, FL 34983
(561) 967-3871

Gamblers Anonymous® (GA)
International Service Office
PO Box 17173
Los Angeles, CA 90017
(213) 386-8789
gamblersanonymous.org

Gam-Anon/Gam-A-Teen
for friends and family members of problem gamblers
Gam-Anon® International Service Office, Inc.
PO Box 157
Whitestone, NY 11357
(718) 352-1671
gam-anon.org

GreySheeters Anonymous (GSA)
greysheet.org

Methadone Anonymous (MA)
methadonesupport.org/

Marijuana Anonymous World Services (MA)
PO Box 7807
Torrance, CA 90504
1 (800) 766-6779
marijuana-anonymous.org

Crystalmeth Anonymous (CMA)
General Services
4470 W Sunset Blvd Ste 107 PMB 555
Los Angeles, CA 90027-6302
(213) 488-4455
crystalmeth.org

Narcotics Anonymous (NA)
PO Box 9999
Van Nuys, CA 91409
(818) 773-9999
na.org

NAIL - Neurotics Anonymous
See Emotions Anonymous

Nar-Anon
for friends and family members of addicts
Nar-Anon Family Group Headquarters
22527 Crenshaw Blvd Suite 200B
Torrance, CA 90505
(310) 534-8188 or (800) 477-6291
nar-anon.org

NicA - Nicotine Anonymous World Services
419 Main Street, PMB# 370
Huntington Beach, CA 92648
Toll Free: (877) 879-6422

Obsessive Compulsive Foundation
PO Box 961029
Boston, MA 02196
(617) 973-5801
ocfoundation.org

PA - Pills Anonymous
pillanonymous.org

Overeaters Anonymous, Inc. (OA)
PO Box 44020
Rio Rancho, NM 87174-4020 USA

On-Line Gamers Anonymous World Services (OLGA)
104 Miller Lane
Harrisburg, PA 17110
(612) 245-1115

Recoveries Anonymous Universal Services
Box 1212
East Northport, NY 11731

Recovering Couples Anonymous WSO Office (RCA)
PO Box 11029
Oakland, CA 94611
(781) 794-1456
recovering-couples.org

SA - Smokers Anonymous
See Nicotine Anonymous

SA - Sexaholics Anonymous
International Central Office
PO Box 3565
Brentwood, TN 37024
(615) 370-6062
sa.org

ISO of Sex Addicts Anonymous (SAA)
PO Box 70949
Houston, TX 77270 USA
(713) 869-4902
sexaa.org

Sexual Compulsives Anonymous (SCA)
PO Box 1585, Old Chelsea Station
New York, NY 10011

SLAA - Sex and Love Addicts Anonymous
Fellowship-Wide Services
1550 NE Loop 410, Ste 118
San Antonio, TX 78209
slaafws.org

Spender's Anonymous
spenders.org

Survivors of Incest Anonymous (SIA)
World Service Office
PO Box 190
Benson, MD 21018-9998
(410) 893-3322

Workaholics Anonymous (WA)
World Service Organization
Post Office Box 289
Menlo Park, California 94026-0289 U.S.A.
Phone: (510) 273-9253
workaholics-anonymous.org

Parents Anonymous (PA)
Parents Anonymous® Inc.
675 West Foothill Blvd., Suite 220
Claremont, CA 91711-3475
(909) 621-6184
parentsanonymous.org

Submit corrections, additions or deletions to Sponsormagazine@gmail.com

The Sponsor Magazine Symbol

USE THE STEPS
TRAVEL BEYOND THIS POINT
W/O SPONSOR NOT ADVISED

When we started the Anonymous Review project, it became clear that we needed to change the name. Sponsor Magazine was a thought, but we wanted a simple graphic that would convey the idea of sponsorship.

This graphic came from consideration of several idea.

- A Warning Sign (in Black and Yellow)

- The Steps

- Each one following the one before him

- The one in front carrying a light

In the original, square version it was clear there were two other peope on the steps - the one the man on the Steps was following, and someone following the first follower.

We have used the two-person symbol in the diamond 'warning sign' style, a circle, and the original square. It may show up in other forms in the future.

Original Graphic

.

Printed in Great Britain
by Amazon